W9-ATK-460

Measurement Investigations

Tamara J. Drean
Vista Unified School District

Randall J. Souviney
University of California, San Diego

Dale Seymour Publications

For Michelle,
in her first year of teaching

Tamara J. Drean is a teacher who has taught at the elementary level for over 15 years. As a professional concerned with improving the quality of education for children, she has presented mathematics teaching workshops throughout North America and Europe. Tamara has also been a trainer for Learning Forum/SuperCamp instructors specializing in learning modalities and presentation skills. In her current position, she is providing district-wide leadership for professional and school restructuring, particularly in the areas of mathematics and science education.

Randall J. Souviney grew up in a family of teachers. He has taught mathematics, science, and computer education at the elementary, secondary, and university levels. He received his PhD in Mathematics Education from the Arizona State University. For the past ten years, he has served as the Associate Coordinator of Teacher Education at the University of California, San Diego. He has been the recipient of several research grants, including the Indigenous Mathematics Project in Papua, New Guinea (UNESCO). He has written over 50 articles on mathematics and computer education and has published a dozen books for teachers and teacher educators, the most recent of which is *Mathematical Investigations,* published by Dale Seymour Publications.

This revised publication was originally published under the title of *Measurement and the Child's Environment,* published by Goodyear Publishing Company, Inc., with original design and illustrations by Karen McBride.

Many of the designations used by manufacturers and sellers to distinguish their products are claimed as trademarks. Where those designations appear in this book, and the publisher was aware of a trademark claim, the designations have been printed in initial caps (e.g., Nerf ball).

Limited reproduction permission: The publisher grants permission to individual teachers who have purchased this book to reproduce the blackline masters as needed for use with their own students. Reproduction for an entire school district or for commercial use is prohibited.

Copyright © 1980, 1992 by Dale Seymour Publications. All rights reserved. Printed in the United States of America. Published simultaneously in Canada.

Order number DS21121
ISBN 0-86651-591-7

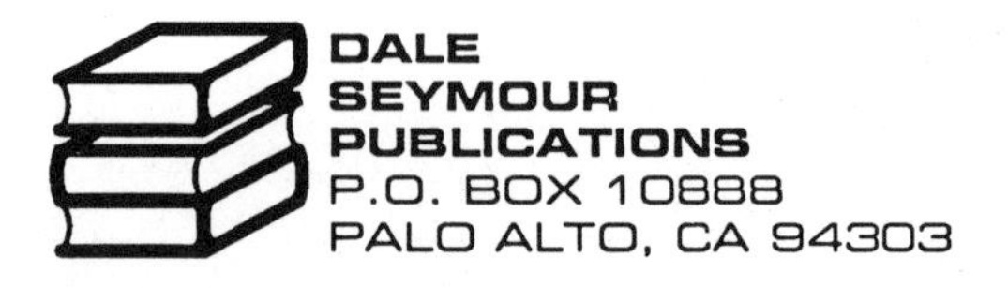

4 5 6 7 8 9 10-MA-96 95 94

CONTENTS

SI METRIC PREFIXES AND SYMBOLS

Factor	Prefix	Symbol
10^{-12}	pico	p
10^{-9}	nano	n
10^{-6}	micro	u
10^{-3}	milli*	m
10^{-2}	centi*	c
10^{-1}	deci	d
10^{0}	Base Unit	
10^{1}	deka	da
10^{2}	hecto	h
10^{3}	kilo*	k
10^{6}	mega	M
10^{9}	giga	G
10^{12}	tera	T

*Most commonly used prefixes

PREFACE

Historically, there has been confusion surrounding techniques of measurement of objects and events due to the way units of measure were invented. Units based on body measures (cubit, inch, foot, yard, hand) were regionally defined and subject to misinterpretation. As people developed a need for cross-cultural communication, more universal measurement units became a necessity.

By exploring the history of measurement, we discovered that the sequence in which our ancestors developed measuring techniques parallels the way measurement is taught today. Children first define measurable attributes through direct comparison. Then, as more accurate measures are required and the need for communication increases, locally known nonstandard units are introduced. Standard units become important when accurate communication between groups of people is necessary.

Of all topics commonly included in the mathematics curriculum, few are more important or more neglected than measurement. The development of sound measurement skills helps children make the world more predictable and provides a basis for the development of number and geometry. Measurement also provides the tools for gathering data often needed for solving complex problems. We hope you and your students enjoy using the activities presented in this book as much as we enjoyed developing and using them in our classrooms.

T. J. D.
R. J. S.

INTRODUCTION

What Is Measurable?

The following story by Alexander Calandra[1] offers insight into the measurement process. A student was asked on an exam how to use a barometer to measure the height of a tall building. To impress her teacher she gave the following answer:

> Take the barometer to the top of the building, attach a long rope to it, lower the barometer to the street, and then bring it up, measuring the length of the rope. The length of the rope is the height of the building.
>
> Take the barometer to the top of the building and lean over the edge of the roof. Drop the barometer, timing its fall with a stop watch. Then, using the formula, $S = \frac{1}{2} at^2$, calculate the height of the building.
>
> Take the barometer out on a sunny day and measure the height of the barometer, the length of its shadow, and the length of the shadow of the building, and by the use of a simple proportion, determine the height of the building.
>
> There is a very basic measurement method that you will like. In this method, you take the barometer and begin to walk up the stairs. As you climb the stairs, you mark off the length of the barometer along the wall. You then count the number of marks, and this will give you the height of the building in barometer units. A very direct method.
>
> Of course, if you want a more sophisticated method, you can tie the barometer to the end of the string, swing it as a pendulum, and by determining the value of "g" the height of the building can, in principle, be calculated.
>
> Finally, there are many other ways of solving the problem. Probably the best is to take the barometer to the basement and knock on the superintendent's door. When the superintendent answers, you speak to him as follows, "Mr. Superintendent, here I have a fine barometer. If you will tell me the height of this building, I will give you this barometer.

Measurement is a procedure that enables the comparison and quantification of objects and events in the world. The woman's answer to the exam question showed considerable understanding of measurement processes because she avoided giving the "expected" answer of calculating the height from the change in air pressure at the bottom and top of the building.

By looking carefully, it is possible to imagine a number of ways to quantify things. Children are interested in these notions at a very early age. They know that older sisters and brothers get to stay up later than they do, or that the neighborhood bully is bigger than they are. Soon the need arises to know "how much later" or "how much bigger."

Most events in the child's world are measurable in some way. By involving students in measuring their environment, you are fostering their ability to "see" the world in a more quantitative way. This perspective is not necessarily a rigid or inflexible view, but one that provides the individual with a more predictable basis for making decisions and solving problems.

Measurement makes mathematics real and tangible

---

[1] Alexander Calandra, "Angels on a Pin: Excerpts from the Teachings of Elementary Science and Mathematics," Saturday Review, Vol. 51 (December 21, 1968), p. 60.

for the individual; it gives children a handle on their world. Most everything is measurable.

The first step in measuring is to decide exactly what property to attend to—in other words, what attribute to measure. For example, take an orange. How many ways can you measure an orange? You could measure its height and width, naturally, but how else might you interpret the notion of length? How about finding the circumference or diameter? One way to pose this problem to students is to ask, "How many ways can you measure an orange using a string?"

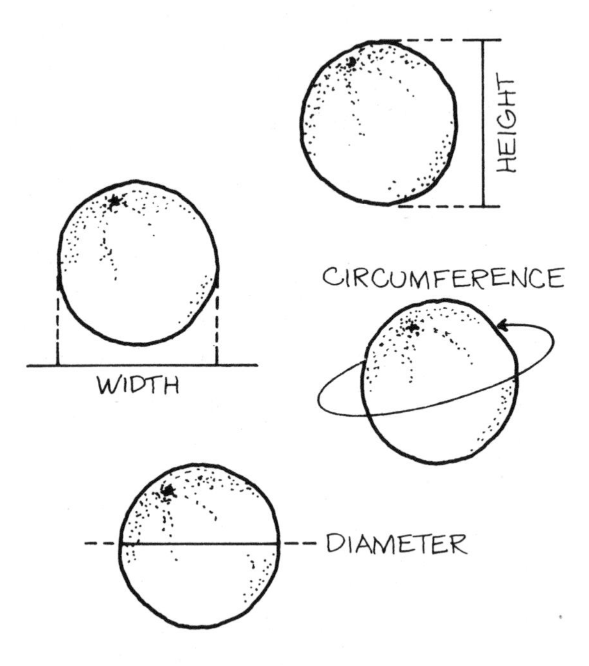

Next, you need to decide what tool you are going to use to measure the orange. In this case, a piece of string is a convenient device for finding length. String allows us to directly compare the circumferences of two or more oranges. If we want to know "how much more," unit lengths need to be used. Almost any set of uniform objects can be used as a measurement unit: pencils, paper clips, grains of rice, stamps, or even popcorn. Imagine measuring the circumference of an orange in stamps.

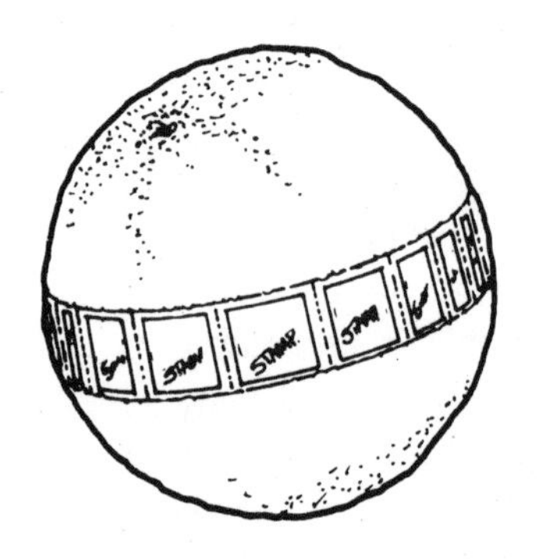

To measure an object, first identify an attribute (length), select a measurement device (string, stamps, and so on), and then measure the object by comparing it with the device (pieces of string) or counting the units (stamps).

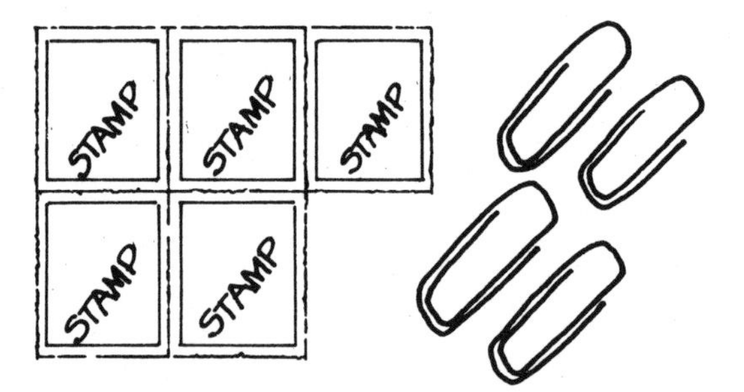

How would you find the mass (weight) of an orange? Following the procedure outlined earlier, first identify the attribute (mass) and select a measurement device. Typically, to find the mass of an object, we simply put it on a scale and read the number of units.

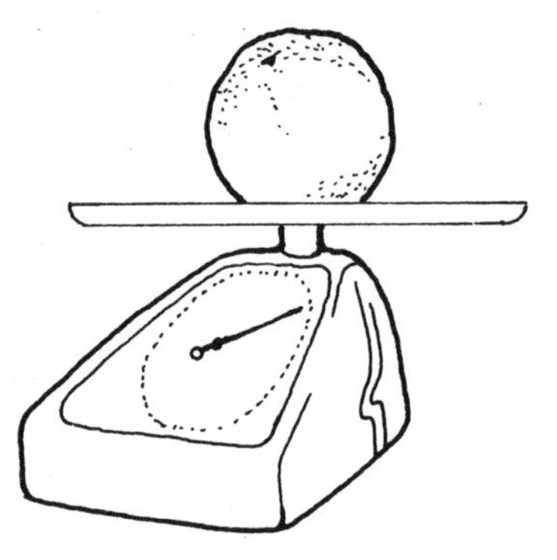

A pan balance can help children to understand better what attribute is being measured.

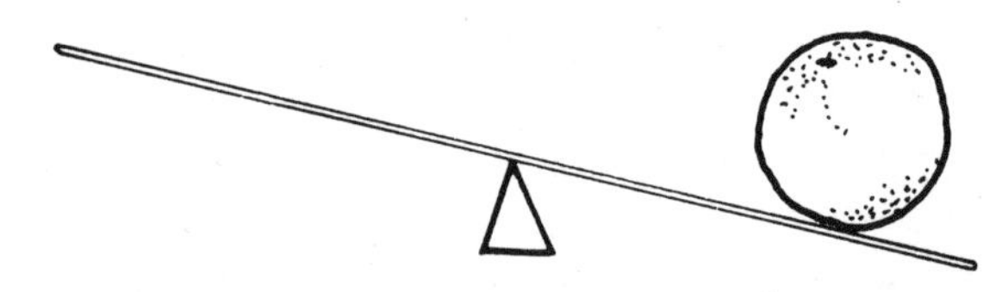

Try finding the mass of an orange in marbles or split peas. What other nonstandard units could be used?

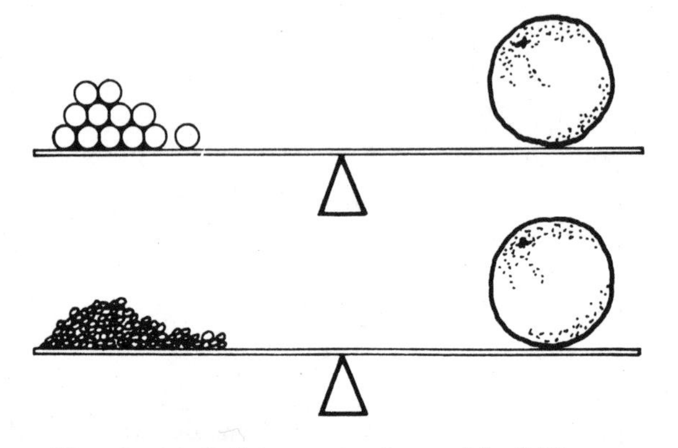

How heavy is this orange in marbles? How many split peas balance the orange?

How many other ways can you measure this marvelous fruit? Peel an orange very carefully so that the skin is removed in one piece. Put the peeling back together and fill the peeling with lima beans.

How many lima beans does it take to fill the orange? You have just found the capacity of the orange using lima beans as a unit of measure. How many oranges would it take to fill up you classroom? How many lima beans? This problem is a good application of large numbers and for calculators.

Now spread the peel flat and closely pack lima beans over the entire surface. The surface area of this orange is 89 lima beans.

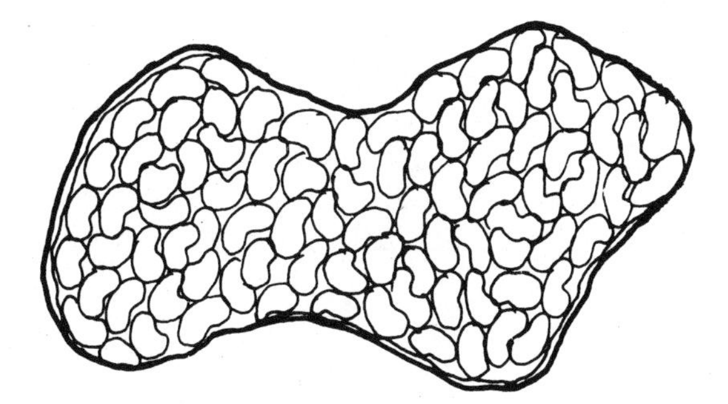

Other attributes that could be measured include the amount of juice in the orange and the angle formed by a section.

We can count the sections or the seeds as a measure of an orange. Do all oranges have the same number of sections? Do bigger ones have more? How many other ways can you imagine an orange to be measurable? Give this problem to your class and watch the imaginations blossom.

Understanding the concept of a *unit* is fundamental to the measurement process. Nonstandard units include marbles, split peas, lima beans, shoes, and thumb prints. The invention and manipulation of nonstandard units build a foundation for the use of customary or metric units.

Children learn that the more uniform their units, the more precise their measurements will be. Paper clips are uniform in length and are therefore more accurate units of measurement than pieces of popcorn. As students begin to communicate measures, it is important that they share common units to avoid confusion. If one student describes to a classmate the length of a soccer field in spelling book units, the classmate will likely understand because they both use the same book. However, a grounds keeper who is used to measuring in yards might not chalk the lines properly if he was given the dimensions of the field in spelling books.

Students discover that as units become shared knowledge, communication is more accurate. This leads into the natural adoption of customary or metric units for standard measurement.

Measurement also helps students learn computation skills and geometry. As teachers, we have traditionally recognized the need for "reading readiness" activities to prepare the child for reading, yet "computation readiness" is often assumed. Measurement gives children tools to compare and quantify objects and events. Addition and subtraction develops naturally from combining and comparing measures.

For example, a balance can be used to model addition.

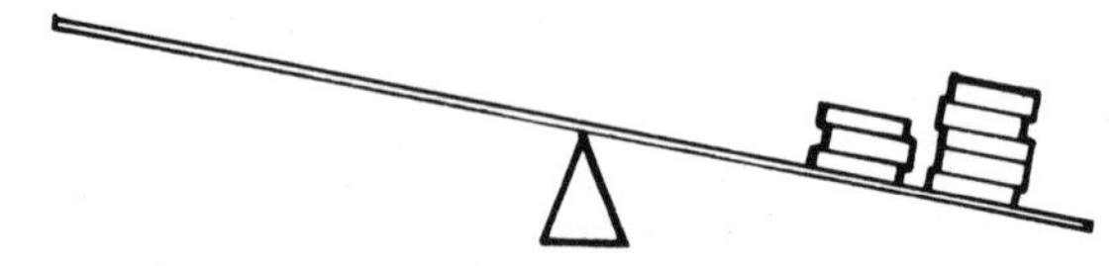

WHAT BALANCES THE COMBINED BUNDLES OF 3 AND 5 HOUSEHOLD WASHERS?

Eight washers placed on one side balances three and five washers on the other. By measuring mass, a student can have a concrete experience showing that 3 + 5 = 8.

Learning to Measure

It is important for children to develop a thorough understanding of measurement concepts. Simply learning the unit names and how to use measurement instruments is not sufficient. Children can develop measurement concepts in three distinct stages: comparison, nonstandard units, and standard units.

STAGE ONE

Children engage in comparison activities as the first step in a sequence of activities, and thus gain understanding of measurement attributes and procedures. They *directly* compare heights, masses, speeds, and temperatures: "I'm taller than you," "Jose is heavier than both of us," "I can run faster than my brother," "How come I have to go to bed earlier than Michelle?"

STAGE TWO

This stage involves *indirect* comparison using a "unit" to determine a number associated with a certain attribute of an object. When it is important to know *how much more* rather than simply comparing the relative size of two objects, nonstandard units are introduced. If two objects cannot be placed near each other, it is necessary to use a mutually agreed upon unit of measure to make a meaningful comparison.

STAGE THREE

The last stage in this learning sequence involves using a standard unit of measure to insure that no misunderstanding occurs. For example, if we decide to weigh two pigs using bricks as unit mass pieces, some confusion would ensue unless we use the same size bricks.

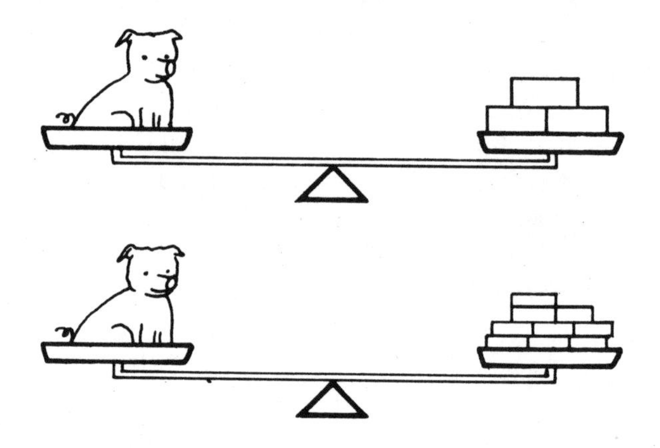

The desire for unambiguous communication necessitates the universal acceptance of standard units. Universal conversion to the metric system can be viewed as an attempt to accomplish this feat on a global scale. Although customary units are still in common use in the USA and are therefore included in this book, a gradual conversion to metric units seems inevitable.

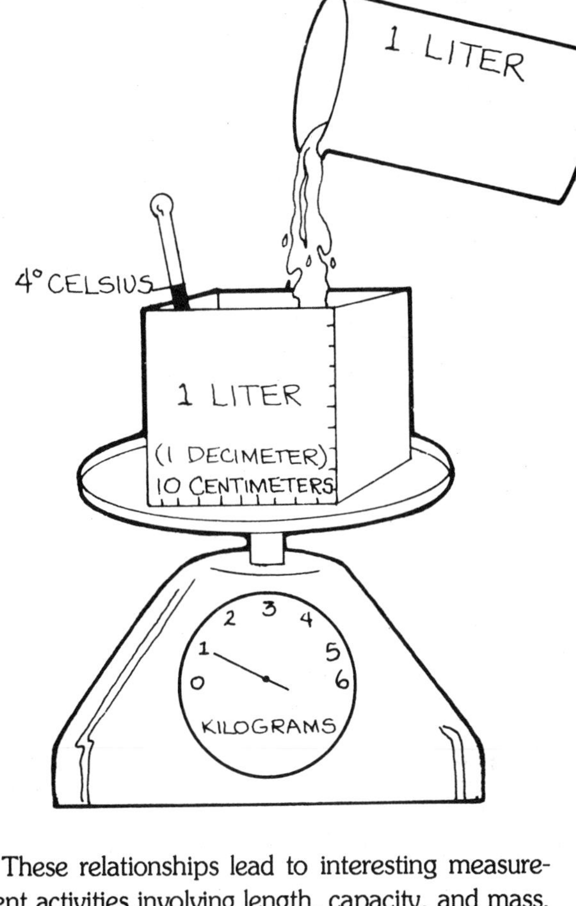

Advantages and Disadvantages of the Metric System

The United States is the last industrialized nation to convert to the metric system and its foreign trade continues to suffer partly because of not converting to it sooner. For years, companies in the United States have had to maintain two sets of inventories and machinery, one meeting customary standards and another meeting international metric standards. Conversion to metric standards allows a significant reduction in inventories of parts manufactured by companies. For example, General Motors reduced the number of types of fan belts it manufactures from 500 to about 50 when it converted to metric standards. The automobile, beverage, and electronic industries are among the major USA manufacturers who have switched to metric standards.

The SI Metric System (International System of Metric Measures) also affords opportunities to improve our techniques for teaching measurement. The basic metric units are related to each other in a concrete way. For example:

- 10 centimeters equals 1 decimeter
- 1 cubic decimeter essentially equals 1 liter
- 1 liter at 4°C has a mass of 1 kilogram

These relationships lead to interesting measurement activities involving length, capacity, and mass. The Celsius temperature scale is somewhat easier to use than the Fahrenheit scale because the distance between the freezing and boiling points of water on a thermometer (0°C–100°C) is broken into 100 equal segments, each being one degree Celsius. The very nature of such relationships encourages an activity-oriented style of instruction. Hands-on experiences designed to familiarize students with the relative size of each unit encourage them to think in metric units. Measures of body parts and common objects can be used to provide a relative benchmark for each unit.

Metric units involve identical prefixes (kilo, hecto, deko, deci, centi, milli), which simplifies learning the metric unit names. Also, the metric units are related by multiples of 10, which invites comparison with the base-10 number system. For example:

- 10 millimeters equal 1 centimeter
- 10 centimeters equal 1 decimeter
- 10 decimeters equal 1 meter

We have included metric and customary unit tables in the appendix for your convenience.

Measurement Activity Sequences

Measurement, like other areas of mathematics, requires a variety of experiences that allow development from concrete manipulation of objects and measurement devices to symbolic understanding of formulas. In order for children to effectively develop measurement skills, each measurement attribute should be addressed using activities for the comparison, nonstandard unit, and standard unit steps. Each step can be addressed as a concrete, representational, or symbolic level activity. In practice, a teacher can develop an activity for each of the nine cells (*A* through *I*) in the Measurement Activity Sequence chart.

Measurement Activity Sequence

	Concrete	Representational	Symbolic
Comparison	**A**	**B**	**C** 
Nonstandard Unit	**D**	**E**	**F** 
Standard Unit	**G**	**H**	**I** 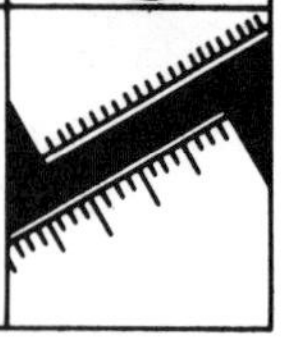

Learning theory suggests that instruction for a novice should begin at activity type *A* and move either across or down. Experience suggests that participation in *all* nine types of activities may be unnecessary. Any arrangement of *adjacent* types leading to type *I* is appropriate. For example, one activity sequence might be *A, B, E, H, I* as shown.

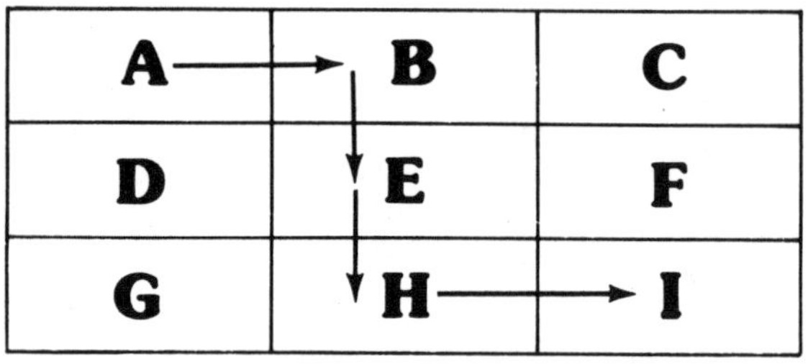

A →	**B** ↓	**C**
D	**E** ↓	**F**
G	**H** →	**I**

If a child is having difficulty, appropriate corrective instruction can be planned by looking for prerequisite activities. For example, by moving to the *left* or *up* in the grid, prerequisite instruction for concept *E* would be either *B* or *D*.

At the elementary level, measurement topics include length, mass, area, capacity, temperature, and time. A series of appropriate activities may be set up in a learning center or developed as a small or whole-class lesson depending on your teaching style. Activities (*A* through *I*) should be selected based on the grade level, learning readiness, and student interests. Begin with hands-on experiences with real objects, followed by representational activities using pictures or drawings, and finally with symbolic activities involving operations using numbers or formulas. Although all novice measurers will benefit from participating in all five activities, some students will progress more rapidly through the learning sequence. It is important to note that many K-1 children should not be expected to measure and do computations involving standard units. Additional activities of type *A, B, D,* or *E* would be appropriate for these students.

An example of a Length Activity Sequence is shown in the following chart. The arrows indicate one path of five activities that would guide the learner from a comparison/concrete experience to a standard unit/symbolic understanding of length.

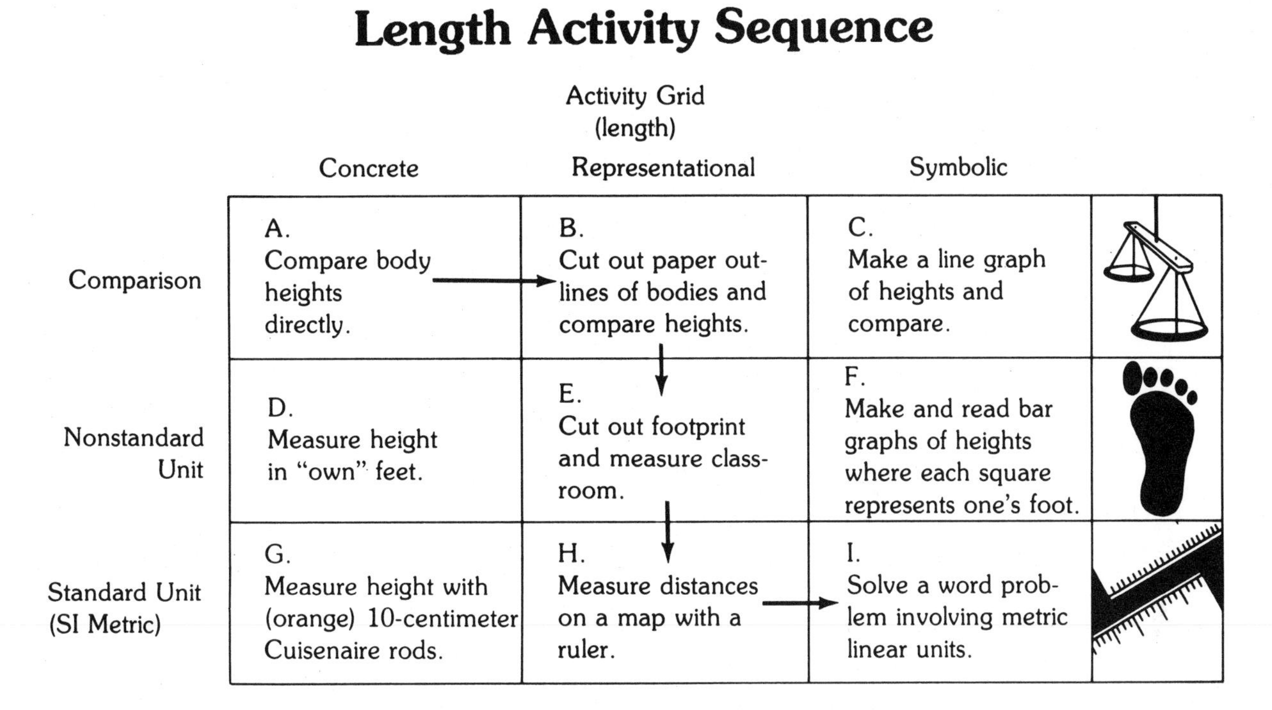

Length Activity Sequence

Activity Grid
(length)

	Concrete	Representational	Symbolic
Comparison	A. Compare body heights directly. →	B. Cut out paper outlines of bodies and compare heights. ↓	C. Make a line graph of heights and compare.
Nonstandard Unit	D. Measure height in "own" feet.	E. Cut out footprint and measure classroom. ↓	F. Make and read bar graphs of heights where each square represents one's foot.
Standard Unit (SI Metric)	G. Measure height with (orange) 10-centimeter Cuisenaire rods.	H. Measure distances on a map with a ruler. →	I. Solve a word problem involving metric linear units.

The activities in this book provide detailed descriptions of measurement activity sequences for primary (K-3) and intermediate (3-6) students. These activities integrate measurement instruction into school life that should help your students develop a deeper understanding of what is measurable and how to measure it.

HOW TO USE THIS BOOK

The most important component of any curriculum is you, the teacher. In order to use the activities presented in this book most effectively, it is important to first try them out yourself. Choose the sequence you plan to introduce, collect the necessary materials, and try to do the activity to work out any problems that may arise. Section II contains student worksheets, rulers, squared paper, and other tools to help with your planning. This section also explains how to construct most of the measurement materials needed to conduct the activities in this book. If you're not familiar with the metric measures, Section II also contains a review of the SI Metric System of Measures.

Before beginning each measurement sequence, you may wish to use the introductory warm-up activity to help you assess your students' understanding of conservation of the relevant measurement attribute. For example, children who do not readily conserve area may need to spend more time doing comparison and nonstandard unit activities before introducing computation and area formulas involving standard units.

As you will see, an *icon* is printed in the upper left-hand corner of each activity in the sequence. These symbols are included to remind you that an activity involves comparison, nonstandard, or standard units of measure. The scales indicate comparison, the footprint represents nonstandard units, and the rulers denote standard units.

Note that some standard activities may be too difficult for many K-1 children. These activities have been included for those students who you feel are ready for them. Some students may need to spend additional time with the comparison or nonstandard unit experiences.

Generally, all students should begin with the comparison activity in each sequence and progress through the five activities. Children who are more capable may wish to progress through the beginning activities quickly and spend more time working with the standard units. This process fosters a better understanding of each concept, building a stronger foundation for the use of standard units of measure.

The activities presented in this book can be introduced through small group instruction, whole class activities, or learning centers. We have included record-keeping charts for both upper and lower grades to help you monitor progress. Several games in Section II can be used to help children memorize the metric unit terminology. *Measurement Checks* are also included at the end of the upper-grade activity sheets to help you assess student understanding of metric units.

Measurement Activity Sequences

CHAPTER 1

Length

OVERVIEW

Length is one of the first measurement attributes discovered by children. Many objects in their environment are better understood if the concept of length can be explored. How far? How high? How far around? and How tall? are questions that require an understanding of length. Length can be measured along a straight or curved path. Length is generally defined as the number of equivalent units, nonstandard or standard, laid end to end that make up the distance from one point to another. Lengths can also be compared without employing a unit of measure.

Five activities are provided for the primary grade levels and five for the intermediate grade levels. Throughout this book, the grade levels are identified as P-L (primary level) or I-L (intermediate level). The length activity sequence charts show the sequence of activities based on the instructional model presented in the Introduction. Begin with Activity 1 and progress through the sequence, allowing sufficient time at each level to insure understanding. Remember, all children may not progress at the same rate, and everyone cannot be expected to reach the final stage of abstraction in the time available.

LENGTH ACTIVITY SEQUENCE 1

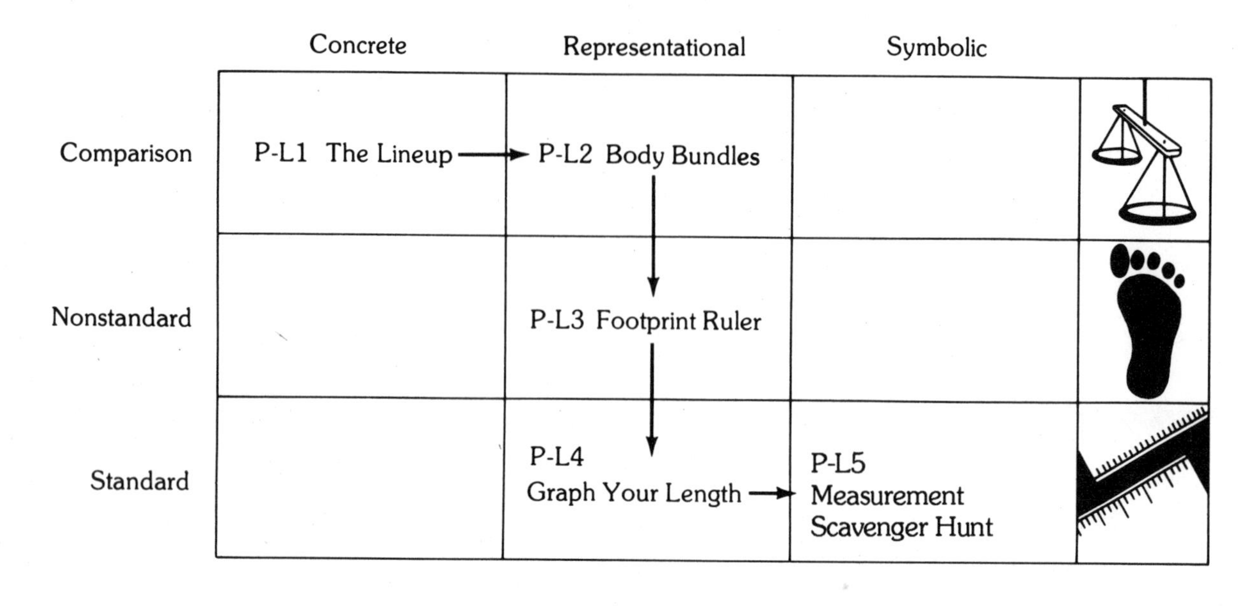

	Concrete	Representational	Symbolic
Comparison	P-L1 The Lineup →	P-L2 Body Bundles ↓	
Nonstandard		P-L3 Footprint Ruler ↓	
Standard		P-L4 Graph Your Length →	P-L5 Measurement Scavenger Hunt

WARM-UP ACTIVITY

What You Need: Two equal pieces of string and two drawings of ants (see below).

How to Do It: Using an overhead projector, let a student examine the two pieces of string. Lay them out parallel to each other on a table or desk and ask if they are equal. Once the student has agreed that both strings are the same length, tell them to imagine placing an ant on one end of each and ask the following question: "If each ant had to walk along this string, would each have to travel the same distance?"

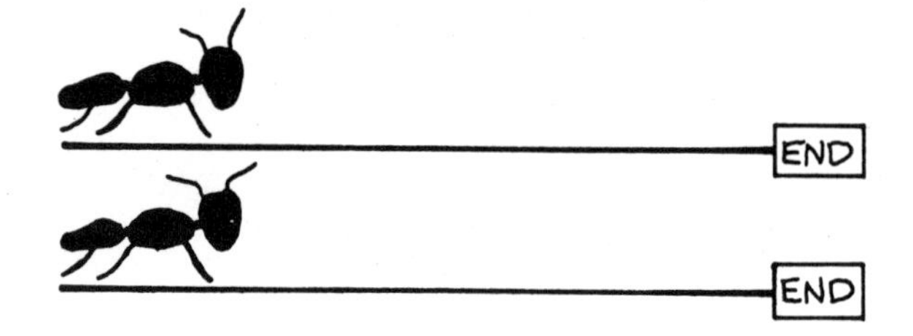

Once children have answered *yes*, change one string so that there is a bend or loop in it, and then repeat the question.

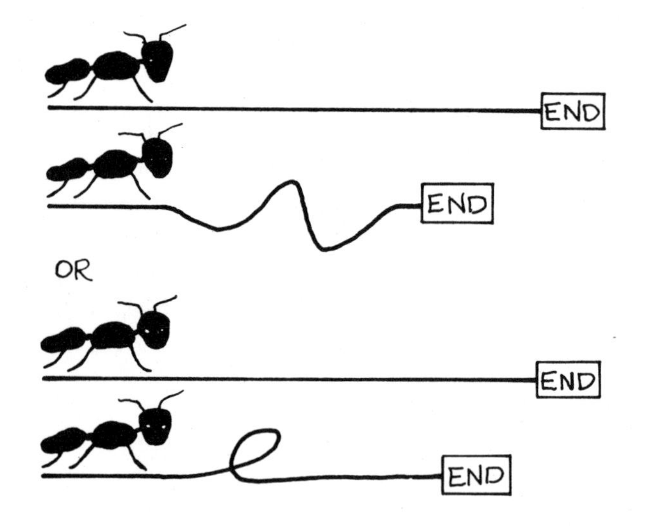

Return the second string to its original position and repeat your question, always asking the students to justify their answers.

TEACHING IMPLICATIONS

Some students will think that the length of an object does not remain constant when its shape or position changes. Because in the second situation the shape of the path has changed and may appear shorter, some students may think that the ant on this string has a shorter path to walk. These students should be encouraged to focus on the comparison and nonstandard unit activities in the length measurement sequence. Such experiences will provide a concrete basis for understanding that length of an object does not change when it is moved.

DEVELOPMENTAL ACTIVITY SEQUENCE

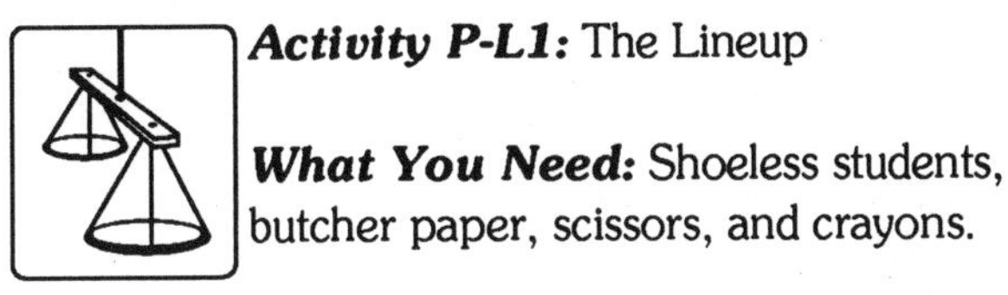

Activity P-L1: The Lineup

What You Need: Shoeless students, butcher paper, scissors, and crayons.

How to Do It: Ask students, "Who is the tallest in the class? Who is the shortest? Who comes in between?" Have the students arrange themselves from shortest to tallest in one line.

Next, pose this problem: "How can we make a record of our line and remember where everyone fits?" Students will suggest various ways such as taking a picture. At this point, show them an example of a "body cutout." These will be made by all students and can then be lined up on a classroom wall as a "record" of the actual body lineup. Have students pair up and take scissors, crayons, and two lengths of butcher paper slightly longer than they are. One student lies down on the paper while the other traces around his or her body; they then switch places. These outlines can be colored in by the students themselves. Once every student has a "body cutout" finished, the class should line up against the wall by height again. This time they can leave a "record" by pinning up their cutouts.

NOTE: Children must be cautioned about the importance of accuracy when tracing each other. For young children to avoid having the cutouts misrepresent their heights, it's helpful to have a parent or older student assist with the tracing.

Activity P-L2: Body Bundles

What You Need: This can be a lesson on body parts as well as measuring. To stimulate student thought, ask questions such as the following: "If you're taller than your friend, do you think your arms are longer than his or hers too?" "Are your feet bigger?" "Is your head bigger around than your waist?" After this discussion, students should measure the following body parts with string: arm (from shoulder to wrist), leg (from hip to floor), foot (from heel to toe), waist, arm span, circumference of head, hand span, and height. Each piece of string should be labeled with the child's name and body measure:

With these "body bundles" children can now compare their respective body lengths. A "garden of body measurements" bulletin board can be made, using the string as flower stems. A cut-out flower can be placed at the top of each, labeled with the child's name and body part. The final board might look like this:

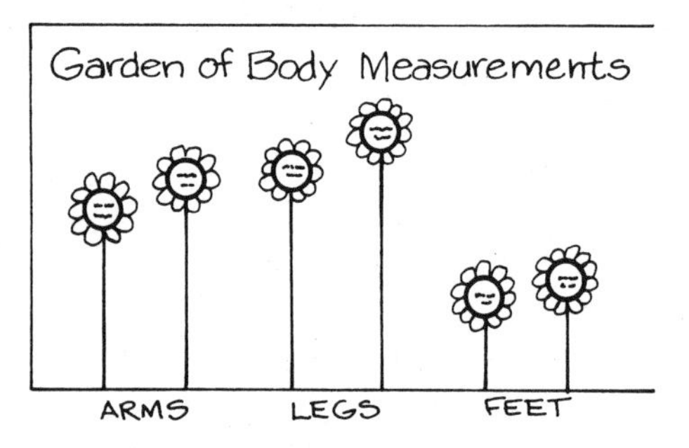

EXTENDED ACTIVITY:

Are you a square or a rectangle? Have students compare the strings for their height and for their arm spans. Is there a big difference, or are they almost equal? If they are equal, have the students cut out a square of construction paper and paste it on the "square" side of a graph like the one below:

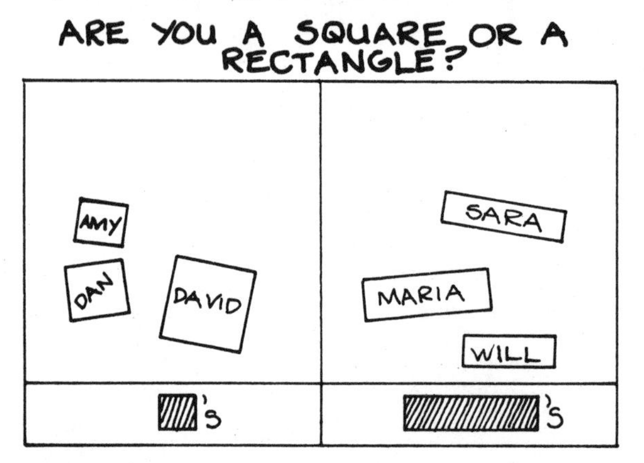

If they are unequal, the students should cut out a rectangle and glue it in the appropriate spot. Is the class mostly squares or rectangles?

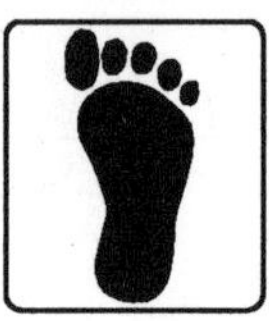

Activity P-L3: Footprint Ruler

What You Need: Tempera, long rolls of paper approximately 15 cm wide, objects to measure, and Record Sheet P-L3 (p. 83).

How to Do It: Children soon find that simply comparing objects is not accurate enough for their measuring needs. They will naturally begin to use their hands or feet to measure objects in their world. Have students measure things in the room and around the school using any nonstandard unit they wish (pencils, books, shoes, etc.). After students are comfortable with the concept of unit measure, let them make a representational nonstandard "ruler" using the following method:

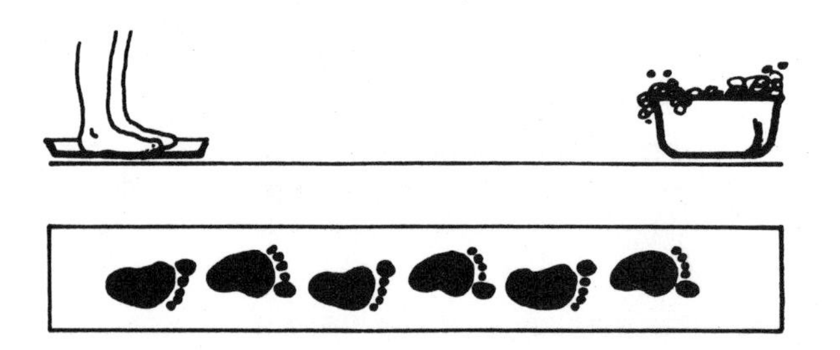

Give students paper strips about the same lengths as their bodies. Place a tub of tempera at one end of the tape and a tub of warm soapy water at the other (this should be done outdoors). Ask students to take off their shoes and step into the tempera. When the bottoms of their feet are completely covered with paint, ask students to walk heel-to-toe down their paper strip and into the tub of warm soapy water. (Have them be careful, since this is slippery!) Each student now has a Footprint Ruler! Now send the kids on a measurement hunt, using Record Sheet P-L3.

This is a good time to introduce the idea that everyone needs to use a "standard" unit of measure. Find a child who is 8 to10 times his own "feet" tall. Find a taller child who is fewer of his own "feet" tall. Then ask students to explain this. You can direct this discussion into the next lesson that uses inches as a standard unit of measure.

Activity P-L4: Graph Your Length

What You Need: A roll of adding machine tape (or long strips of paper), scissors, and masking tape.

How to Do It: On an empty wall in your classroom, construct a giant graph.

At this point it is appropriate to compare the feet cutouts to an inch scale on the graph. This will help children develop a sense of how nonstandard units relate to standard units. It is not necessary to make inch-to-foot conversions.

Have the students work in pairs, and give each pair a sufficient length of adding machine tape to measure their heights. As one child lies on the floor, the other places a piece of masking tape on the floor directly beneath the bottom of the heel and at the top of the head.

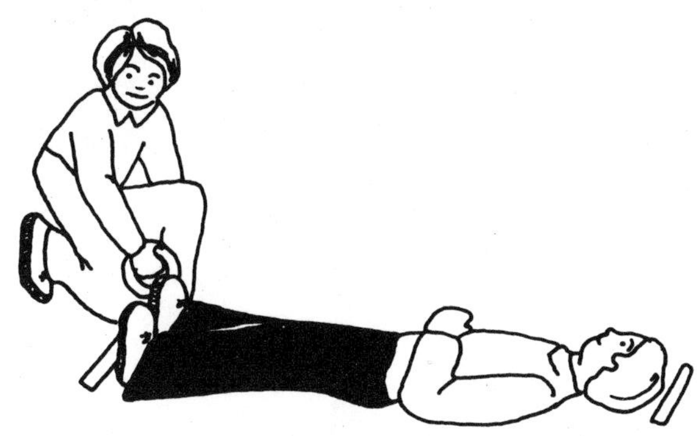

The child lying down can then get up and roll out a strip of adding machine tape, cutting it off at the appropriate length. After reversing the procedure, each child should have a piece of paper tape representing his or her height.

They can then measure their "length strips" by placing them next to the inch ruler on the graph. The students can then write their names and lengths on their strips and pin them onto the wall. (Make sure each strip starts at the floor line.) If you wish to organize the strips from shortest to longest, the children should hold their strips and order themselves by height. They can then pin the strips on the wall in order.

Teacher's Note:
This graph should be to scale 1" = 1"

FEET

GRAPH YOUR LENGTH

4
3
2

CRAIG 42 in.
MARTA 40 in.
JAMIE 36 IN.
DONNA 39 in.

EXTENDED ACTIVITIES:

Remember, most activities in this book can be easily converted from customary to metric units, or vice-versa. The following Body Bundle activity can be done with standard 12" rulers.

Body Bundle Measure and Fancy Meter Measure

Have the students use 25-centimeter rulers to measure and record various lengths in their Body Bundle (from Activity P-L2). Record the results on Record Sheet P-L4 (p. 84).

The following activity can be easily converted to a "fancy yardstick." If you wish to continue with customary units, simply cut the cardboard 36" long!

To practice measuring longer distances, have each student construct a "Fancy Meter Measure." Each student will need a piece of cardboard (15 cm x 100 cm), some heavy string, a piece of aluminum foil big enough to cover the cardboard, glue, black shoe polish, and some steel wool. Have each student make a design by gluing heavy string on the cardboard. Then cover the whole piece with aluminum foil, wrap the foil around the edges, and press it down around the string design. Cover the surface with shoe polish, let it dry, and lightly rub with steel wool.

Use the Fancy Meter Measure to find and record objects larger and smaller than a meter as well as things about a meter long. To measure longer distances, count the number of Fancy Meters required to measure the length. (A 10-meter rope could be constructed to simplify measuring long distances on the playground.)

Activity P-L5: Measurement Scavenger Hunt

What You Need: yardstick (or fancy yardstick from previous activity) and a 12" ruler.

How to Do It: Tell the students they are going on a Measurement Scavenger Hunt. The objects to be found are in the classroom and can be identified by their length. Prior to the beginning of this activity, find objects of appropriate lengths in your room. Make a secret list to compare with the students later. The children will then look for objects of each length, providing practice estimating as well as measuring with inches, feet, and yards. You might try an outdoor "hunt" for longer lengths. Younger children may experience difficulty estimating; let them check their measures with their measurement tools.

LENGTH ACTIVITY SEQUENCE 2

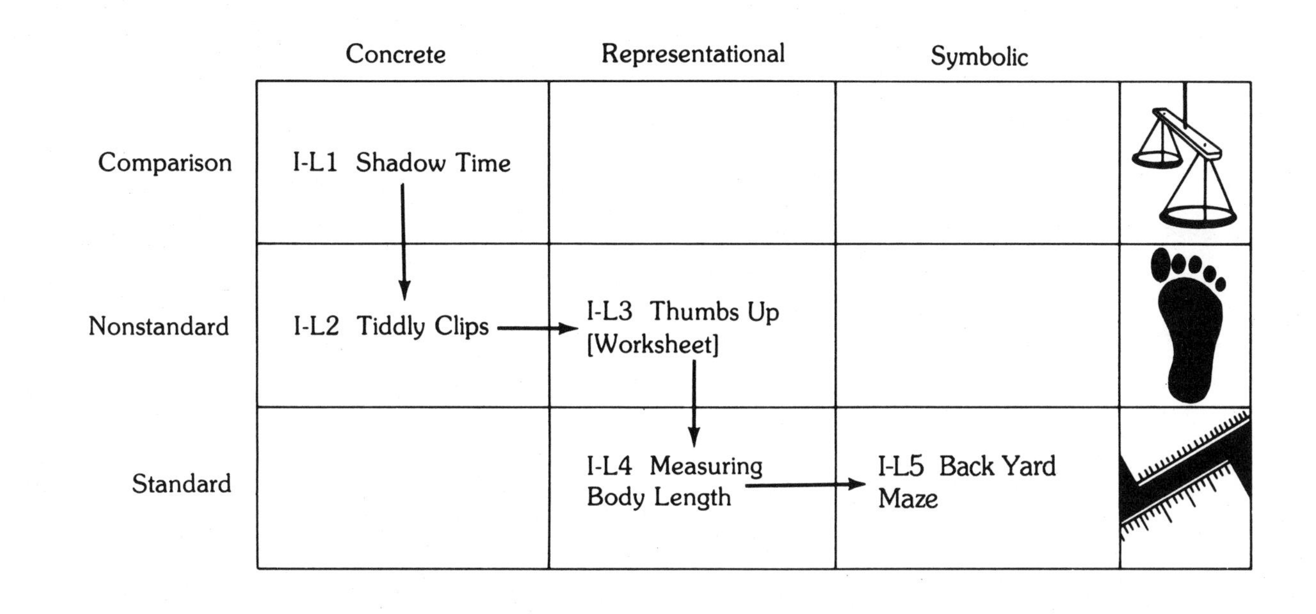

	Concrete	Representational	Symbolic
Comparison	I-L1 Shadow Time		
Nonstandard	I-L2 Tiddly Clips	I-L3 Thumbs Up [Worksheet]	
Standard		I-L4 Measuring Body Length	I-L5 Back Yard Maze

WARM-UP ACTIVITY

What You Need: Mealworm, construction paper, pencil, and string.

How to Do It: Place a mealworm on a piece of construction paper and trace its trail with a pencil. You may need to "warm up" your mealworm by holding it in your hand. This makes it crawl faster.

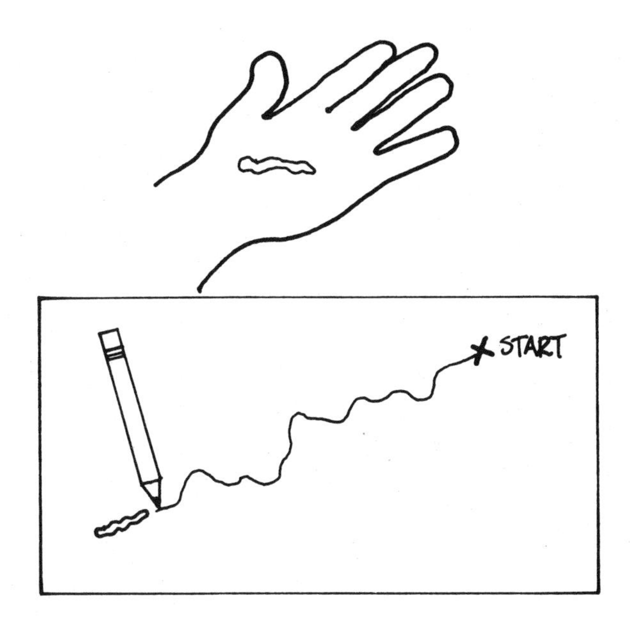

Have the student cut a piece of string the length of the worm trail. (Place the string along the traced pencil track and cut the appropriate length.) Ask if the piece of string is equal to the distance the worm has traveled. After the student answers *yes*, ask for justification. Now, stretch out the string next to the original trail.

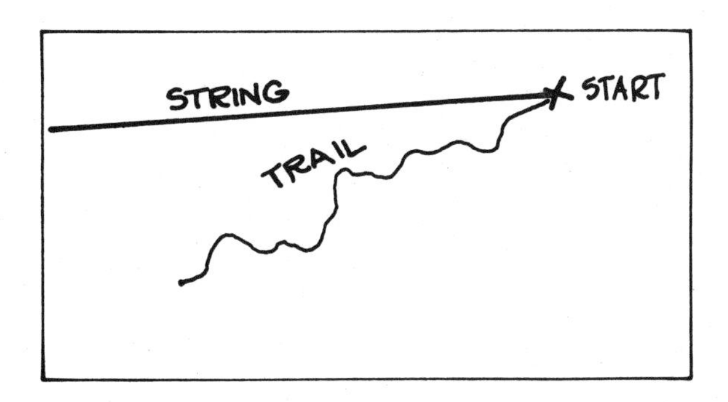

Ask if the worm would have to travel further on the trail or on the string, or would both journeys be the same distance? Again, ask for justification.

TEACHING IMPLICATIONS

A child who does not correctly answer this question probably does not understand that the length of an object remains constant even though its shape or position may change. Because, in the second situation, the string appears to be longer, this student is unable to reverse the transformation of the worm's path and allows perception to become the basis for reasoning.

These students should be encouraged to focus on the comparison and nonstandard unit activities in this measurement sequence. These experiences will provide a concrete basis for understanding that length of an object does not change when it is moved.

DEVELOPMENTAL ACTIVITY SEQUENCE

Activity I-L1: Shadow Time

What You Need: Sun, blacktop or sidewalk, and chalk.

How to Do It: Have students work in groups of four to five and go outside on a sunny day supplied with chalk. Let them experiment with their shadows. Can they make funny scenes by tracing around their shadows on the ground?

After allowing for a period of exploration, stimulate thought by asking questions such as the following: "Is your shadow the same length as you are?" "Can you make it longer or shorter?" "If you have a friend who is taller than you, will his shadow be longer?" "How can we find out?" Have students compare their shadow lengths and make a class "lineup" from shortest to tallest, outlining them in chalk.

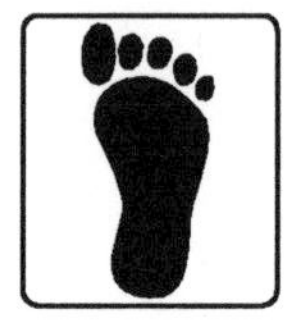

Activity I-L2: Tiddly Clips

What You Need: Paper clips and Record Sheet I-L2 (p. 102).

How to Do It: A student is not satisfied with knowing only that his or her big sister is taller; they want to know how much taller she is or how much longer her hair is, etc. This curiosity develops into the need for a unit concept. A unit is something of a given size used to measure a specific attribute of another object. It could be almost anything—a pencil, a piece of chalk, shoes, a ruler, a smile—you name it! In this activity we are going to use paper clips to measure length (the large ones work best). To accustom your students to the idea of using paper clips as a unit, have them measure all their books, finding each dimension in "paper clip lengths."

A fun way to practice this technique is to play "Tiddly Clips." Each student gets to tiddly-a-clip to see how far it goes (just like tiddlywinks). Use both a large and small clip, as shown below.

This distance is then measured in clip lengths and recorded on the graph.

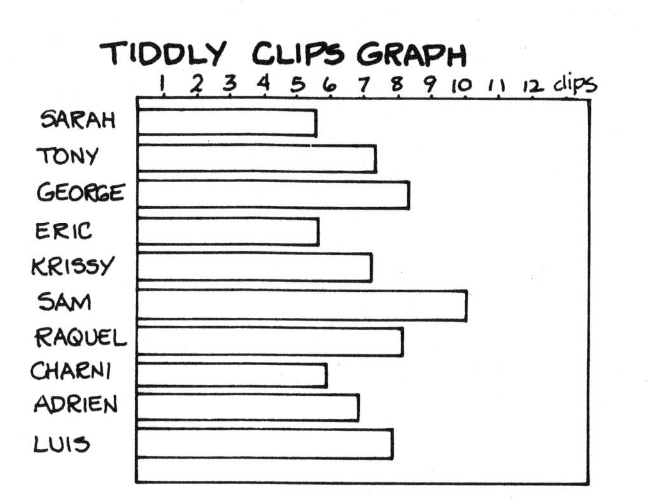

Save this graph so that when you introduce standard units you can have your students measure their records.

EXTENDED ACTIVITY:

Pace-On Paper clips and other small units become very cumbersome when measuring long distances. A convenient unit for measuring length is the "pace," or the distance of a normal footstep. This could be used for measuring longer distances. Make a chart like the one below (based on Record Sheet I-L2A, p. 103) for your classroom wall and have children pace off some lengths. Remember, ask them to estimate first!

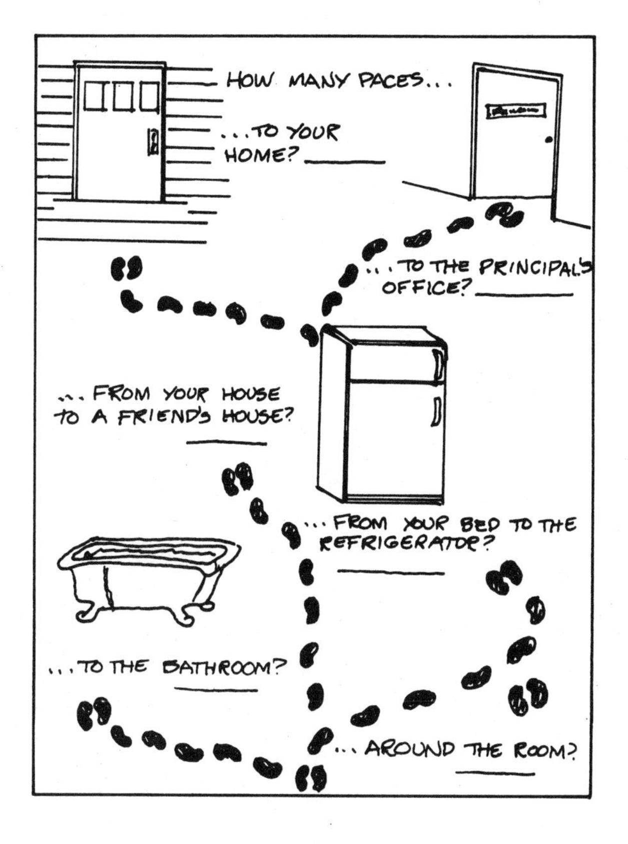

EXTENDED ACTIVITY:

Mealworm Mania You will need mealworms, a racetrack (use a sheet of 8 1/2 x 11 construction paper), string, glue, and Record Sheet I-L2B, p. 104. Working in pairs, have students select a mealworm and place it on the racetrack (a piece of construction paper).

As one student looks at a watch, his or her partner traces the worm's path with a pencil. At the end of one minute, the worm is removed from the "racetrack" and the distance the worm has traveled is measured by laying out the string along the path and cutting it to an appropriate length. Several strings, representing the distances traveled by the various worms, can then be glued onto a graph and compared.

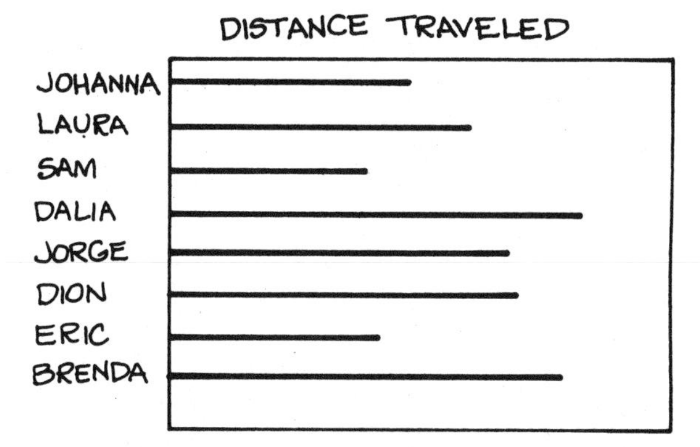

Save this graph so that when you introduce standard units you can have your students measure their records.

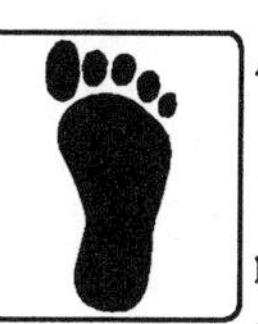

Activity I-L3: Thumbs Up!

What You Need: Tempera, adding machine tape, scissors, objects to measure, and Record Sheet I-L3 (p. 105).

How to Do It: After extensive experience utilizing actual concrete nonstandard units, students should be ready to make more abstract rulers. Pass out pieces of paper tape about one meter long. Instruct students to dip their thumbs in tempera and make successive thumbprints side by side down their lengths of paper tape.

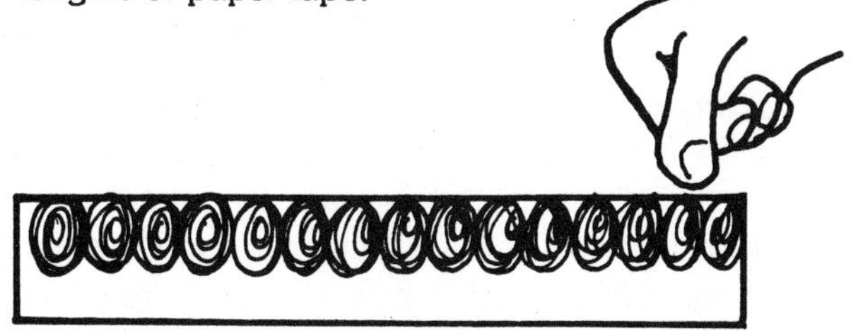

This ruler can then be used to complete Worksheet I-L3.

Activity I-L4: Measuring Body Length

What You Need: Strips of poster board or wood about 2 inches wide and longer than a yard, several yardsticks marked off in inches, fine-point felt pens, roll of adding machine tape, scissors (or saws), and masking tape.

How to Do It: First, have the students construct their own personal yardsticks. Have them measure their poster board (or wood) strips to a length of one yard and cut them off at that point. Using a commercially made yardstick as a standard, have them mark off inch units with each 12th line (foot) a bit longer to assist with counting. Numbering each mark will ease the process of measuring inch lengths.

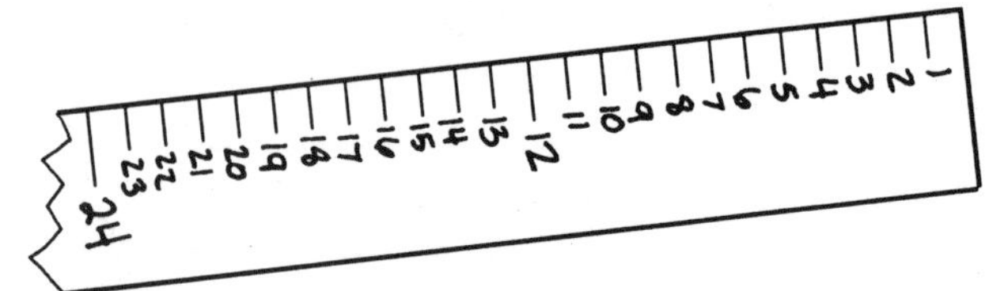

Next, have the students pair off. Have one lie on the floor while the other places a piece of masking tape on the floor at the base of his or her heel and the top of his or head. A piece of adding machine tape should be cut to the appropriate body length by measuring the distance between the two pieces of tape. After changing places, each child should have a paper strip which represents his or her height.

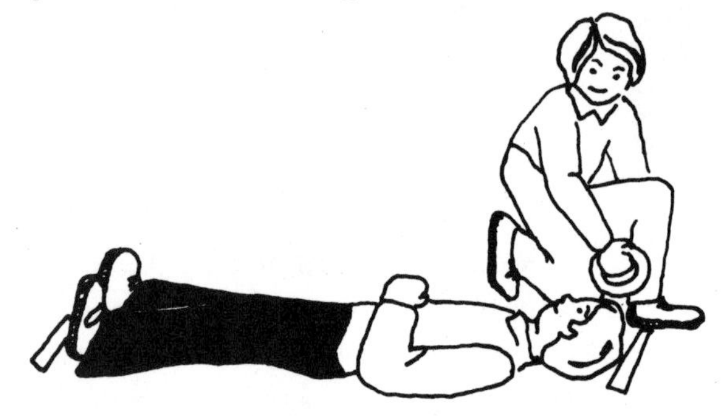

Finally, have the students measure their body-length tapes in feet and inches, put their names on them, and pin them on the wall to make a graph. Try having the students order their lengths from shortest to longest to make it easier to read the graph. Interesting questions to ask include: "Who is the tallest person in the class?" "Who is the shortest?" "Who is in the middle?" "What is the greatest difference in heights?" If you were going to pick one person to represent the height of the whole class, who would be the most appropriate [the median]?

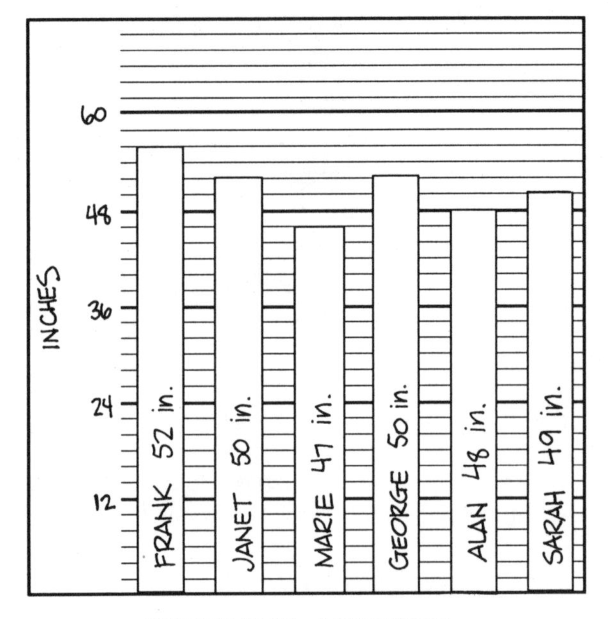

EXTENDED ACTIVITY:

Remember, any of these activities can be done using customary or metric units. The following activity uses metric units but can be easily adapted by using a standard 12" ruler with smaller units markings of 1/4" or 1/16".

Treasure Map For practice measuring with centimeters and millimeters, give each student a Treasure Map, some string, and a 25-centimeter ruler with millimeter markings. By laying string along each route from the landing to the treasure and measuring each accurately, the shortest trail can be determined.

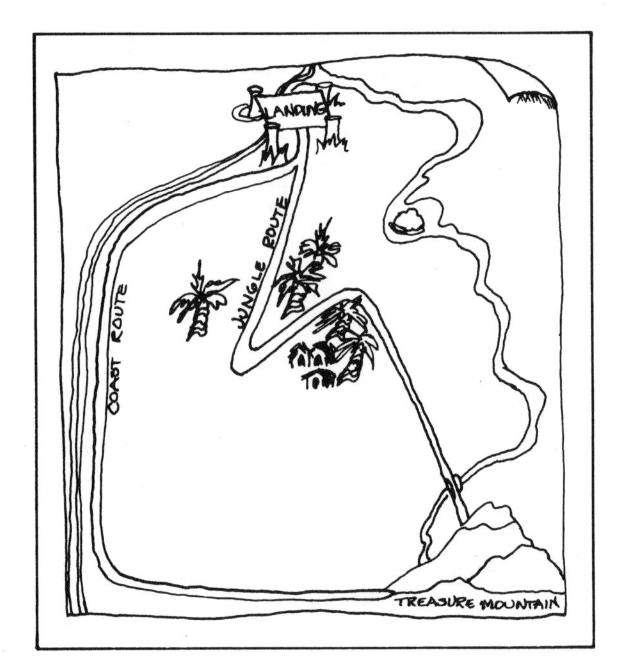

Similar measurement activities can be constructed on a larger scale outdoors on the playground. Divide the class into pairs and give a written set of directions beginning at the classroom door to some destination point (such as the flagpole on the principal's desk). Have each pair estimate the distance and then accurately measure the path. Encourage the use of various measurement techniques—such as laying a string path and measuring the resulting length, using a trundle wheel (see Section III), measuring with a knotted 10-meter rope or meter ruler. You might try developing more than one path or see who can devise the shortest route.

Activity I-L5: The Back Yard Maze

What You Need: Yardstick, paper, and pencil.

How to Do It: On a piece of paper, have each student attempt to draw a Maze similar to the one below. It must consist of a single continuous line the length of which should be as close to 1 yard as students can estimate.

Have the children start in the middle of the page and without measuring, spiral outward, stopping when they think they have traveled one yard. Then, laying string along the path, have them measure the length and record the actual measure on the maze. Have each child repeat this process three times and observe if his or her estimation skills improve.

Some children may wish to attempt to draw a single-line yard sketch, forming a single line approximately one yard long.

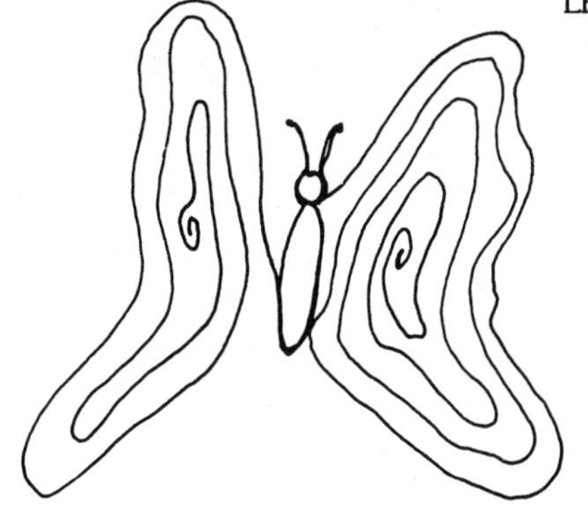

This activity helps children develop estimating skills.

EXTENDED ACTIVITY:

Metric Scavenger Hunt: Find a set of mystery objects in the classroom that corresponds to the lengths given on Record Sheet I-L5 (p. 107). This will be your Mystery Length List. Then tell your class they are going on a Metric Scavenger Hunt. Each student should try to find an object in the classroom for each length indicated on the record sheet. Students should use their rulers to measure various objects. Then they can record the findings and discuss the results with the class. Several objects will inevitably be found for each indicated length, and equivalent lengths should be explored.

This activity can also be done very effectively with customary units.

CHAPTER 2

Mass

OVERVIEW

The mass of an object refers to the amount of force required to move it. *Mass* and *weight* refer to similar properties of an object and can commonly be used interchangeably. Under water or in outer space, however, the weight of an object changes while its mass remains constant. We use the term *mass* when referring to the heft of an object. As long as your classroom is not on the moon or flooded, *weight* will work just as well.

Five activities are provided for both the primary grade levels and the intermediate grade levels. The mass activity sequence charts show the sequence of activities based on the instruction model presented in the Introduction. Begin with Activity 1 and proceed through the sequence allowing sufficient time at each level to insure understanding. Remember, all children may not proceed at the same rate and some may not reach the final stage of abstraction in the time available.

MASS ACTIVITY SEQUENCE 1

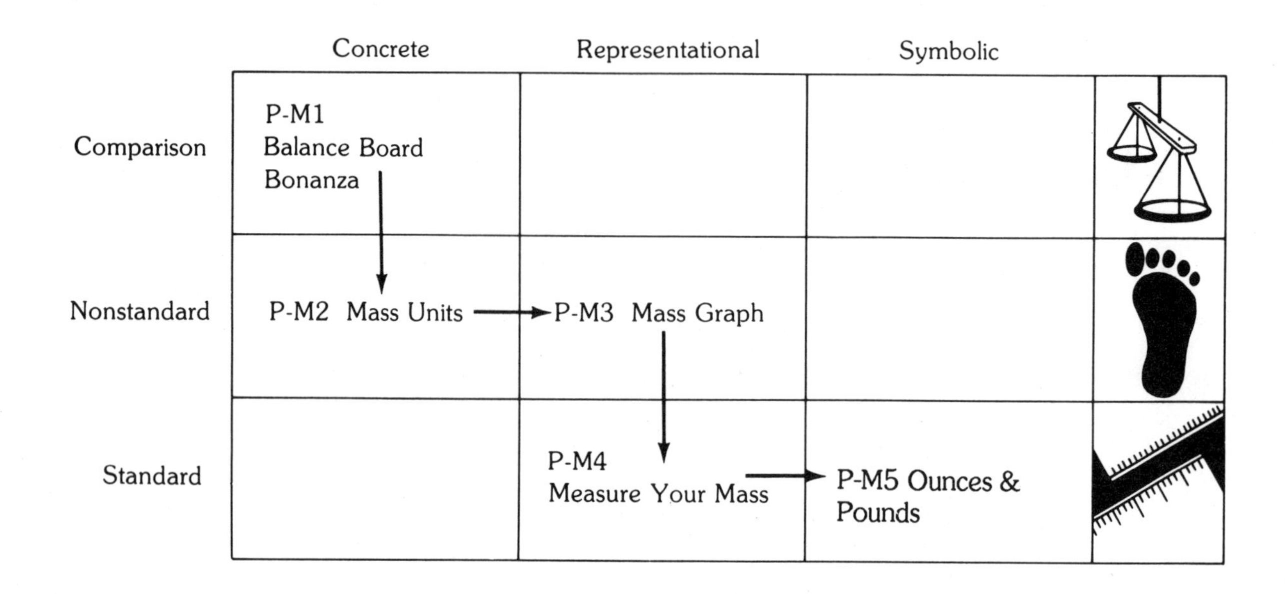

WARM-UP ACTIVITY

What You Need: Clay and a balance.

How to Do It: Give the students a piece of clay and tell them to break it into two equal pieces. After the children have carefully adjusted both pieces (using the balance), ask if both pieces weigh the same. Have each child continue the process until satisfied that both have the same mass. Now have them roll one piece into a ball and the other into a long snake.

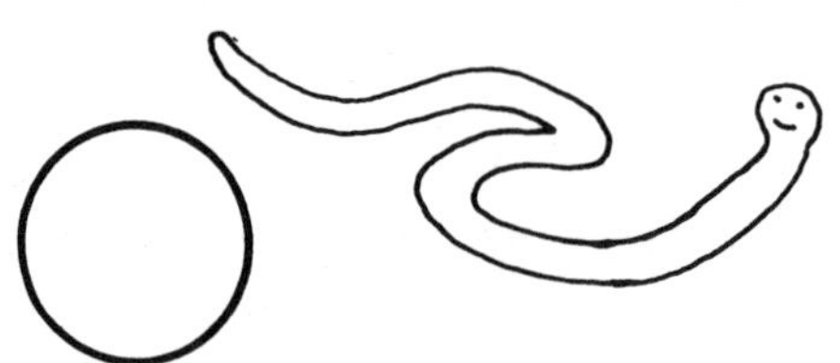

Ask if the two pieces still weigh the same or if one is heavier than the other. Have several children justify their answers. Have them roll the pieces back into similar balls and ask if they are now the same weight. Again, ask for justification.

TEACHING IMPLICATIONS

A child who is unable to answer this question correctly probably does not understand that the mass of an object remains constant even though its shape may change. Since the ball appears to be larger, the child's perception becomes the basis for his or her reasoning. When the snake is rolled back into a ball, the two objects are "magically" the same mass again. Due to lack of experience and ability to reason logically, this contradiction goes unnoticed by the child. These children should be encouraged to focus on the comparison and nonstandard unit activities. These experiences will provide a concrete basis upon which an understanding of mass may be built.

DEVELOPMENTAL ACTIVITY SEQUENCE

Activity P-M1: Balance Board Bonanza

What You Need: Large balance boards (see Section III for construction plans), double pan balance, objects to compare, and Activity Sheet P-M1 (p. 86).

How to Do It: In order to provide students with a variety of comparison experiences, pose a sequence of problems similar to this: "Do you know anyone who weighs the same as you do?" "Do you know anyone who weighs more?" "Less?" Encourage students to talk about their ideas. It is important that everyone become comfortable with a specific vocabulary: mass (or weight), heavier, lighter, balanced, not balanced, etc. These concepts should become clear to the students in the following activity. Have a balance board set up in the classroom and ask the students how they could find someone lighter, someone heavier, and someone the same weight as themselves. When they suggest using the balance board, let them experiment with it until they become comfortable with the vocabulary discussed earlier. Now, ask them to actually find the students who are lighter, heavier, and at least one who is the same weight as themselves. The person they find who has the same mass will be their "partner" for the rest of the mass activities.

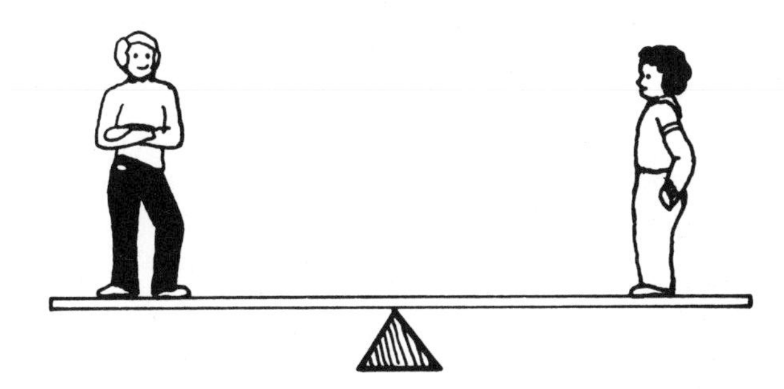

NOTE: Teachers should be sensitive to any children in their classroom who have a weight problem. Two classes might work together to ensure pairing by all students. This could also be made into a cross-curricular activity by using this process as an "opener" 'or a values-clarification lesson. Students' attitudes and feelings about physical attributes (and prejudices surrounding them) can be explored and discussed.

After students have found a partner, ask them to join with one or two other pairs of students. Ask, "Who is the heaviest?" "Who is the lightest?" Have them order themselves by mass—lightest partners to heaviest partners. To introduce the concept of transitivity, ask children "If you are heavier than Jason, will your partner be heavier or lighter than Jason?" Because partners have the same mass (or are very close), children soon realize that if they are heavier or lighter than someone else, their partner will be also.

EXTENDED ACTIVITY:

Mysterious Mass Once children are comfortable comparing their own "masses," they should begin to compare other objects by weight. Small balances can be used for comparing shoes, lunches, books, blocks, guinea pigs, Cuisenaire rods, etc. The results can then be recorded on Record Sheet P-M1A, (p. 87). Objects of varying densities can eventually be used to separate the notions of size and mass. For example, a large styrofoam shape and a small lead ball could be compared:

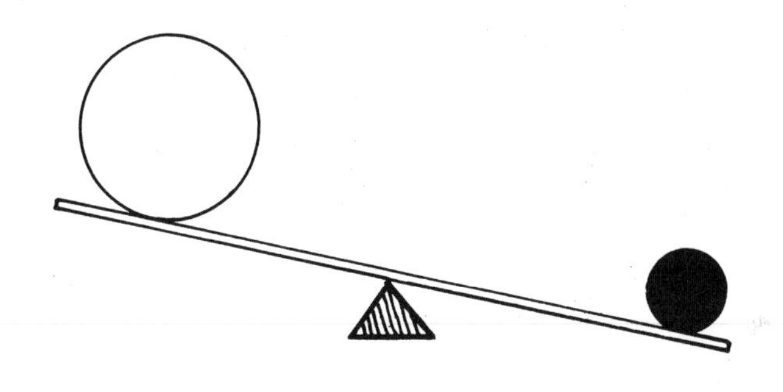

Just for fun, ask students to explain the above drawing. Similar activities using Object Pictures P-Ml and Record Sheet P-M1B (p. 88) might be appropriate.

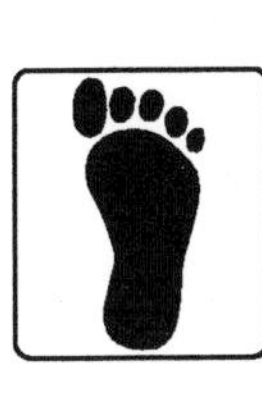

Activity P-M2: Mass Units

What You Need: Small balances, large washers, objects to weigh, and Record Sheets P-M2A and P-M2B (pp. 90 and 91).

How to Do It: Discuss what a nonstandard unit could be and ask what set of objects students can find in their classroom that could serve as nonstandard units of mass. With a balance in front of the group, ask someone to find the mass of a dictionary using one of the nonstandard units they have suggested (for example, math books, journals, pencils, chalk, scissors, etc.). Students can then break up into pairs, choose a nonstandard unit, and find the mass of five to ten specified objects. For very young children, the number of objects should remain small. Give students Record Sheet P-M2A (p. 90) to keep track of their measurements.

Group I

OBJECTS	ESTIMATE IN SCISSORS	MASS MEASURE IN SCISSORS
Dictionary	30	20
Math Book	10	15
Globe		
Chair		
Your Shoes		

Group II

OBJECTS	ESTIMATE IN READERS	MASS MEASURE IN READERS
Dictionary	1	2
Math Book	1	1
Globe		
Chair		
Your Shoes		

Groups should compare their answers. How will one group understand another's "record" if they have used a different nonstandard unit? Ask students how they could solve this problem. Suggest adopting a class standard, and in that way everyone will be able to communicate their measurements to each other. A good unit to use is a common household washer:

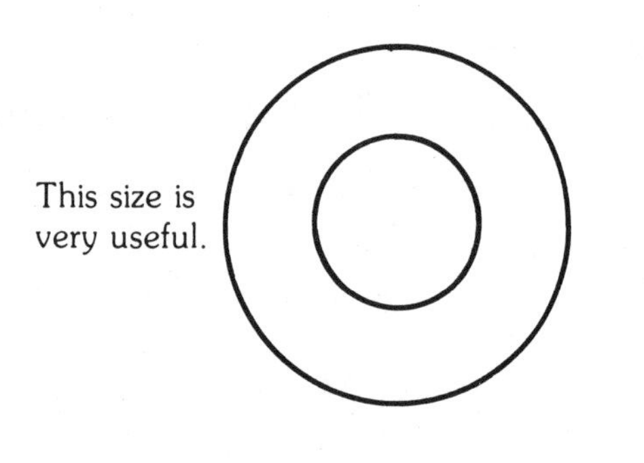
This size is very useful.

Household washers are inexpensive and make great nonstandard units for measuring mass. Other possibilities include marbles or paper clips. Start asking children to guess how many "washers heavy" certain objects are. Give students Record Sheet P-M2B and ask them to measure the mass of the objects of their choice. Be sure to have students estimate first, record their guess, and then measure. To insure estimation, you might have students pick the objects, then estimate their masses before you give them any balances. They should have access to washers, however, so that their guesses will be "educated" ones. Have groups compare their measurements. This time communication is easier because everyone is using the same *unit of measure.*

OBJECTS	NUMBER OF WASHERS TO BALANCE OBJECT	
	ESTIMATE	MEASURE
1. Shoe	10 washers	25 washers
2. Pencil	5 washers	1 washer
3.		
4.		
5.		

NOTE: This becomes a good argument for moving into the metric system!

EXTENDED ACTIVITY:

Washer Mania: Have each student estimate his or her own mass in washers, and then devise some way to actually measure it. One way students might solve this problem is to find out how many washers are in one larger unit (e.g., a dictionary, a pound, etc.) and then to do the appropriate multiplication once they determine how many of the larger units it takes to balance their own weight.

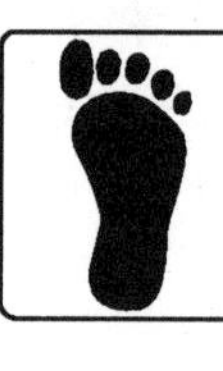

Activity P-M3: Mass Graph

What You Need: Records from Activity P-M2, 2-cm graph paper cut into strips, glue, and Record Sheet (p. 92)

How to Do It: Have the students make a graph from the information that they compiled in Activity P-M2. For each object ask your students to color in one square on a strip of graph paper for each washer heavy they measured it to be. For example:

OBJECT	ESTIMATE	MEASURE
Math Book	15	13

OR (WASHERS)

After students have completed all five strips, ask them to arrange the strips from lightest to heaviest (i.e. shortest to longest), and glue them on a Record Sheet P-M3 in that order, as shown here.

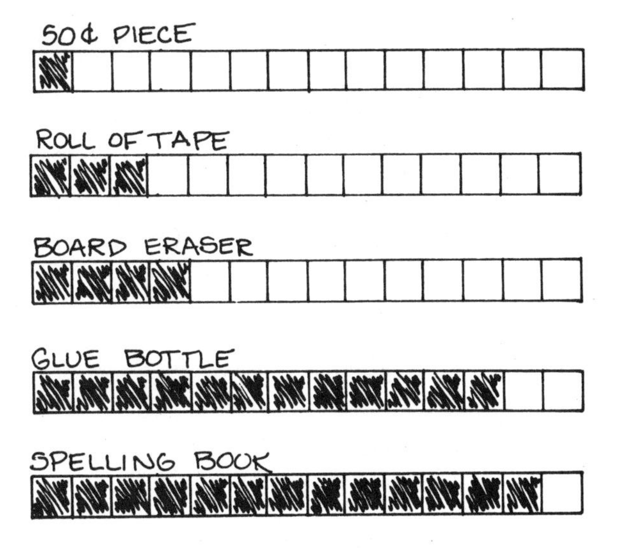

EXTENDED ACTIVITY:

Washer Cooking *What You Need:* Pan balance, large and small washers, paper clips, appropriate ingredients.

How to Do It: As children become familiar with the concept of using some sort of *units* for measurement, they are able to deal with their world more effectively. The benefit of this concept can be made real to children through this activity. Have students follow these recipes using only nonstandard units.

PEANUT BUTTER

No cooking: use grinder or blender
43 large washers of peanuts in the shell
2 large washers of salad oil
Crackers

Directions

Shell nuts and put through grinder or blender. Add oil until spreadable. Spread mixture on crackers.

Activity P-M4: Measure Your Mass

What You Need: Bathroom scale marked in pounds, construction paper strips, scissors, glue, and Record Sheet P-M4 (p. 93).

How to Do It: Have each child find his or her mass in pounds on the bathroom scale. Have them cut strips of paper the proper length by measuring along the vertical axis (on the graph) and pin their strip on the graph.

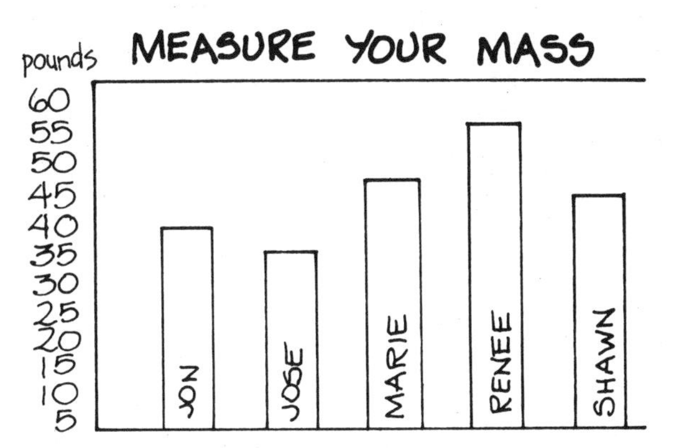

The strips should then be ordered according to length. Children can now easily compare their masses. They can also determine how much more they weigh than someone else by overlapping their two strips and measuring the part that sticks out (using the vertical scale).

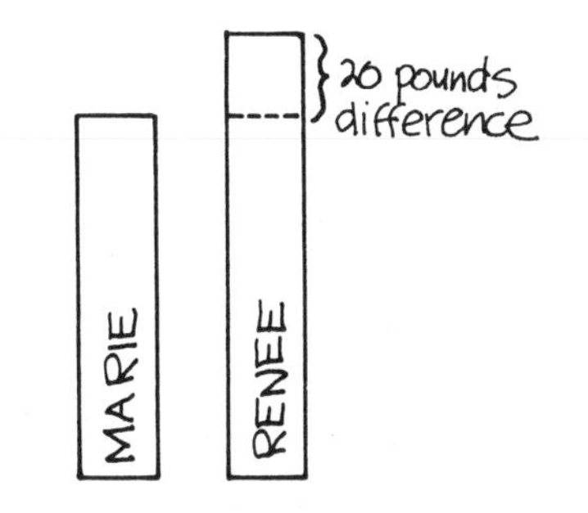

Activity P-M5: Ounces and Pounds

What You Need: Several 1 oz and 1 lb mass pieces, pan balance (see Appendix II), objects to weigh, and Record Sheet P-M5 (p. 94).

How to Do It: Using a pan balance, have each child weigh several small common objects, counting the ounces and recording the results. Have students estimate first!

OBJECT	OUNCE ESTIMATE	OUNCE MEASURE
chalk	14 oz.	10 oz.
board eraser	30 oz.	38 oz.

Heavier objects weighing several pounds each should then be introduced. Each object should be carefully chosen so that it may be balanced evenly with one or more whole pound mass pieces. (Measuring objects that require mixed unit representation [e.g., 2 pounds, 5 oz] should be introduced at a later time):

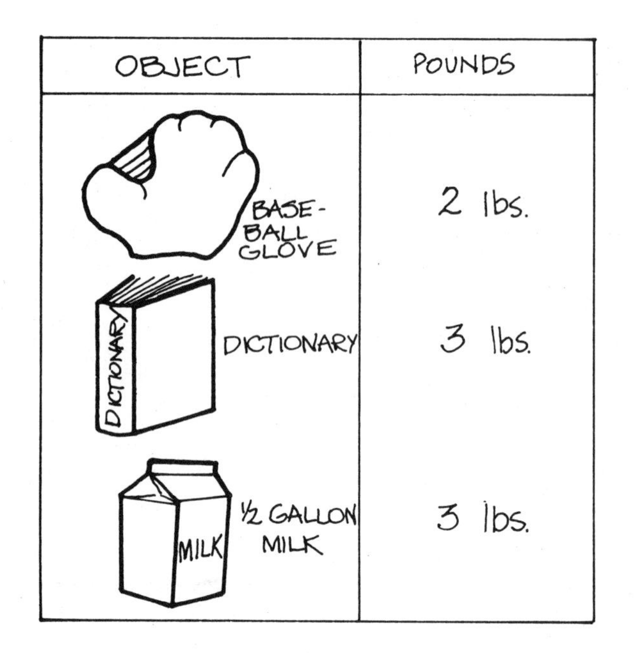

OBJECT	POUNDS
BASE-BALL GLOVE	2 lbs.
DICTIONARY	3 lbs.
½ GALLON MILK	3 lbs.

NOTE: As with nonstandard units, any measurements made with standard units are only approximate in nature. Therefore, any measurement made should be to the nearest whole unit. With older children, more accurate measures may be made by utilizing both pounds and ounces.

EXTENDED ACTIVITY:

NOTE: We have included the following activity to help you familiarize your students with metric units. Remember you may easily change this activity to customary units by using ounces instead of grams and pounds instead of kilograms.

Mystery Mass List Prepare a Mystery Mass List by weighing several objects throughout the classroom and recording the mass of each. The list should be put away for later use. Give the children only a list of the masses as shown and have them try to find the matching mystery objects.

Children should be encouraged to estimate the masses of various objects and validate their guesses on a scale. Choose objects that differ significantly in mass to make the task easier. If children are unable to write the name of an object, have them make a sketch.

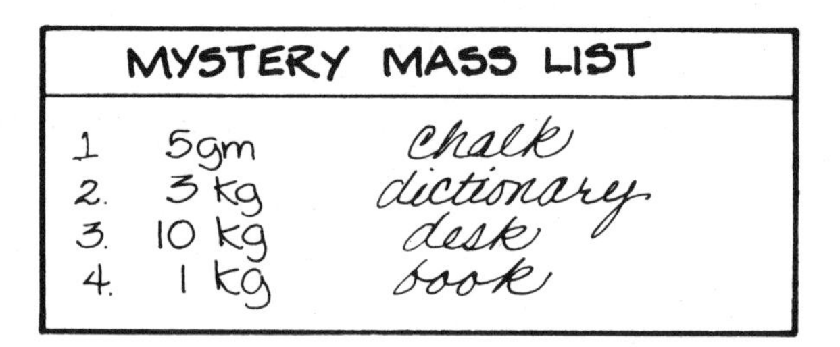

MYSTERY MASS LIST

1	5gm	chalk
2.	3 kg	dictionary
3.	10 kg	desk
4.	1 kg	book

MASS ACTIVITY SEQUENCE 2

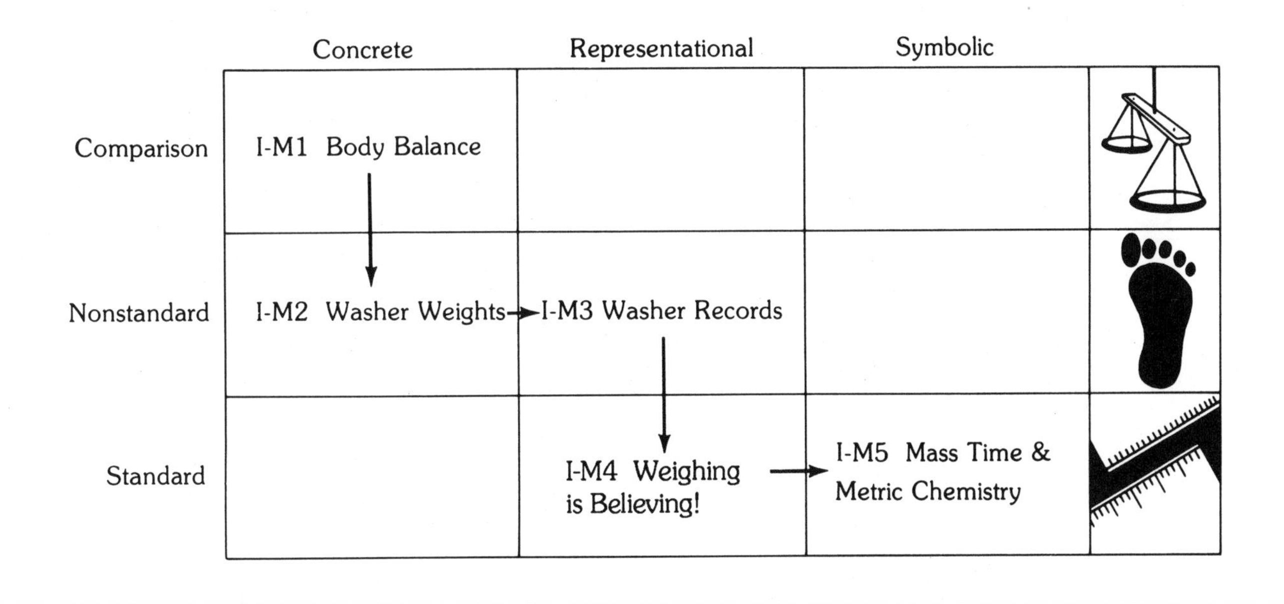

WARM-UP ACTIVITY

What You Need: Heavy aluminum foil, scissors, and a container of water.

How to Do It: Give each student a piece of heavy aluminum foil. Have them fold it in half and cut out identical rectangles.

Ask if both pieces weigh the same. Have them trim the pieces until they are satisfied that they have the same mass. Have them roll one piece up into a very tight ball, taking care to remove all air pockets, and fold the other piece into a boat that will float. Drop the ball into the water (if they followed instructions, it should sink) and put the boat on the surface (it should float). Remove both from the water and ask if the two pieces of foil still have the same mass. If a student responds that one piece is now heavier, ask why. Have the student remove both pieces of foil, unfolding and smoothing them into the original rectangles and ask if they have the same mass. Again, ask for justification.

TEACHING IMPLICATIONS

A child who is unable to answer this question correctly probably does not understand that the mass of an object remains the same even when it changes shape. Instead, the student relies on perceptual cues (i.e., if the ball sinks it must be heavier) rather than logically reversing the folding process and realizing that the mass must remain constant because nothing was added or subtracted by transforming the shape. These students should be encouraged to focus on the comparison and nonstandard unit activities. These experiences will provide a concrete basis upon which an understanding of mass can be built.

DEVELOPMENTAL ACTIVITY SEQUENCE

Activity I-M1: Body Balance

What You Need: Large and small balances and objects to compare (see Section III for construction plans), and Activity Sheet I-M1 (p. 108).

How to Do It: Set up large balance boards in the room. Ask students to find someone lighter and someone heavier than they are, proving it on a balance board. The children should divide up into pairs with each child having the same mass as his or her partner.

NOTE: Teachers should be sensitive to any children in their classroom who have a weight problem. Two classes might work together to insure pairing by all students. This could also be made into a cross-curricular activity by using this process as an "opener" for a values-clarification lesson. Students' attitudes and feelings about physical attributes (and prejudices surrounding them) can be explored and discussed.

In doing the above tasks, students have "measured" their own masses by comparison alone. To give children more experience with comparing objects, provide small balances and many sets of smaller objects to order by mass. These can be containers filled with approximately the same amount of sand, varied enough to be distinguishable on a balance. The students must do a series of physical comparisons in order to complete this task.

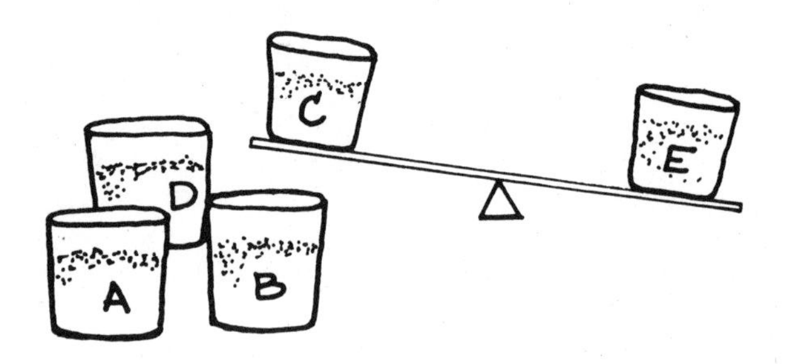

When students have finished, ask them: "What is the least number of weighings (comparisons) necessary to order five boxes?" (This is assuming that you have no lucky guesses!)

A similar problem involves six mystery-mass boxes: five of these boxes have the same mass, while the sixth is slightly heavier. What is the minimum number of weighings it would take to find the heavier box? Try it yourself; the answer is less than three!

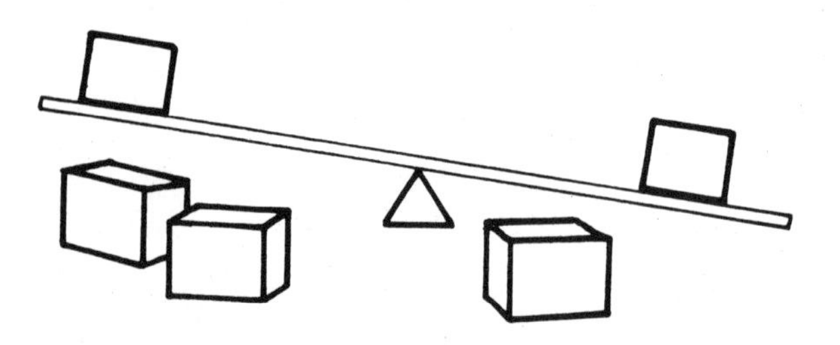

EXTENDED ACTIVITY:

Fulcrum Move When the children are comfortable with balancing and ordering two or more objects, ask them what happens when someone moves the fulcrum on the balance, or what happens when the position of the object is moved.

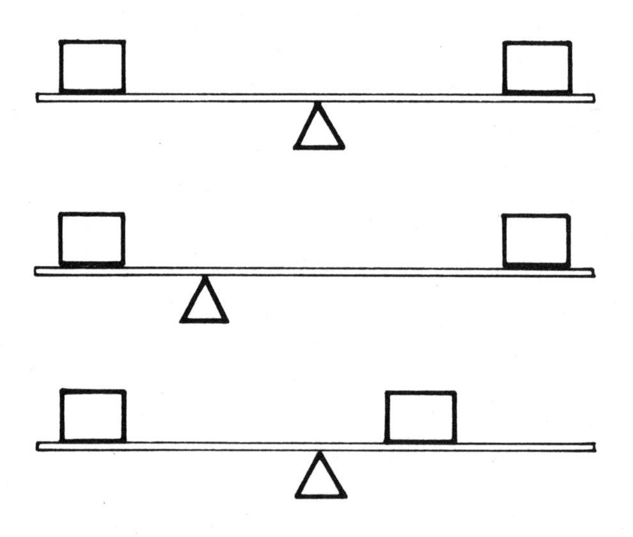

Pose this problem: Show how every student can "balance" the teacher on the large balance board. Have students draw the solution to this problem.

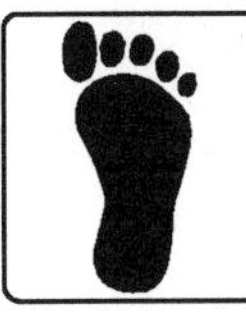

Activity I-M2: Washer Weights

What You Need: Small balance boards, multiple sets of objects to use as nonstandard units, e.g., scissors, readers, pencils, large and small washers, paper clips, and Record Sheet I-M2, (p. 109).

How to Do It: Talk about what a nonstandard unit is and ask students what they could find in their classroom to use as units of mass. Using a balance, ask someone to find the mass of a dictionary, utilizing one of the nonstandard units they have suggested (i.e., math books, spellers, pencils, chalk, etc.).

Students can then break up into pairs of partners (groups of four), choose a nonstandard unit, and find the mass of five to ten specified objects. Give students record sheets to keep track of their measurements. For example:

OBJECTS	ESTIMATE IN SCISSORS	MASS MEASURE IN SCISSORS
Dictionary	30	20
Math Book	20	15
Globe		
Chair		
Your Shoes		

OBJECTS	ESTIMATE IN READERS	MASS MEASURE IN READERS
Dictionary	3	2
Math Book	2	1
Globe		
Chair		
Your Shoes		

Groups should compare their answers. How will one group understand another's "record" if the groups have used different nonstandard units?

Ask students how they could solve this problem. Suggest adopting a class standard, since in that way everyone will be able to communicate their measurements to one another. A good unit to use is a common household washer:

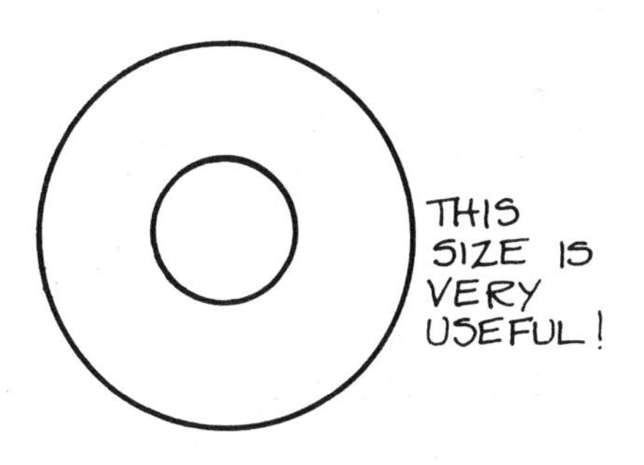

These are inexpensive, and the large ones make great nonstandard units for measuring mass (other possibilities are marbles, paper clips, etc.). Start asking children how many "washers heavy" certain objects are.

Give students recording sheets and ask them to measure the mass of ten objects of their choice. Be sure to have the students estimate first! (To insure estimation, you might have the students pick ten objects, then estimate their masses before you give them any balances. They should have access to washers, however, so that their guesses will be "educated" ones.) Then instruct students to record their estimates:

OBJECTS	NUMBER OF WASHERS HEAVY	
	ESTIMATE	MEASURE
1.		
2.		
3.		
4.		
5.		
6.		
7.		
8.		
9.		
10.		

Have groups compare their measurements. This time communication is easier because everyone is using the same unit of measure.

Students will find that not all objects will balance evenly with groups of large washers. Ask the students to discover solutions to this problem. They should suggest using a lighter nonstandard unit in conjunction with the large washers. By doing this, they can become more accurate in their mass measurements. Smaller washers make excellent lighter units and paper clips are good for even smaller and more accurate divisions.

To demonstrate this principle to your students, clarify by means of one or more concrete examples. Explain to them that if an object, say a baseball, weighs between 34 and 35 large washers, it is possible to estimate which measure it is closer to. By using smaller measurement units in combination with larger ones, they can now say, "A baseball has a mass equal to that of 34 large and two small washers.

Give students recording sheets and have them take some more measurements:

OBJECT		BASEBALL
ESTIMATE		30 WASHERS
MEASURE	LARGE WASHERS	34
	SMALL WASHERS	2

For even more accuracy:

OBJECT		BASEBALL
ESTIMATE		30 WASHERS
MEASURE	LARGE WASHERS	34
	SMALL WASHERS	1
	PAPER CLIPS	2

NOTE: Discuss this process of adding smaller nonstandard units as measurement tools. Why are they necessary? Students soon realize that *all* measurements are really only approximations, and the smaller the unit one uses, the more accurate one can be.

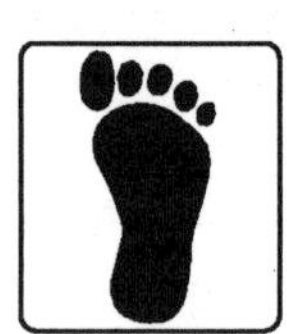

Activity I-M3: Washer Records

What You Need: Records from Activity I-M2 (p. 109), centimeter graph paper cut into strips, glue and Record Sheet I-M3 (p. 110).

How to Do It: In this activity, students will make a graph from the information that they compiled in Activity I-M2. For each object measured, ask students to color in one square on a strip of graph paper for each washer heavy they found the object to be.

For example:

OR (WASHERS)

OBJECT	ESTIMATE	MEASURE
Spelling Book	15	13 Washers

After the students have filled in all ten strips, ask them to arrange the strips from lightest (shortest) to heaviest (longest) as shown here and either glue them on Record Sheet I-M3 or fill in the appropriate number of squares on their graph.

50¢ PIECE

MAGIC MARKER

ROLL OF TAPE

ROCK

BOARD ERASER

STICK

CUP

WALLET

GLUE BOTTLE

SPELLING BOOK

After the partners have arranged their objects from lightest to heaviest, ask them questions like these: "How much heavier is your second object in line than your third?" "What is the difference in mass between your lightest and heaviest object?" "Compare your graph with another group's—who weighed the lightest object?" "The heaviest?" "Add up the masses of all your objects—whose group had the heaviest combined total?" "The lightest?" Ask students to discuss the benefits of using nonstandard units instead of a comparative method alone.

EXTENDED ACTIVITY:

Washer Cooking ***What You Need:*** Pan balance, large and small washers, paper clips, appropriate ingredients.

How to Do It: As children become familiar with the concept of using some sort of units for measurement, they are able to deal with their world more effectively. The benefit of this concept can be made real to children through this activity. Have students follow these recipes using only nonstandard units.

PEANUT BUTTER

No cooking: use grinder or blender
43 large washers of peanuts in the shell
2 large washers of salad oil
Crackers

Directions:
Shell nuts and put through grinder or blender. Add oil until spreadable. Spread mixture on crackers.

EXTENDED ACTIVITY:

Washer Cooking As children become familiar with the idea of using some sort of units for measurement, they are able to deal with their world more effectively. The benefit of this concept can be made real to children through this activity. You will need a pan balance, large and small washers, paper clips, and the ingredients listed in the recipes given below. Have students follow the recipes using only nonstandard units.

ALPHABET BREAD STICKS

Oven: set temperature at 300°F or 150°C.
45 large washers of flour
2 large washers of sugar
1 large washer of salt (or 18 paper clips)
2 pkgs. yeast
4 large washers of salad oil
30 large washers of hot water

Directions:
Stir 14 washers of flour, all sugar, all salt, and yeast together. Gradually add hot water. Beat 2 minutes with electric mixer or 300 strokes by hand. Add 7 washers of flour and beat 300 more strokes. Add the remaining flour to form a soft dough. Turn onto a floured board. With floured hands, knead into a smooth ball. Shape into a log, then divide into 20 pieces. Roll each piece into a rope. Place ropes on greased pan and roll to grease all sides. Arrange in alphabet letter shapes, leaving 3 cm of space on all sides of each-letter. Let rise 15 minutes or until puffy. Bake 25–30 minutes.

ORANGE JUICE GOODIES

15 large washers of frozen orange juice concentrate
1 box of vanilla wafers
3 large washers of grated coconut
20 large washers of powdered sugar

Directions:
Thaw orange juice concentrate but do not dilute it. Crush wafers into crumbs with rolling pin in a plastic bag. Mix crumbs, coconut, and only 10 washers of powdered sugar, and stir orange juice into mixture. Form this mixture into 3 cm balls. Roll these balls into the remaining 10 washers of powdered sugar. Voila!

PUMPKIN BREAD

2 eggs
25 large washers of brown sugar
8 large washers of oil
20 large washers of pumpkin
25 large washers of flour
3 paper clips of baking powder
6 paper clips of baking soda
13 paper clips of salt
9 paper clips of pumpkin pie spice
chopped nuts
raisins

Directions:
Grease and flour loaf pan. Beat eggs until foamy, add sugar, oil, and pumpkin. Mix well. Sift all dry ingredients together, add to pumpkin mixture, and mix until just blended. If desired, stir in nuts and raisins, pour into loaf pan and bake for 45 minutes at 350°F or 177°C.

Activity I-M4: Weighing is Believing!

What You Need: Balance scale, spring scale or 5 lb food-type scale with ounce calibrations, bathroom scale, 3 or 4 sets of a variety of objects to weigh (include objects that are visually deceiving such as large styrofoam or *Nerf* balls, lead sinkers, golf balls, etc.), two large graphs (see below) and Record Sheet I-M4.

How to Do It: In order to help students distinguish between the attributes of mass and volume, select 4 or 5 objects that do not appear to weigh as much or as little as they seem. For example, you could have students estimate the weight of a piece of styrofoam painted like a rock, a very heavy fishing sinker, or a *Nerf* -type basketball. Place one set of these objects in front of the room so that students can see but not touch them. Have the class tell you which object they think is the heaviest, and have them sequence the entire set from heaviest to lightest. After the objects have been visually ordered, select two objects that are in the incorrect order and place them on the balance scale. Ask students to try to explain the discrepancy. Next, send students into small groups to estimate and then measure the mass of a variety of objects (allow them to pick up the objects to help with their estimation). Have each student use two copies of record sheet I-M4 to record the estimated mass and weighed mass of their objects. To insure that the students estimate first, do not pass out scales until estimates are recorded. Remember—only weighing is believing!

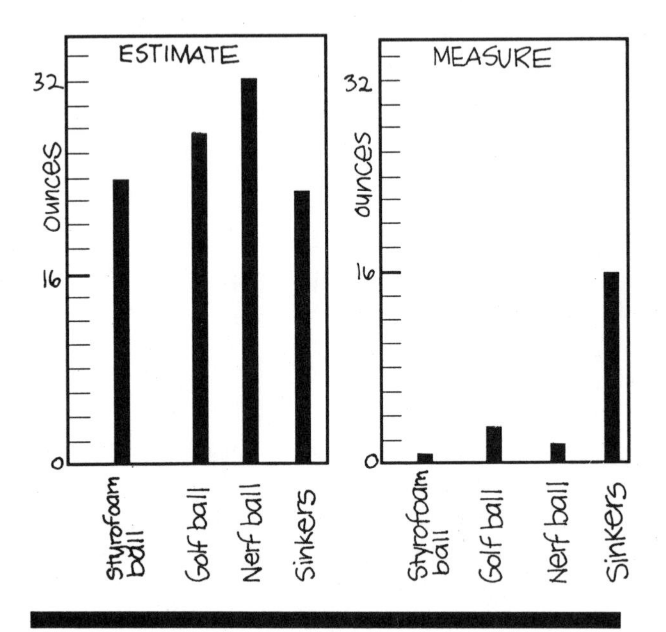

Activity I-M5: Mass Time

What You Need: Set of metric mass pieces, pan balance and objects to, weigh, and Record Sheet I-M5 (p. 112).

We included the following activity to help familiarize your students with metric units. Remember you may easily change this activity to customary units by using ounces instead of grams and pounds instead of kilograms.

How to Do It: Have each child weigh several common objects using a pan balance and metric mass pieces. The mass of each object should be recorded on a worksheet as shown. Measurements should be made using gram units when an object cannot be balanced using whole kilograms. Each mass should be recorded in mixed kilograms and gram units (when necessary). Remember, when weighing liquids, the mass of the container must be taken into account.

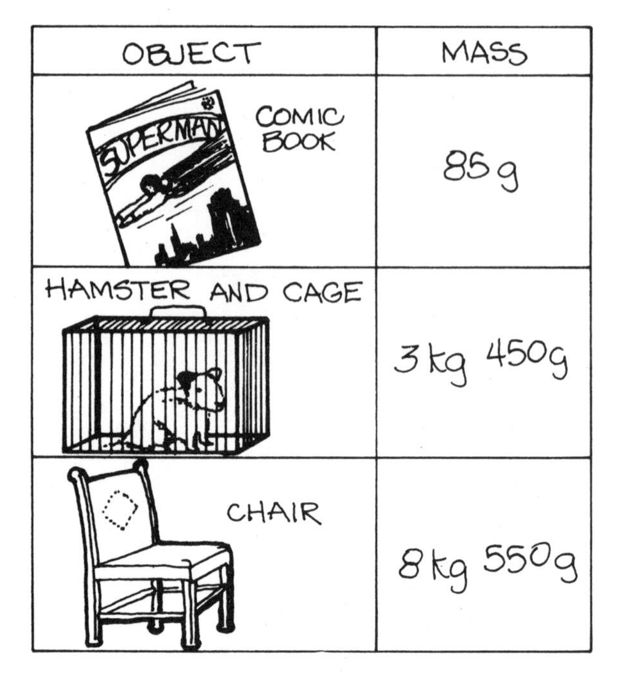

OBJECT	MASS
COMIC BOOK	85 g
HAMSTER AND CAGE	3 kg 450 g
CHAIR	8 kg 550 g

Extensive experience weighing common objects will help children become familiar with the relative mass of the kilogram and the gram units. After plenty of concrete experiences, metric units will become much easier to use than the pound and ounce most of us are familiar with.

EXTENDED ACTIVITY:

Metric Chemistry ***What You Need:*** Flour, salt, cornstarch, water, and cooking oil and food coloring.

How to Do It: Give the students the following recipes for making clay and Glick (commonly known as Silly Putty). Have them use an accurate balance with gram mass pieces when weighing the ingredients for the recipes.

NOTE: In countries that use the metric system exclusively, all ingredients, whether liquid or solid, are measured by weighing them rather than by their capacity. This process eliminates the density problem involved in cooking. For example, just how tightly do you pack down your brown sugar when measuring? By weighing ingredients one doesn't have to worry about it. The clay and Glick may subsequently be used for art activities such as modeling and science activities such as trying to make a clay boat that floats. Remember, when weighing ingredients, the mass of the container must be taken into account.

BAKERS' CLAY

960 grams of salt
150 grams of flour
30 grams of cooking oil
2 grams of food coloring
100–300 grams of water

Directions

Mix the flour and salt in a bowl Mix water, cooking oil, and food coloring, adding this mixture to the salt/flour mixture until it reaches the right consistency. The clay can be used for modeling and should dry without many cracks. For larger amounts of clay, have the students double or triple the recipe.

GLICK

80 grams of cornstarch
60 grams of water

Directions

Put the cornstarch in a bowl, carefully mix in a little water at a time until the whole mess can be picked up and kneaded with your hands. The proper consistency should allow you to hold a ball of putty in your hands as long as you keep moving them. As soon as you stop moving the ball, it will run through your fingers like a liquid. If you pull it quickly, it will break into two pieces very neatly. If the putty is too runny, sprinkle on a little cornstarch and knead it into the ball. If it gets too dry, wet your fingers and rub the surface of the ball. Clean up is a snap! A moist cloth quickly cleans up hands, clothes, and spills. HAVE FUN!

Area

OVERVIEW

Area, as a measurement attribute, describes the amount of surface an object or region occupies. Traditionally, area is defined using rectangular regions. The concept of area is better developed when irregular regions are measured using thumb prints or centimeter graph paper. Area is therefore the number of units required to cover the surface of an object or region. Through this process, not only does the notion of area take on meaning, but also the approximate nature of measurement is more clearly demonstrated. No measure is exact. If more accuracy is desired, one must use a more accurate instrument.

Five activities are provided for both the primary grade levels and the intermediate grade levels. The area activity sequence charts show the sequence of activities based on the instructional model presented in the Introduction. Begin with Activity 1 and proceed through the sequence, allowing sufficient time at each level to insure understanding. Remember, all children may not progress at the same rate and some may not reach the final stage of abstraction in the time available.

AREA ACTIVITY SEQUENCE 1

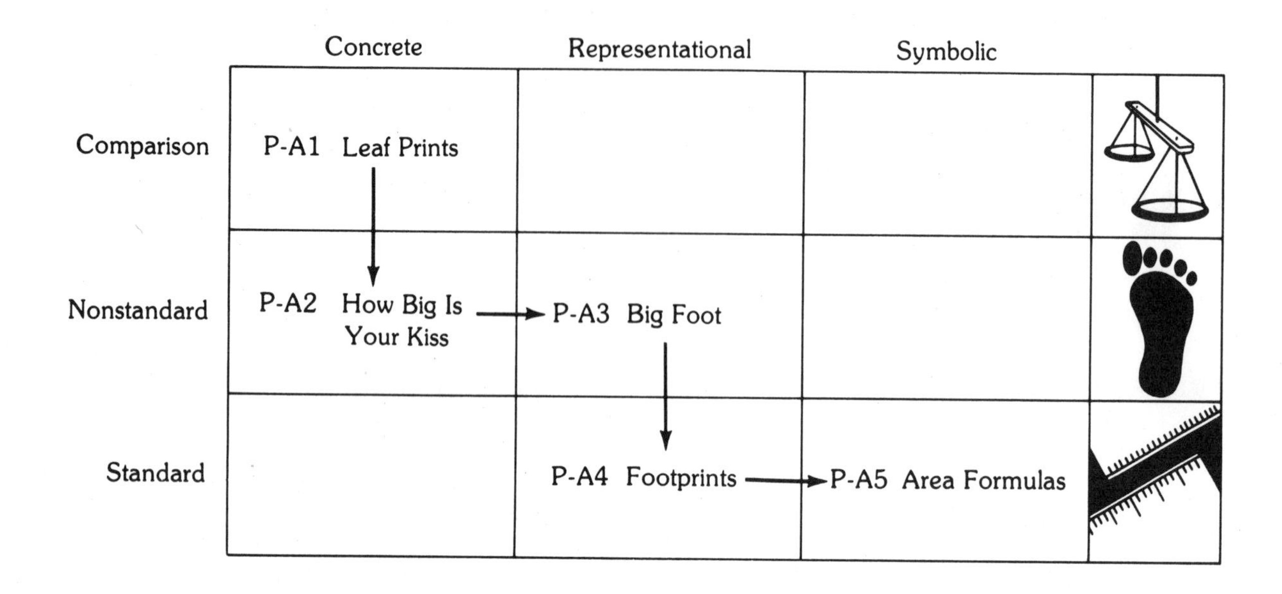

WARM-UP ACTIVITY

What You Need: Paper rectangles and scissors.

How to Do It: Ask the children to pretend that a paper rectangle is a cake that needs its top frosted.

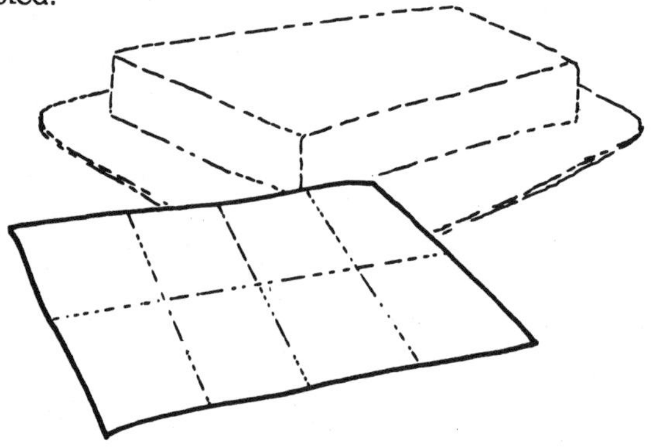

Next, have them cut the "cake" into two pieces, moving the pieces apart. Now ask if it would still require the same amount of frosting to cover the tops of the two pieces as it did the original cake. Always ask students to justify their answers. Push the pieces back together and repeat the question. Again, ask for justification. Repeat this process, cutting the cake first into four and then eight pieces, and asking the same questions.

TEACHING IMPLICATIONS

A child who cannot correctly answer this question probably believes that the surface area of the "cake" changes when it is divided into pieces. These students do not fully understand the invariance of the area, relying instead on perceptual cues to make decisions about the amount of frosting needed. He or she sees more pieces (quantity) or smaller individual pieces and cannot logically reverse the part-whole relationship. These students should be encouraged to focus on the comparison and nonstandard unit activities in the area measurement sequences. These experiences will provide a concrete base upon which an understanding of area can be built.

DEVELOPMENTAL ACTIVITY SEQUENCE

Activity P-A1: Leaf Prints

What You Need: If you are in an environment that will provide the raw materials for this lesson, take your students for a "leaf collecting" walk. If not, bring in sufficient leaves for your class. Once students have a variety of leaves, they can make leaf prints. This activity provides for the introduction of the concept of area. Students are instructed to cover the *surface area* (one side) of each leaf with tempera paint:

They can then arrange their leaves painted side down from smallest to largest on a piece of construction paper:

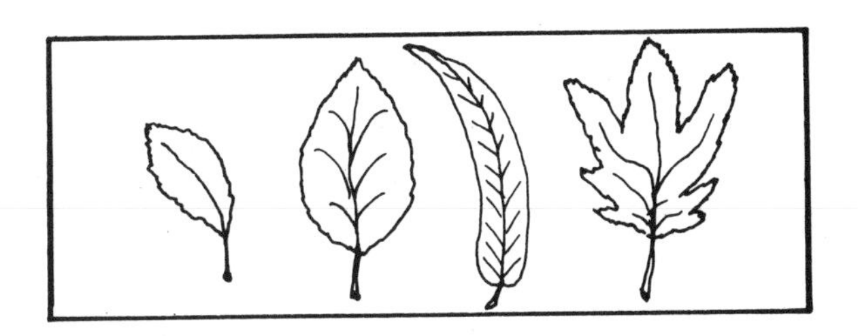

By placing another sheet of construction paper over this and rubbing carefully, students will have a record of their leaf areas! As this activity progresses, the teacher should ask questions similar to the following: "Which of your leaves has the greatest surface area?" "Does a long skinny one take as much paint as a short fat one?" "Do the biggest leaves use the most paint?" "Why?" Hang the leafy constructions around the room or send them home to adorn the refrigerator door.

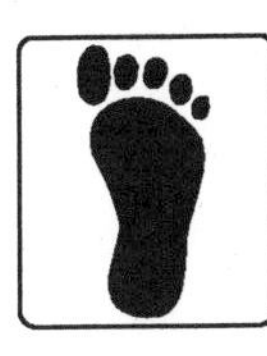

Activity P-A2: How Big Is Your Kiss?

What You Need: Paper, pencils, split peas, Record Sheet P-A2 (p. 95), and class graph on construction paper.

How to Do It: To introduce the notion of a unit of area, have the children moisten their lips and kiss a piece of paper. They can then outline their kiss with a pencil:

This outline can then be covered with split peas. Make sure children lay the peas flat, edge to edge, as they cover their kiss. Some may be tempted to pile them up, which does not represent the concept of area units. The peas are then counted to determine the area of each kiss. This number can then be graphed on "The Big Kiss," a large class graph taped to the wall.

Young students may need some help counting their peas, or perhaps larger units such as dried beans could be used. Older children might enjoy completing Record Sheet P-A2 as an extended experience.

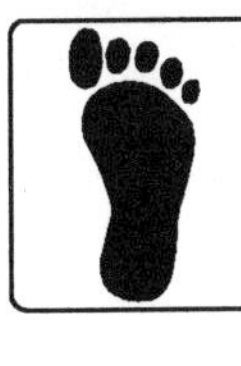

Activity P-A3: Big Foot

What You Need: Tempera, construction paper, pencils, paper towels, scissors, Record Sheet P-A3 (p. 96), and class graph on construction paper.

How to Do It: To have students find the area of their footprints, have them trace around a shoeless foot on construction paper and then cut out their footprints. This time have students use their thumb prints as a unit of area measure. Ask them to dip their thumbs in tempera paint and fill their cutouts with thumb prints. Make sure children use the flat surface of their thumbs and not just the tip. Also make sure that their thumb prints do not overlap—they should just barely touch. Have fun!

Next, have children count these thumb prints and record their foot area on the "Big Foot" class graph:

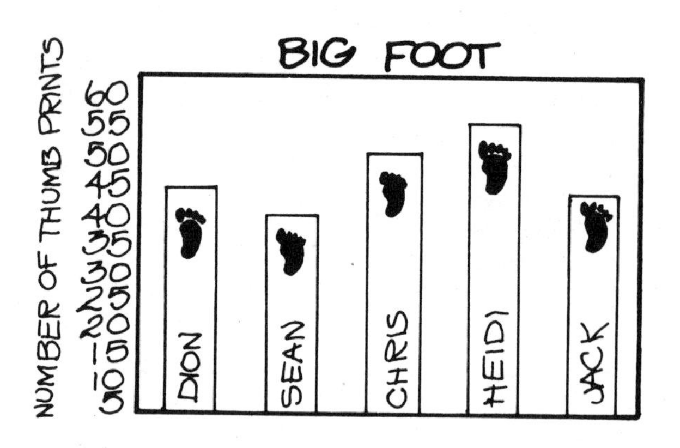

Older students might try ordering their classmates by foot area on Record Sheet P-A3 (p. 96).

Activity P-A4: Footprints

What You Need: Activity Sheet P-A4 (p. 97), and pencil.

How to Do It: Have each student make an outline of his or her foot on activity sheet P-A4. To determine the area of their footprints in square inches, have students simply count the squares inside the region, combining parts of squares in an approximate manner to arrive at the final total.

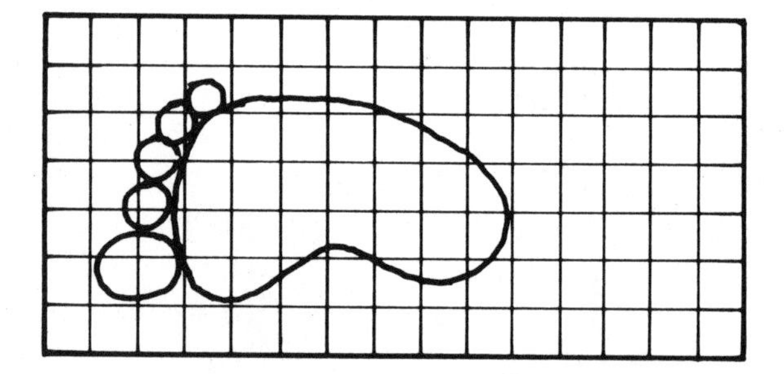

Try the same activity with a "hand print."

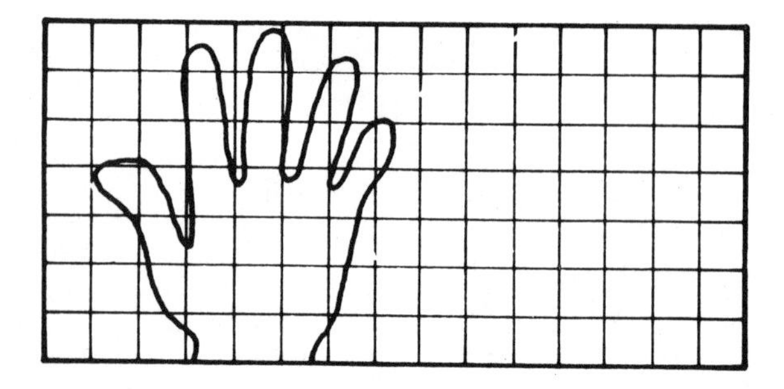

Does it matter if the fingers are together or spread out?

These activities develop the notion that area is determined by the *total number of unit squares that cover the region*. Later, the area "formulas" will be seen as a convenient way of counting the number of unit squares that cover a figure.

Activities of this type also demonstrate the approximate nature of measurement. No measure is exact. If a more accurate measure is desired, a more accurate measuring instrument is required. For example, to find a more accurate measure of a hand print, older children might substitute 1/4-inch^2 graph paper for inch^2 graph paper.

Activity P-A5: Area Formulas

What You Need: Activity Sheet P-A5 (p. 98), and pencil.

How to Do It: In order to develop the concept of area as the number of unit squares required to cover a figure, as well as lay a foundation for the area formula for rectangular regions, ask your students to try Activity Sheet P-A5.

First, students can find the area of a rectangular figure by counting the unit squares (in^2).

1	2	3
4	5	6

Next, working with examples in which not all of the squares have been drawn in (see P-A5), older students will discover that multiplying the length by the width is an efficient way of counting the squares.

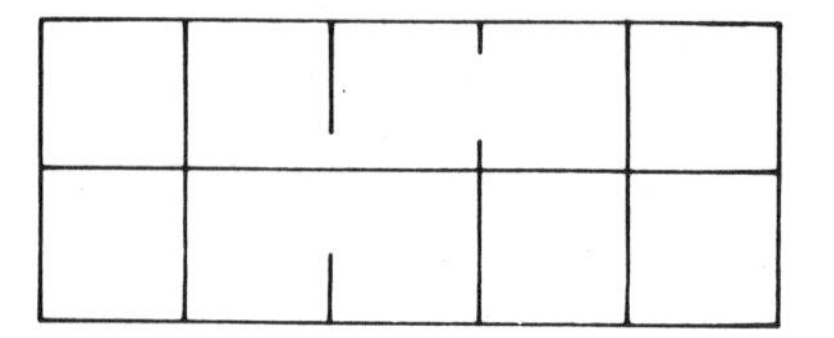

Students should be allowed to use a calculator to find the area products. This will minimize the interference between any lack of multiplication skills and the development of the area concept.

For older children (grades 2-4) additional rectangles without any lines etched in complete the sequence. An inch ruler should be used to measure the length and width. Children should be provided with semitransparent square inch graph paper if they need to check their answers. They can lay it over the region and count the squares, validating their products and insuring understanding. (Putting it up against a window can help.)

These activities should not be attempted until children have had considerable success with previous area experiences. Additional experiences with larger rectangles on the playground might also be attempted. Using a cardboard square yard to "cover" the region or a yardstick to measure the length and width, children can have a great time determining how much carpet would be necessary to cover the basketball court, parking lot, lunch area, sidewalk, or playground.

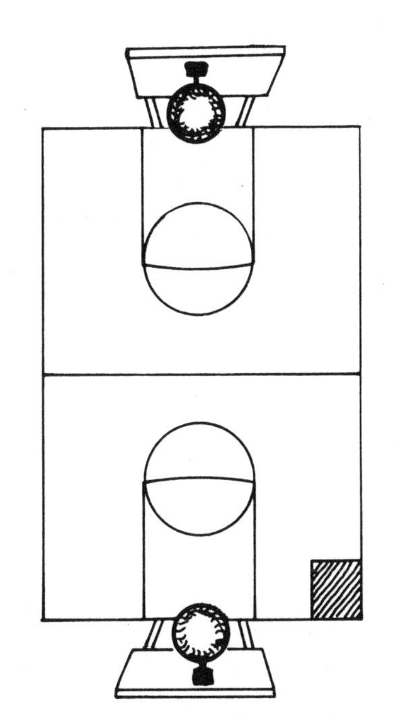

EXTENDED ACTIVITY:

The following activity will help familiarize your students with metric units. Remember you may easily change this activity to customary units by using ounces instead of grams and pounds instead of kilograms.

Big Books ***What You Need:*** cm^2 paper, a variety of books from the classroom, pencils, 3 × 5 cards.

How to Do It: Establish teams of 4 or 5 students. Have each team collect ten books from the classroom. Have them trace the surface area of each book cover on cm^2 paper and calculate (or count) the area of each. Then each team makes separate cards showing the area of each book. Two teams compete by trying to match each other's cards and associated books. The team that makes the most matches wins the round. Play several times by pairing different teams.

AREA ACTIVITY SEQUENCE 2

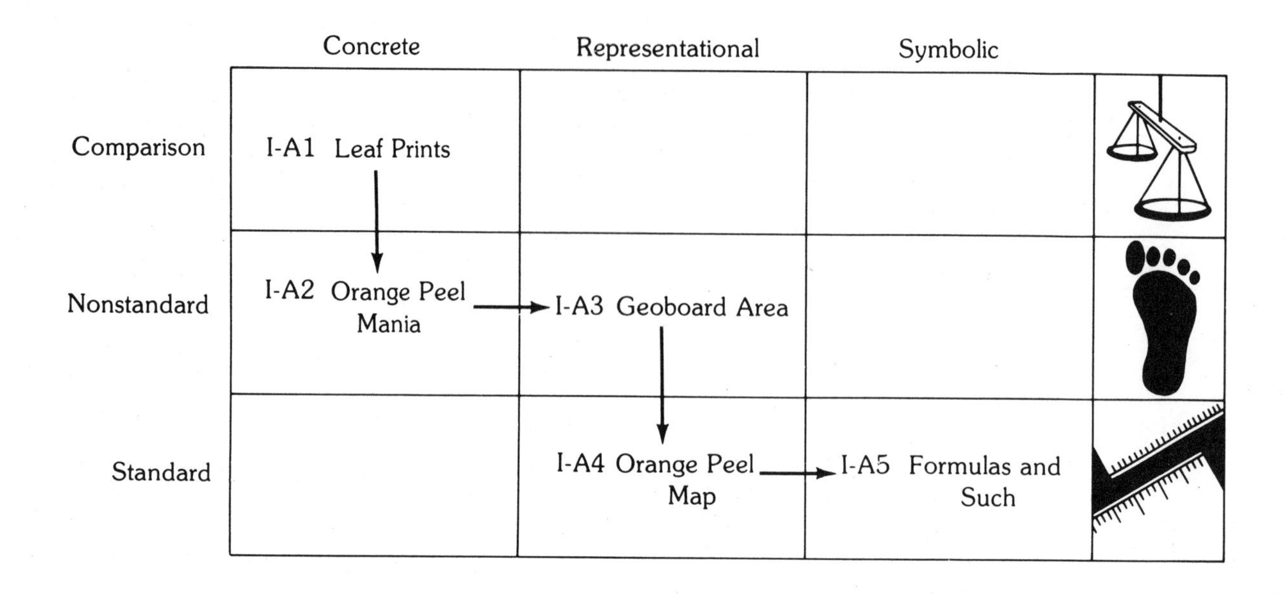

	Concrete	Representational	Symbolic
Comparison	I-A1 Leaf Prints		
Nonstandard	I-A2 Orange Peel Mania	I-A3 Geoboard Area	
Standard		I-A4 Orange Peel Map	I-A5 Formulas and Such

WARM-UP ACTIVITY

What You Need: Pencils and paper.

How to Do It: Have each student trace around their hand (fingers together) on a piece of paper.

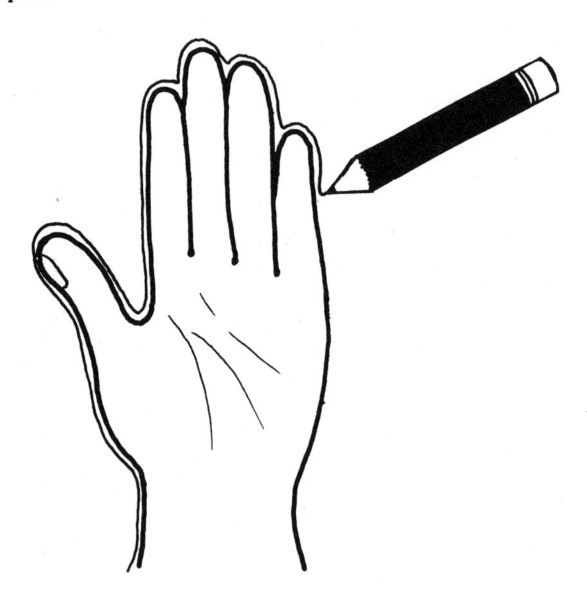

Discuss how much paper a hand print covers. Next, have the students spread out their fingers and trace around their hands.

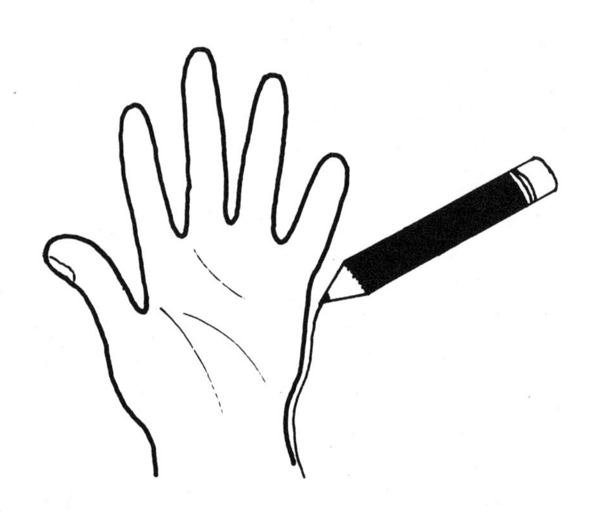

Ask which hand covers up more paper, or if they are equal. (If you have traced carefully, they should be equal.) Ask students to justify their answers.

TEACHING IMPLICATIONS

Students who are not able to correctly answer the above question probably do not understand that the area of an object remains constant no matter how you change its position or divide it. To some, the second hand print appears to cover more area as it is spread out, or they think that the spaces between the fingers "take away" area. These students rely more on concrete perceptual cues than logical reasoning to answer the question. These students should be encouraged to focus on the comparison and nonstandard unit activities in the area activity sequences. These experiences will provide a concrete base upon which an understanding of area may be built.

DEVELOPMENTAL ACTIVITY SEQUENCE

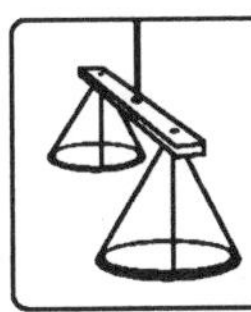

Activity I-A1: Leaf Prints

What You Need: Leaves, tempera, and construction paper.

How to Do It: If you are in an environment that would provide the raw materials for this lesson, take your students for a "leaf-collecting" walk. If not, bring in an approximate supply for your classroom.

Once students have a variety of leaves, they can make leaf prints. This activity provides for the introduction of the concept of area. Instruct your students to cover the surface area (one side) of each leaf with tempera paint.

They can then arrange their leaves, paint side down, from smallest to largest on a piece of construction paper:

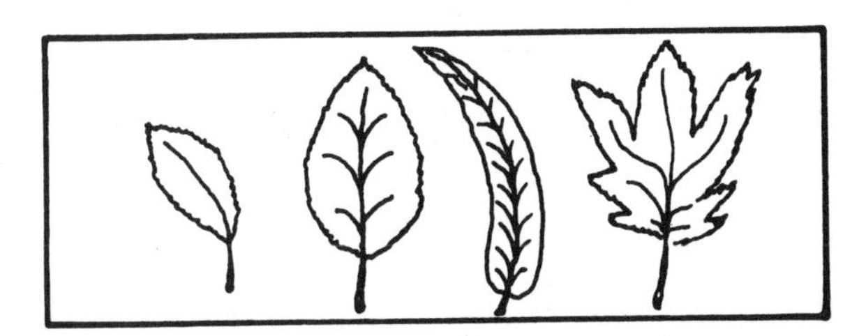

By placing another sheet of construction paper over this and rubbing carefully, students will have a record of their leaf areas.

As this activity is progressing, ask questions similar to the following: "Which of your leaves has the greatest surface area?" "Does a long skinny one take as much paint as a short fat one?" "Do the biggest leaves use the most paint?" "Why?"

EXTENDED ACTIVITY:

Area Mobiles To further develop the notion of surface area, have students cover containers of a variety of shapes and sizes with construction paper. All the surfaces should be covered so that when removed the students will have a duplicate "shell" of the original container. Have students lay out the paper-covering and observe which containers use a greater amount (i.e., have a greater surface area). After the activity is finished, the students can reconstruct their paper containers and make mobiles.

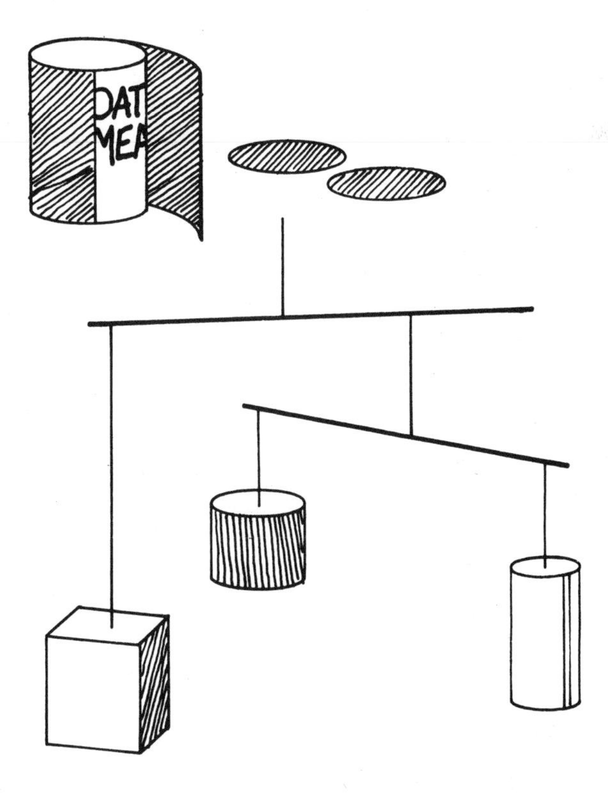

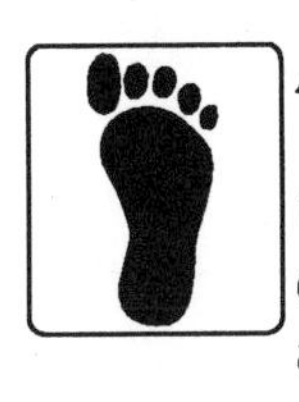

Activity I-A2: Orange Peel Mania

What You Need: Oranges, lima beans, class graph made from construction paper, and Record Sheet I-A2 (p. 113).

How to Do It: Have students attempt to peel an orange in one piece. If the peel is laid out, it looks something like Goode's homolosine world map projection.

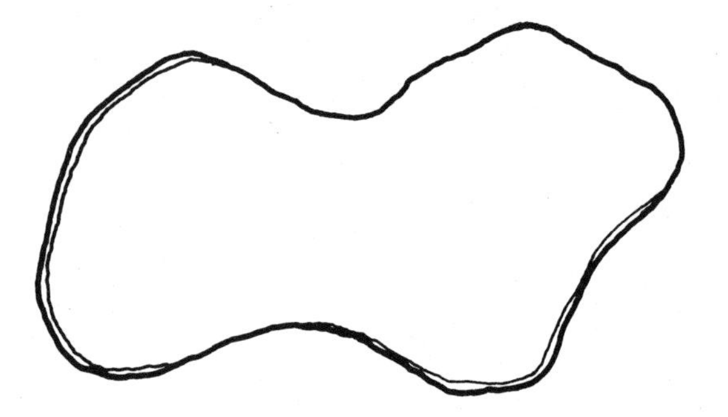

Students can determine the surface area of their orange peels by using beans as their unit of area measure. Have them lay lima beans over the entire orange peel so that very little peel shows through.

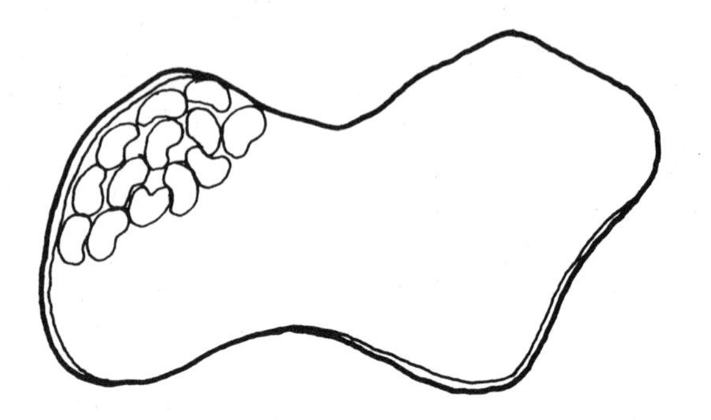

The beans can then be counted to determine the surface area of the orange in bean units. Each student's results can be recorded on a class graph:

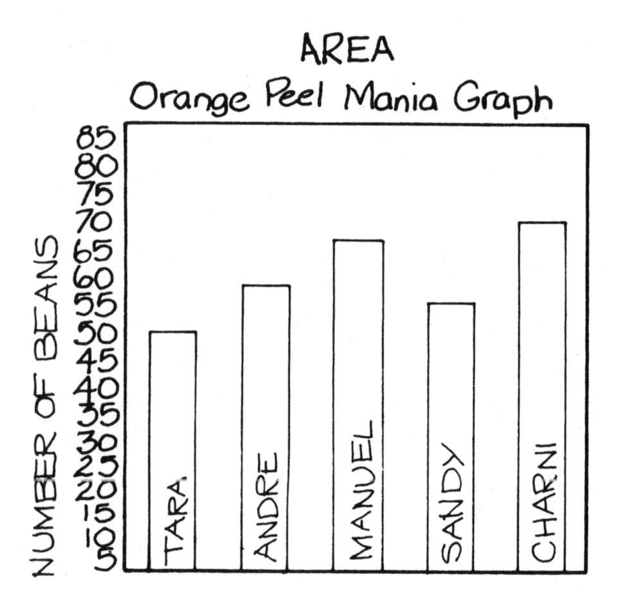

Students may then record all the class information in their record sheet (I-A2), ordering the peels from least surface area to greatest.

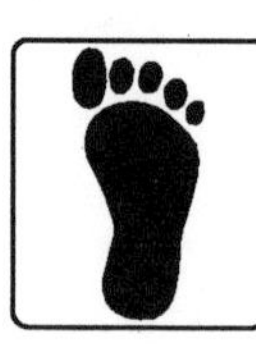

Activity I-A3: Geoboard Area

What You Need: Geoboards, rubber bands, and Record Sheet I-A3 (p. 114).

How to Do It: Give each student a geoboard (see Appendix II) and a supply of rubber bands. Allow a period of free exploration to familiarize students with the materials. Then define one square on the board as a unit area and ask students to find other regions with an area of one.

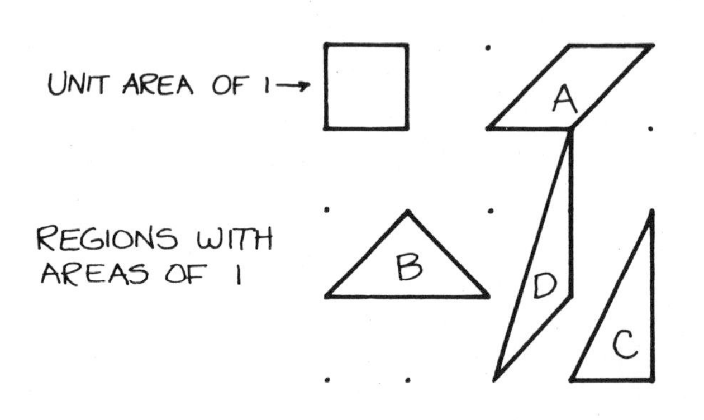

Many different shaped regions have an area of one. Have the children record their shapes on dot paper and collect as many different "units" as possible. Perhaps a class collection could be constructed and displayed.

Insight and facility with problem-solving skills are required in justifying that a region has an area of one. Regions A and B can be divided into two smaller regions, each with an area of one-half. Mentally rearranging these pieces (or physically using dot paper) should clearly show their area to be equal to the unit square.

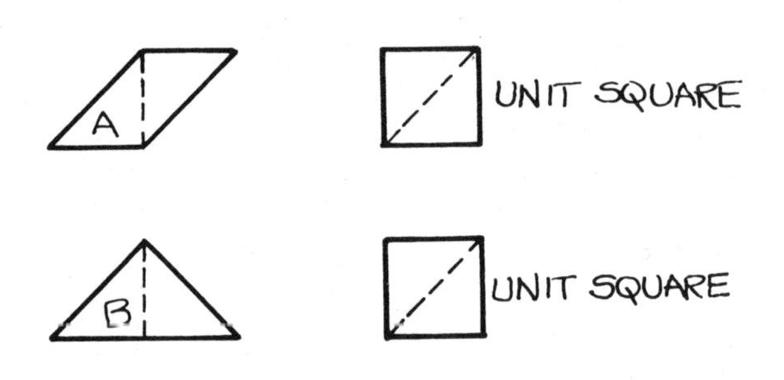

Regions C and D require another problem-solving technique to determine their areas. First, a rectangle can be constructed around the region as shown below.

The area of the rectangle is two unit squares. Since region C is one-half of the rectangle, its area must be one-half of two or one unit square. Similarly, the area of region D can be found as shown below.

RECTANGLE (AREA 3)

SUPERINSCRIBED FIGURE (D)

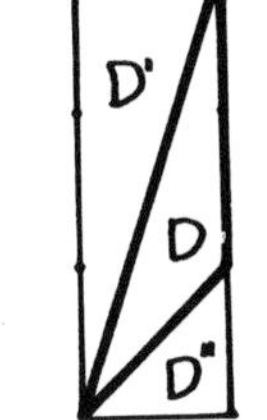

AREA D' IS ONE-HALF OF 3 OR 1½ UNIT SQUARE.

AREA OF D MUST BE 1 UNIT SQUARE BECAUSE THE AREA OF D" IS ½ UNIT SQUARE.

Observing all the regions found to have an area of one unit square, your students may have noticed they all have exactly four nails on their perimeters. It might be fun to try and find a region that "touches" only four nails, but encloses an area other than one unit square. Notice that no nails are included in the interior of the regions. How about these:

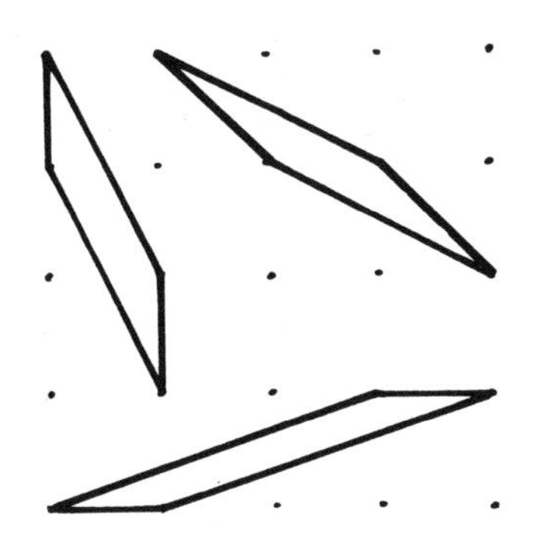

EXTENDED ACTIVITY:

Geoboard Geometry Other interesting questions can be investigated with the geoboard. How does the area "grow" when one nail is included in the interior of the region? How about two nails? Three?

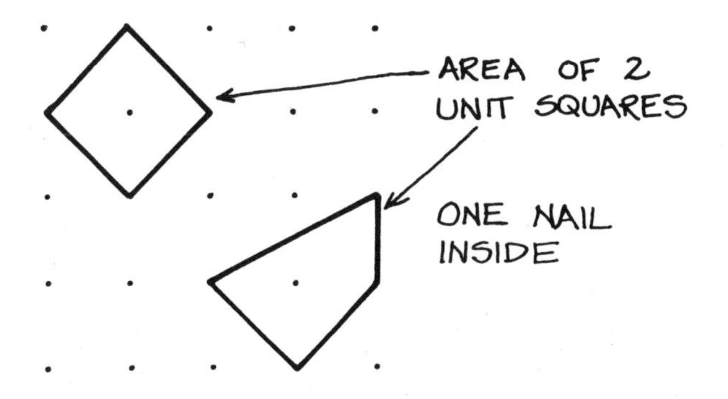

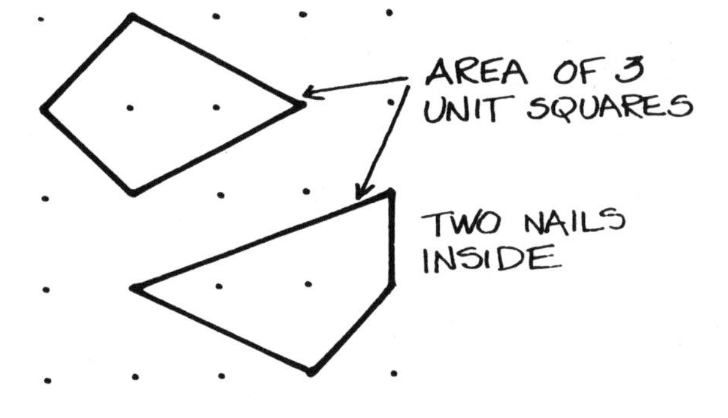

How does the area grow when there are five nails on the perimeter? Six nails? Seven? Can you discover rules that will allow you to predict the area of any region by simply counting the number of nails on the perimeter and on the inside?

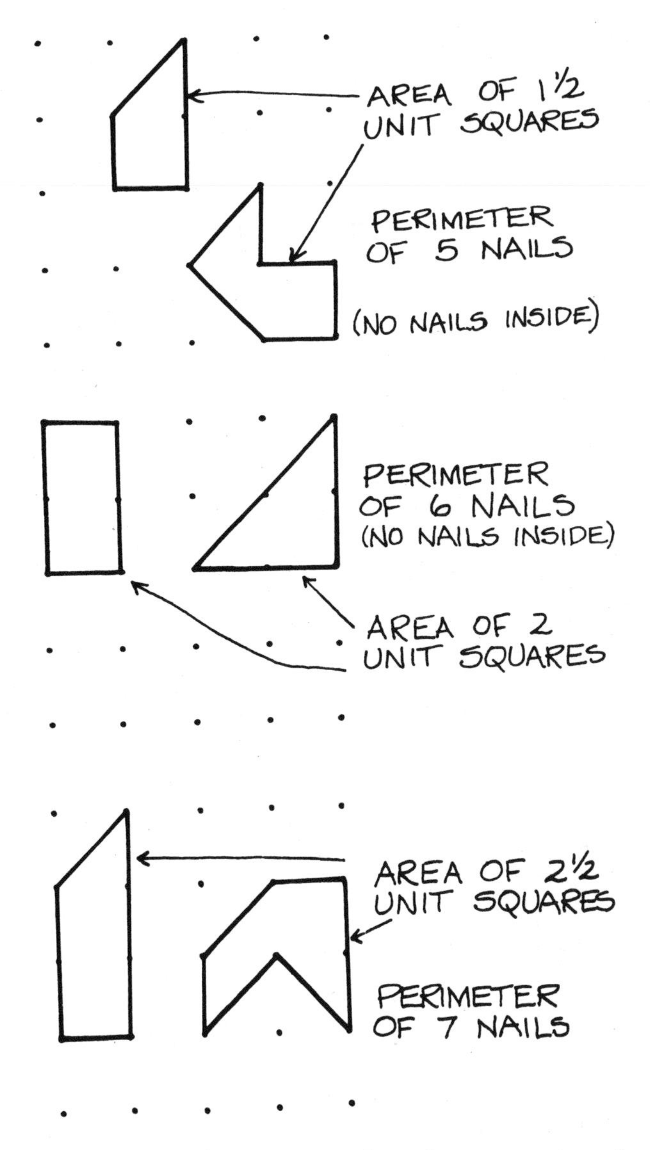

Collecting data from many geoboard experiments and organizing it in tables as below may help students discover patterns and rules. Have fun!

FOUR NAIL PERIMETER EXPERIMENT

NO. OF NAILS INSIDE	AREA
0	1
1	2
2	3
3	4
4	5

NO NAILS INSIDE EXPERIMENT

NO. OF NAILS ON PERIMETER	AREA
0	0
1	0
2	0
3	½
4	1
5	1 ½
6	2
7	2 ½

Activity I-A4: Orange Peel Map

What You Need: Oranges, Record Sheet I-A4 (p. 115), pencils, in.^{2} paper, towels for cleanup.

How to Do It: Distribute oranges to all children; have them carefully remove the peel in one piece. Next, have them carefully flatten out the peel on Record Sheet I-A4.

If this step is done carefully, the shape of the peel should resemble Goode's homolosine world map projection.

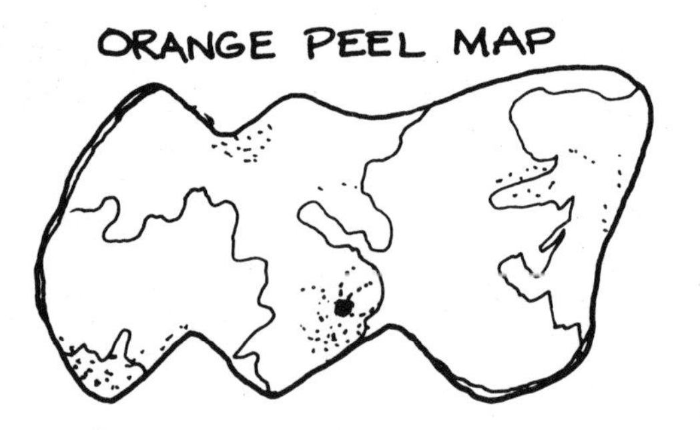

Have the students trace around their orange peels. To determine the surface area of their oranges, have them count the inch squares inside the tracing. Those squares that are not completely inside the region can be totaled up in an approximate manner by mentally combining the partial squares into countable wholes.

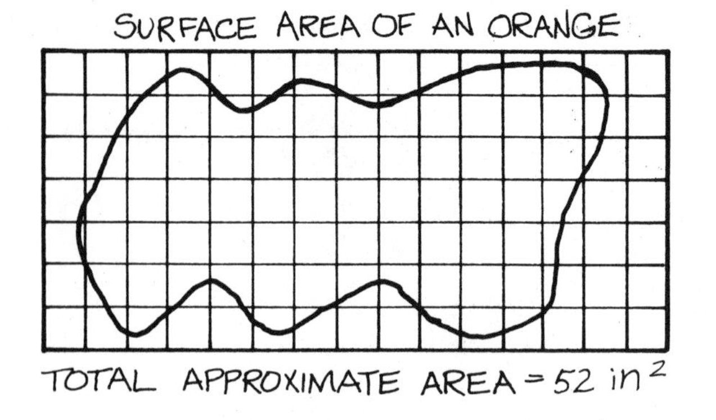

This process points out again the approximate nature of measurement. No measure is exact, yet any measurement can be made more accurate by improving our instrument. For example, by using 1/8 in.^{2} graph paper, a far more accurate measure of the orange peel map's area is possible.

EXTENDED ACTIVITY:

NOTE: We included the following activity to help familiarize your students with metric units. Remember you may easily change this activity to customary units by using ounces instead of grams and pounds instead of kilograms.

Body Prints Have your class find the area of other nonrectangular objects such as a pencil, handprint, or "body" print. Using large sheets of in.^{2} or cm.^{2} paper, a "print" can be made of one surface by tracing around the perimeter. For example, a body print can be constructed as below and the number of square centimeters determined. Students soon discover the efficiency of breaking the body print up into rectangles.

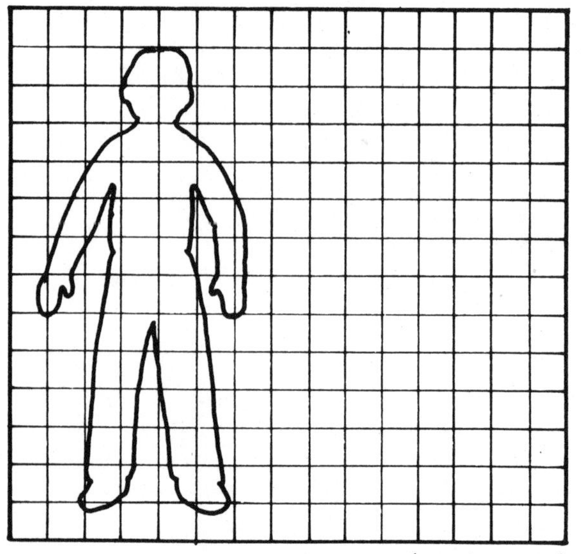

(not to scale)

Using a little multiplication and counting the rest of the squares allows the students to discover their approximate "sleeping" area. Encourage your students to measure any irregular areas using the graph paper technique and other techniques they develop.

Activity I-A5: Formulas and Such

What You Need: Activity Sheet I-A5 (p. 116), ruler, and pencil.

How to Do It: To develop an understanding that the area formula for rectangular regions (Length x Width = Area) is merely an efficient method of counting unit squares, use the following sequence of problems from Activity Sheet I-A5. First, have the students determine the area of rectangles with all the centimeter squares drawn in.

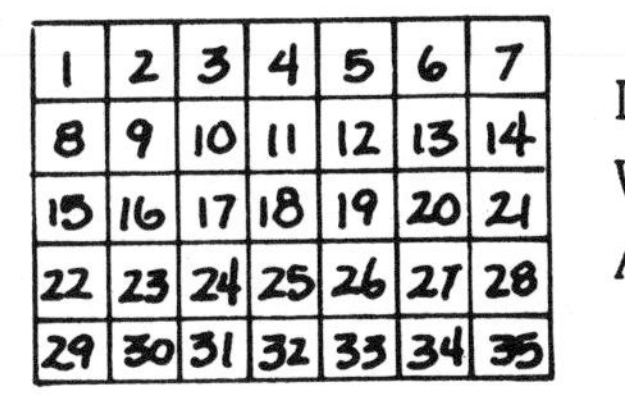

Length – 7 in.
Width – 5 in.
Area – 35 in^2

Length – 10 in.
Width – 3 in.
Area – 30 in^2

In the next example leave out some of the lines.

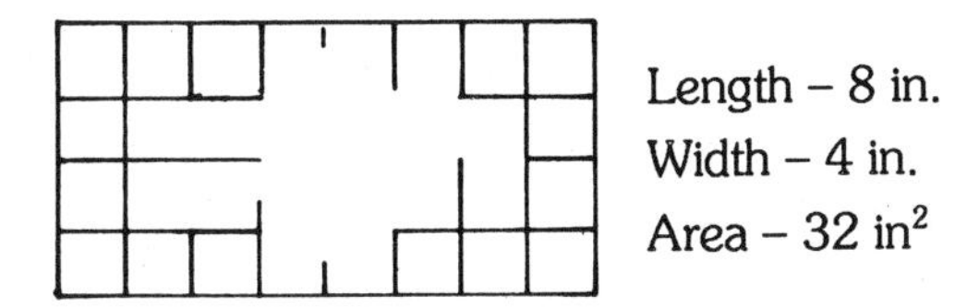

Length – 8 in.
Width – 4 in.
Area – 32 in^2

Then leave out all the lines:

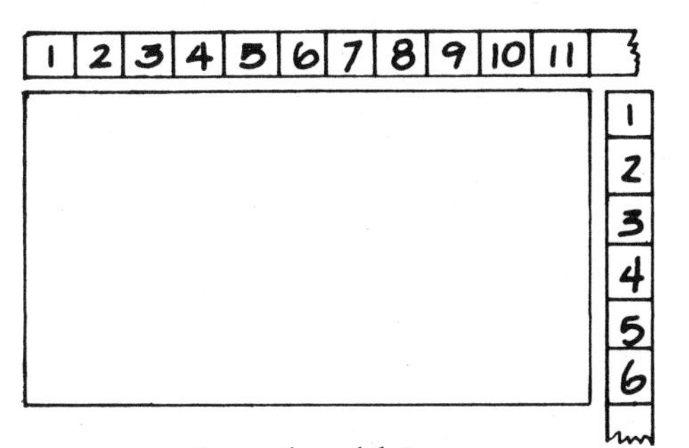

Length – 11 in.
Width – 5 in.
Area – 55 in^2

Use a ruler to measure the length and width. Scale drawings (1 inch represents 1 yard) could be introduced next.

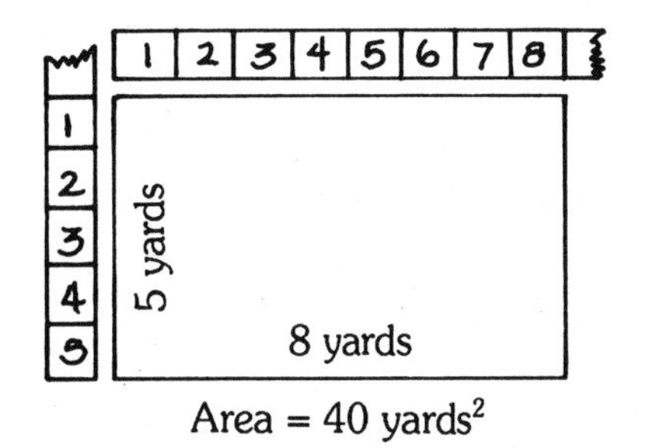

Area = 40 $yards^2$

Word problems involving area should be introduced only after your students have discovered the area formula and demonstrated a facility with its use on problems like those above. Have your students complete Activity Sheet I-A5.

EXTENDED ACTIVITY:

Geometric Shapes Standard formulas for triangles, area formulas, and trapezoids can also be developed from similar experiences.

Using a right triangle (a triangle with a 90° angle), we can see where the formula $A = \frac{1}{2}BH$ comes from. By building an identical triangle onto the original as below (dotted region), we have a rectangle the area of which is equal to the Base times Height. Therefore, the triangle is equal to half that or: Area = $\frac{1}{2}$ Base x Height. Though other triangles are a bit more complicated, this formula works for all cases.

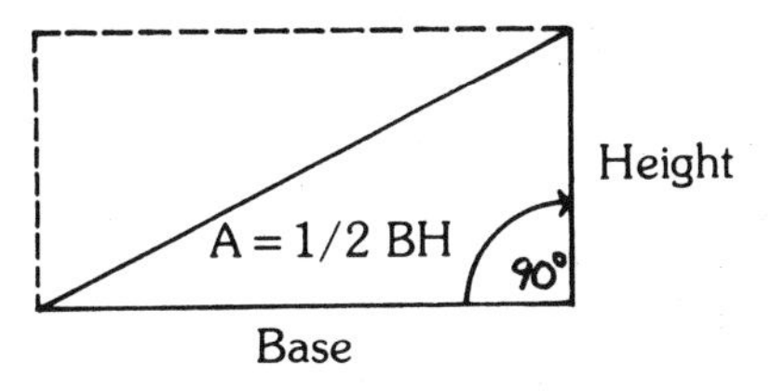

Have those students who are interested try to justify the area formulas for parallelograms and trapezoids.

Parallelogram

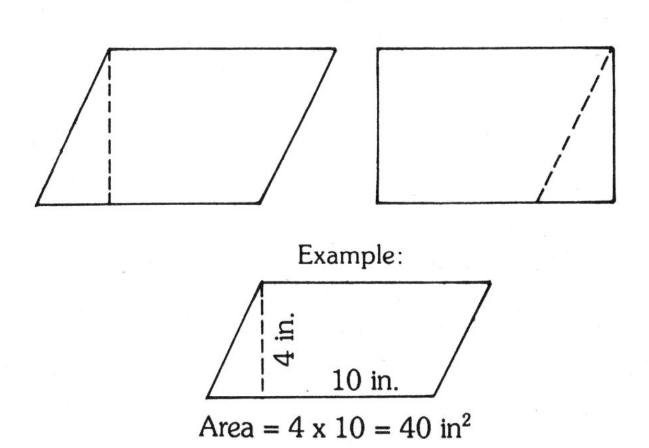

Area = 4 x 10 = 40 in^2

Trapezoid

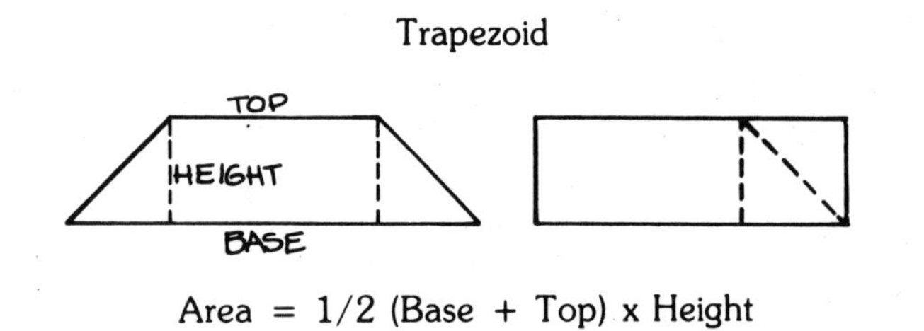

Area = 1/2 (Base + Top) x Height

Example:

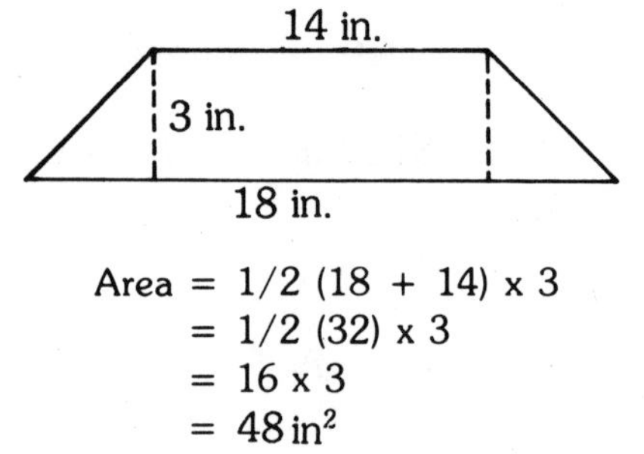

Area = 1/2 (18 + 14) x 3
= 1/2 (32) x 3
= 16 x 3
= 48 in^2

Capacity

OVERVIEW

The measure of the interior of a container is called its *volume* or *capacity*. Volume and capacity have slightly different meanings (i.e., a brick has volume but no capacity); however, both terms may be used to describe the interior measure of an object or container. Objects having three dimensions have a measurable capacity. For example, lung capacity can be measured by blowing up a balloon. You could *compare* lung capacities by seeing who could blow up a balloon the most using one breath. Remember, this type of comparison activity is the first stage of development in the measurement process.

Once it becomes important to know how *much* more, units of capacity must be introduced. Marbles, beans, water, or any other three-dimensional measurement medium that can be counted or measured out in uniform quantities can be used as a unit of capacity measure.

Finally, standard units such as cubic inches or cubic centimeters (milliliters) are used to *measure* capacity. The standard formula for the volume of a box (Length × Width × Height = Capacity) is an efficient way of counting layer after layer of cubic units. Again, the abstract formula should be introduced only after considerable concrete experience with capacity measurement.

The capacity activity sequence charts outline a sequence of capacity measurement activities based on the learning model presented in the Introduction. Five activities each for the primary grade levels and the intermediate grade levels are provided. Begin with Activity 1 and progress through each subsequent experience. Remember, students may not progress at the same rate and some may not be ready to complete the entire sequence.

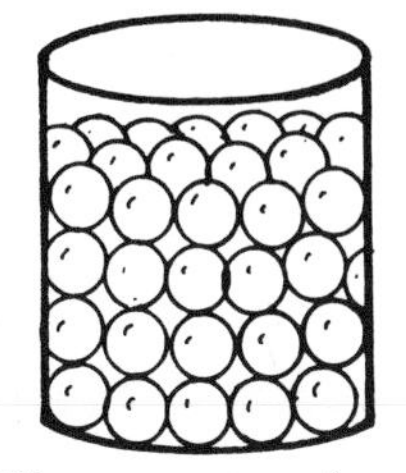

This container has a capacity of 63 marbles

This container has a capacity of 250 thimblefuls of water.

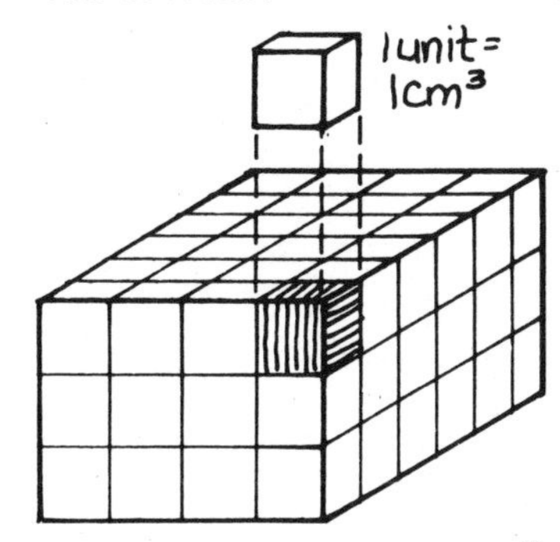

$4\text{ cm} \times 6\text{ cm} \times 3\text{ cm} = 72\text{ cm}^3$

CAPACITY ACTIVITY SEQUENCE 1

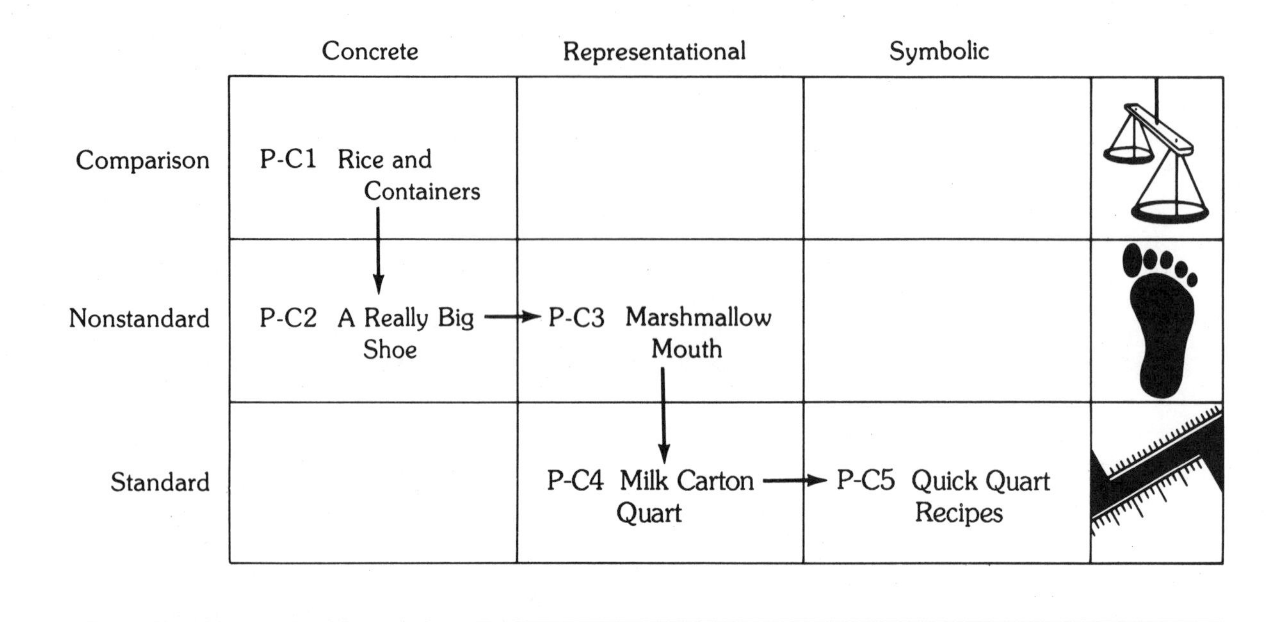

WARM-UP ACTIVITY

What You Need: Water and four containers of shapes similar to these:

How to Do It: *Part I.* Have a volunteer come to the front of the room and fill two identical glasses (containers #4) with the same amount of water. Ask the class if they contain the same amount. If necessary, have the child pour water from one glass to another until they are equal. Next, pour one glass of water into container #3. Ask several volunteers if the two containers (#4 and #3) contain the same amount, or whether one has more now. Have each give justification. Return the water to the empty #4 and repeat with glasses #2 and #5.

Part II. Using one glass of water (#4) and 8 identical small cups (e.g., coffee creamer cups), distribute all the water from the glass to the cups in full view of the class. Ask if there is as much water in all the little cups as there was in the original glass. Reverse the process and ask the same question.

TEACHING IMPLICATIONS

Students who do not answer these questions correctly probably do not understand that capacity remains constant even if the amount is divided among several containers. In Part I, the decision may be based on the height of the water in the glass (container #2 appears fuller than #4, whereas in Part II the decision may be based on quantity (8 cups as opposed to one large container) or individual unit size (each cup is separately smaller than container #4). In all these instances, the notion of the constancy of volume is not clear for these children. They are not able to make decisions based on the fact that capacity does not change although the size and shape of the container may vary; they are relying instead on perceptual cues. These students should be encouraged to focus on the comparison and nonstandard unit activities in the capacity measurement sequence. These experiences provide a concrete base upon which an understanding of capacity can develop.

DEVELOPMENTAL ACTIVITY SEQUENCE

Activity P-C1: Rice and Containers

What You Need: Assorted containers of various shapes, rice, and a funnel.

How to Do It: Provide children with containers marked at different levels for filling with rice:

Children should be allowed to simply explore the process of filling these containers up with rice to the specified levels. Develop appropriate vocabulary during this period of exploration. Words like "full," "empty," "capacity," and "fill" should be explicitly understood. Once children understand the notion of filling up, encourage them to compare quantities of rice. Ask how they could prove to you which container holds the most. Students should order the containers by capacity from smallest to largest:

Fundamental to the student's ability to successfully complete this task is the understanding that if rice from one container is poured into another and overflows (or exceeds the fill line), the first capacity is the greater of the two.

Children should have extensive experience with comparison activities of this sort before proceeding to Activity P-C2.

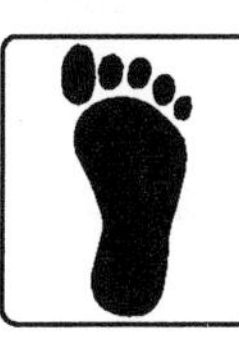

Activity P-C2: A Really Big Shoe

What You Need: 200 marbles and children's shoes.

How to Do It: To introduce the concept of a unit of capacity, have a group of students do the following activity. Take off one shoe and find out just how big it is. Use marbles as the unit of capacity measure. The children can count the number of marbles in their shoe to find its capacity. If students can't count that high, they can simply lay out their marbles in rows, seeing who has the longest row and, therefore, the biggest shoe. This activity works well with students divided into small groups. Within each group one or two shoes can be chosen to be measured. Groups can then compare their results.

Activity P-C3: Marshmallow Mouth

What You Need: Marshmallows, Record Sheet P-C3 (p. 99), class chart, and glue.

How to Do It: Who has the biggest mouth in your room? Have children find the volume of their mouths by using mini-marshmallows as a unit of capacity:

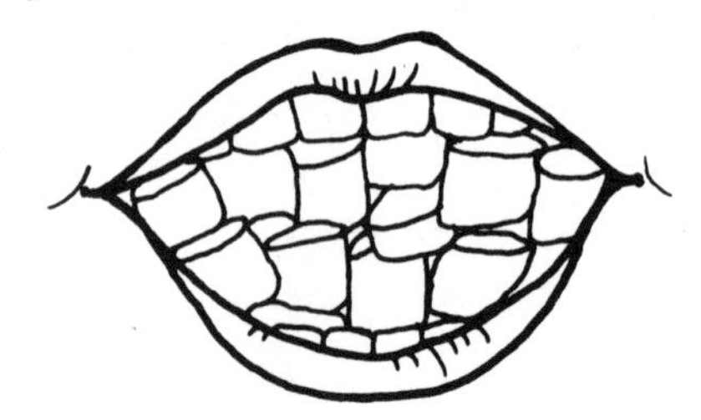

Have the children pair off and graph the size of each others mouths by gluing one marshmallow on the class chart for every marshmallow that goes into their partner's mouth. The children should stuff in only as many marshmallows as they can and still close their mouths. Have one child count as the other stuffs.

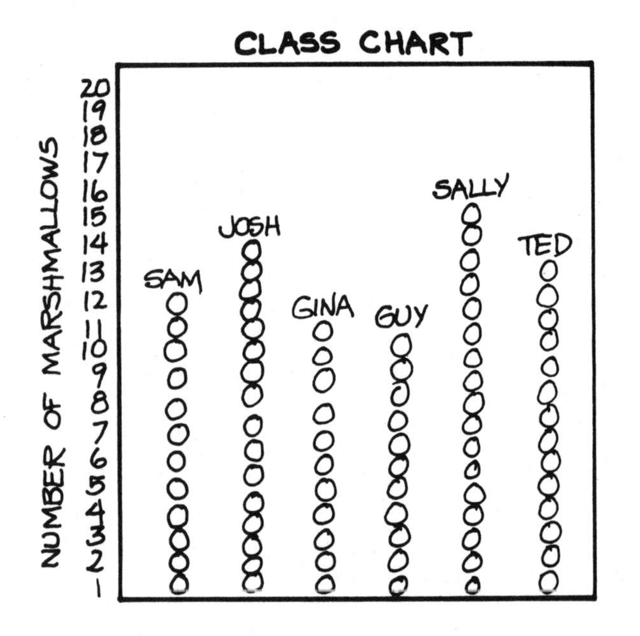

Activity P-C4: Milk Carton Quart

What You Need: Several one-quart milk cartons, water, puffed cereal or rice, scissors, felt pens, large pots or containers for filling, and Record Sheet P-C4 (p. 100).

How to Do It: Give each student a washed, one-quart milk carton and have him or her open the top.

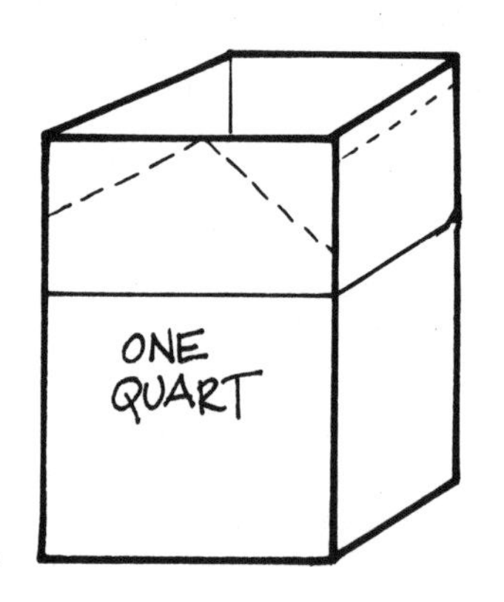

Students can decorate their quart containers and use them as a standard to measure the capacity of any common container. Have the class find out how many quarts of water it takes to fill up a gallon milk container, various pots and pans, the sink, or a hat (put a plastic bag in the hat first). The capacity of nonwaterproof containers can be found by substituting rice or puffed cereal for water. For example, the capacity of a desk drawer, purse, or pair of pants can be found in this manner.

Bar graphs, recording the capacity of various containers, should be made on Record Sheet P-C4 similar to the one shown here.

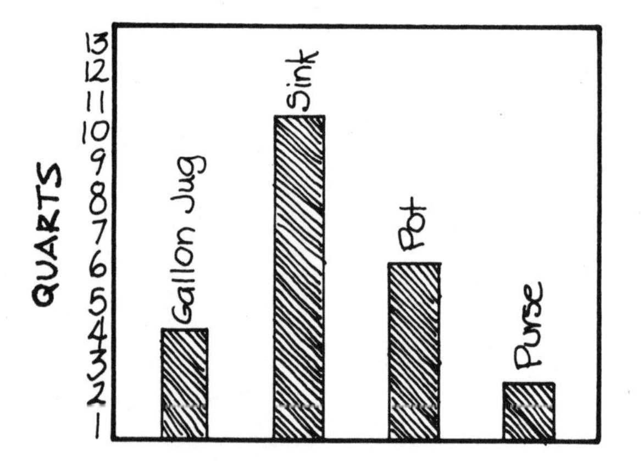

Have the students find the capacities of several containers and fill in squares on the graph with felt pens to the appropriate heights. For larger containers, a bulletin board graph could be constructed. Strips of colored paper cut to the appropriate lengths can be used to construct the large graph.

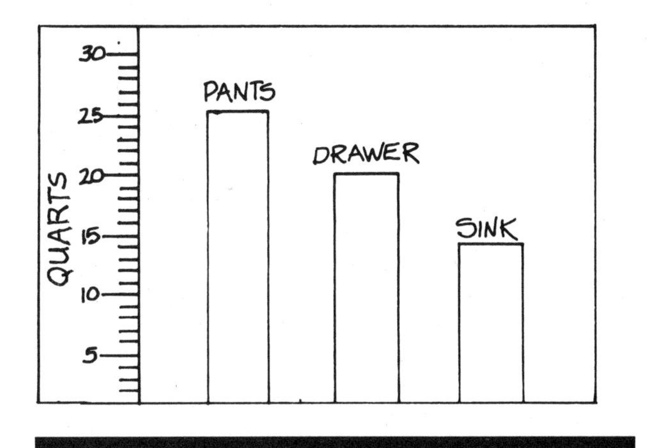

Activity P-C5: Quick Quart Recipes

What You Need: Quart container, paper cups, lemon squeezer, blender, large pot, bowl, ingredients for Lemonade and Strawberry Smoothy recipes, Activity Sheet P-C5 (p. 101).

How to Do It: Using the following recipes for Lemonade and Strawberry Smoothies, organize a group of approximately 15 students. Have each child be responsible for some part of the preparation such as squeezing a lemon or preparing three or four berries. Once the ingredients have been prepared and collected, have one child come up and measure the proper amount of water or milk. Have the entire class count the number of quarts measured out loud as each is being poured into the pot. Complete the steps in the recipe and serve the class a cup of the healthy brew. After they have consumed the product of their efforts, have them draw pictures (on Activity Sheet P-C5) of the steps the class went through in making the recipe. Make sure each picture has a caption.

LEMONADE

15 lemons
4 quarts of water
honey or sugar to taste

Directions:
Step 1. Hand-squeeze lemons and collect juice in a large pot. (Make sure to pick out the seeds). You might try drying the seeds thoroughly to see if they can be encouraged to sprout.
Step 2. Measure 4 quarts of water and pour into pot.
Step 3. Stir in honey or sugar to taste.

STRAWBERRY SMOOTHY

45–50 fresh strawberries
4 quarts of milk
4 eggs

Directions:
Step 1. Carefully clean strawberries and collect in a bowl.
Step 2. Pour one liter of milk into a blender.
Step 3. Crack two eggs into the milk. Save the shells. They can be used to plant the lemon seeds in.
Step 4. Turn on the blender (medium speed) and begin dropping in strawberries until the mixture becomes quite thick.
Step 5. Serve and repeat Steps 2 through 4 until you run out of something.

NOTE: Several excellent metric cookbooks for kids are listed in the bibliography. Once children become familiar with liter measures, we encourage lots of cooking experiences using smaller capacity containers such as 500 and 250 millimeter (one-half and one-fourth liter) measures as well as measurement techniques from Chapter 2.

CAPACITY ACTIVITY SEQUENCE 2

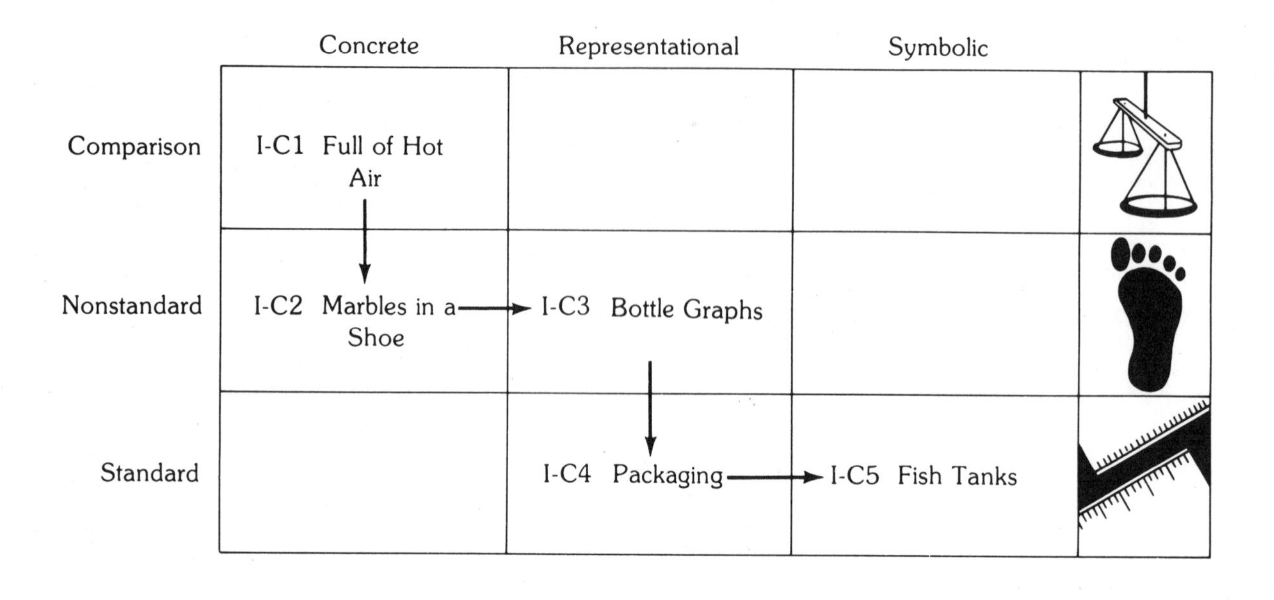

WARM-UP ACTIVITY

What You Need: Water and four containers of shapes and sizes similar to these:

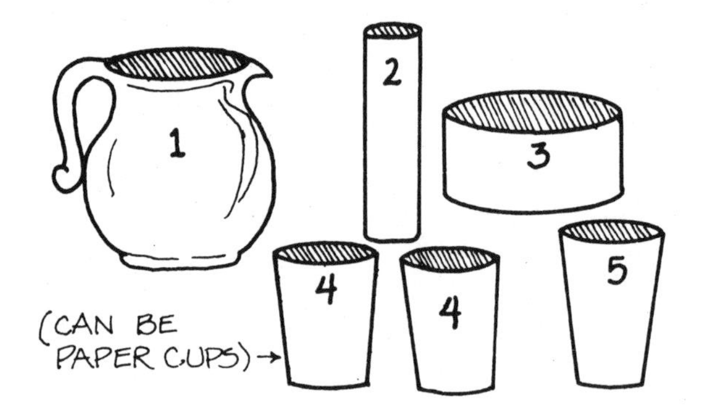

How to Do It: *Part I.* Have a volunteer come to the front of the room and fill two identical glasses (containers #4) with the same amount of water. Ask the class if they contain the same amount. If necessary, have the child pour water from one glass to another until they are equal. Next, pour one glass of water into container #3. Ask several volunteers if the two containers (#4 and #3) contain the same amount, or whether one has more now. Have each give justification. Return the water to the empty #4 and repeat with glasses #2 and #5.

Part II. Using one glass of water (#4) and 8 identical small cups (e.g., coffee creamer cups), distribute all the water from the glass to the cups in full view of the class. Ask if there is as much water in all the little cups as there was in the original glass. Reverse the process and ask the same question.

TEACHING IMPLICATIONS

Students who do not answer these questions correctly probably do not understand that capacity remains constant even if the amount is divided among several containers. In Part I, the decision may be based on the height of the water in the glass (container #2 appears fuller than #4), whereas in Part II the decision may be based on quantity (8 cups as opposed to one large container) or individual unit size (each cup is separately smaller than container #4). In all these instances, the notion of the constancy of volume is not clear for these children. They are not able to make decisions based on the fact that capacity does not change although the size and shape of the container may vary; they are relying instead on perceptual cues. These students should be encouraged to focus on the comparison and nonstandard unit activities in the capacity measurement sequence. These experiences provide a concrete base upon which an understanding of capacity can develop.

DEVELOPMENTAL ACTIVITY SEQUENCE

Activity I-C1: Full of Hot Air

What You Need: Lung capacity measurer (see below), two clothespins, drinking straws, yarn, class chart, Record Sheet I-C1 (p. 117).

How to Do It: First, you will need to construct your measurement device, which should look something like this:

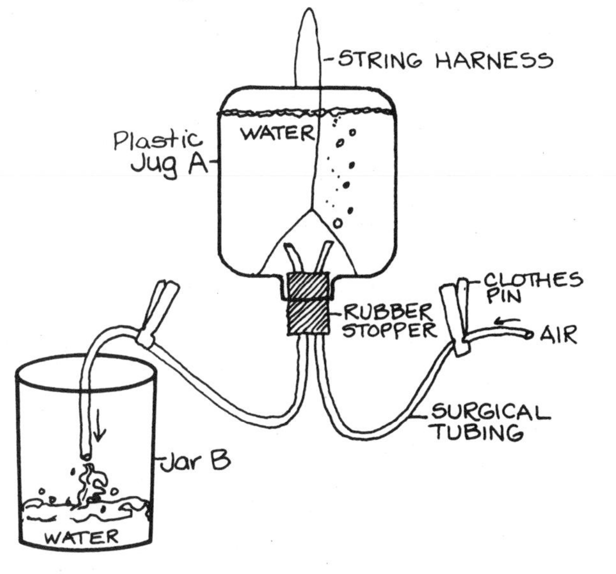

To find each student's lung capacity, have him or her take a deep breath and blow into the air tube. This will displace an equal volume of water from jug A to jar B. After the student has exhaled as much air as possible, the flow of water should be stopped with clothespins attached to both the water tube and the air tube. The water level in jar B can then be recorded by cutting a piece of string the same height as the water level.

This piece of string can then be placed on a class chart over the student's name:

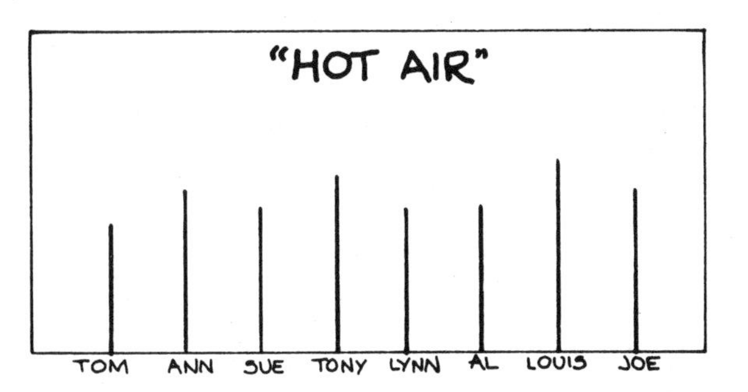

NOTE: To prevent the spread of germs, insert a new drinking straw in the air tube for each child.

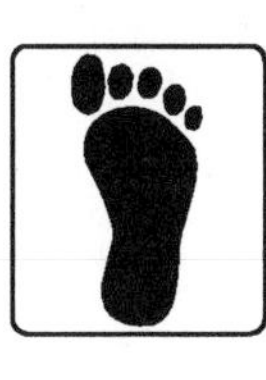

Activity I-C2: Marbles in a Shoe

What You Need: Marbles, shoes, class chart, and Record Sheet I-C2 (p. 118).

How to Do It: To introduce the concept of a unit of capacity, have your students do the following activity. Ask them to take off one shoe and find out just how big it is. Have them use marbles as their unit of capacity measure, filling up one shoe. Have students record on the class chart the number of marbles it took to fill up their shoes.

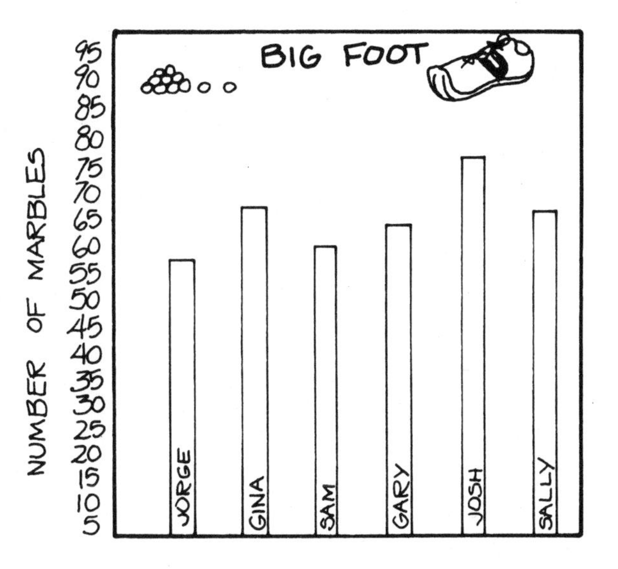

Students can then order these capacities from smallest to largest on their recording sheets.

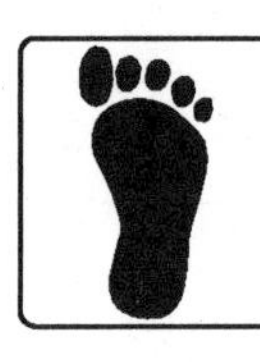

Activity I-C3: Bottle Graphs: Ounces

What You Need: Several odd-shaped bottles, one-ounce cups, graph paper, ruler, and Record Sheet I-C3 (p. 119).

How to Do It: The objective of this activity is to see how the height of the water line in a bottle changes as small units of water are put into the bottle. Where the bottle is narrow, the water line will shoot up much faster than where it is wider, even though equal measures are added every time. First, have students pair up with a partner. Then have one student from each pair pick a bottle and the other fill in the table on Record Sheet I-C3. The height of the water level should be measured and recorded after each measure is added. For simplicity, assume that the height is zero when you begin.

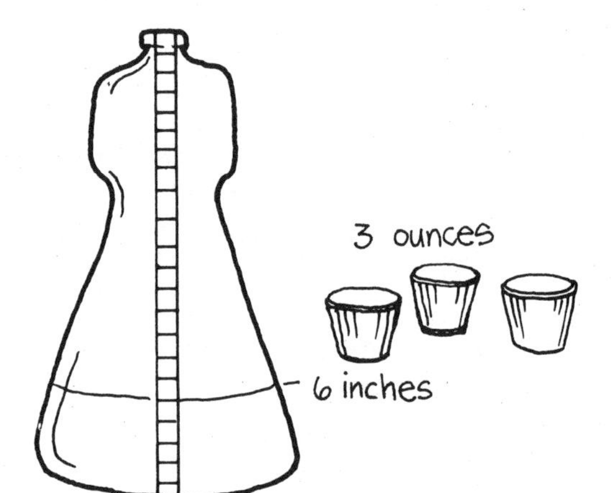

No. of ounces	Waterline Height (in)
0	0
1	1
2	3
3	6
4	
5	
6	
7	
8	
9	
10	

This data can be graphed as below. The shape of the graph can give you information about the original bottle. As the graph gets steep, the bottle narrows; as it flattens, the bottle gets wider. A straight-line graph represents a bottle with parallel sides like a cylinder.

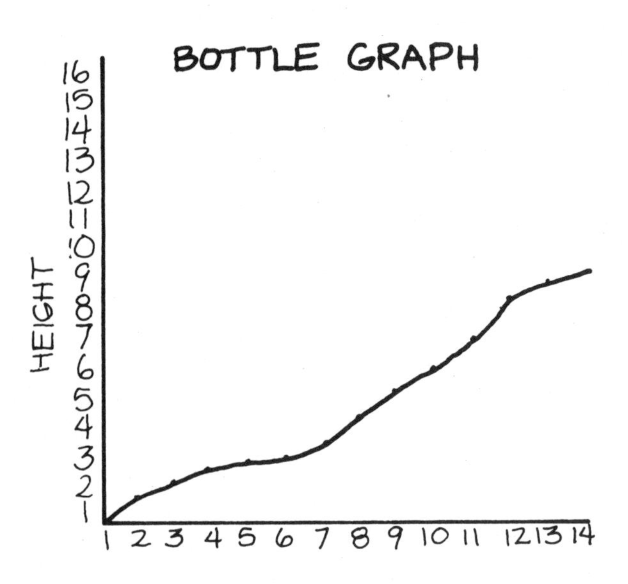

Students might try to match graphs to the appropriate bottle or try drawing the graph by just looking at the bottle. You might also prepare several graphs and have the students try drawing the shape of the bottle. Allow sufficient time for experimenting before you encourage generalizations.

Activity I-C4: Packaging

What You Need: Inch graph paper, scissors, inch cubes, Activity Sheet I-C4 (p. 120).

How to Do It: Give each student five pieces of 10 in x 10 in graph paper (Activity Sheet I-C4). Have the students form an open-top box by cutting a square out of each corner and folding up the edges.

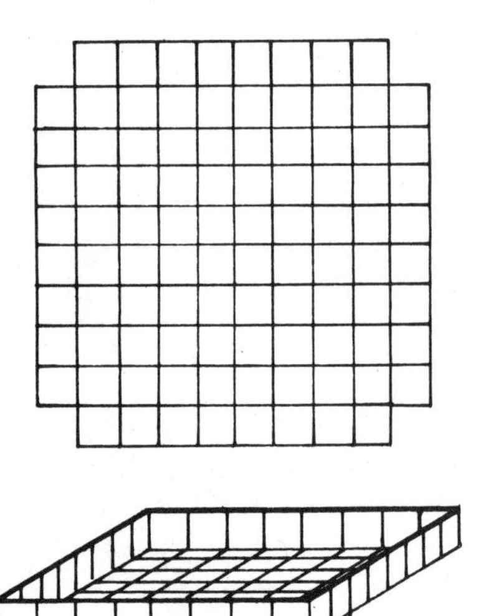

This box can hold 64 inch cubes. Have your students try cutting larger squares out of each corner and construct the resultant boxes. How many inch cubes can be "packaged" in these boxes? What size square must be trimmed from each corner in order to package the greatest number of inch cubes? After each construction, have the students carefully fill each box level with inch cubes to justify their conclusions.

NOTE: We included the following activity to help familiarize your students with metric units. Remember you may easily change this activity to customary units by using inches instead of centimeters and quarts instead of liters.

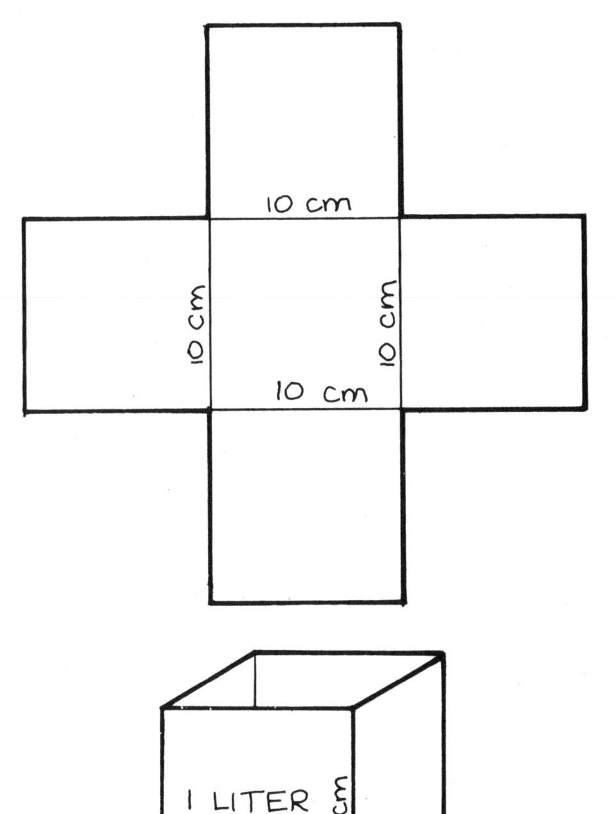

How many centimeter cubes can be packaged in the one liter box? Students should practice measuring the liter capacity of familiar containers, using an easily constructed milk-carton liter container (see Activity P-C4).

EXTENDED ACTIVITY:

Small Packages. Since 100 centimeter cubes can be packaged in a liter container, we sometimes call one centimeter cube a milliliter (1/1000 of a liter). Smaller capacity measures can be constructed from one-quart milk cartons (500, 250, and 100 milliliter) by pouring these measured quantities of water into a milk carton, marking the water line, and cutting along the line. One set of appropriate metric containers will be necessary to provide the initial standard (see Appendix II). Cooking with metric measures affords an excellent opportunity for children to practice using metric capacity measures. See the bibliography for children's metric cookbooks.

Activity I-C5: Fish Tanks

What You Need: Activity Sheet I-C5 (p. 121), pencil, and calculator (optional).

How to Do It: The formula for finding the capacity of a box may have been discovered by some of your students during the Packaging Activity (I-C4). Multiplying the length times the width times the height is a convenient way of counting all those tiny cubes. If this shortcut wasn't discovered, introduce it at this time and review the packaging experiments.

Give each student Activity Sheet I-C5. The fish tank problems will require students to find the capacity of various aquariums. Each fish requires 1 liter (1000 milliliters) of water to live. For example, how many fish can live in this tank?

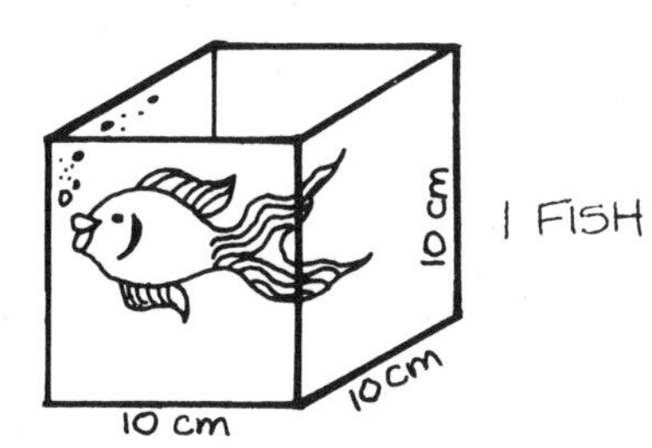

10 cm x 10 cm x 10 cm = 1000 cm^3 or
1000 ml or 1 liter

How about this one?

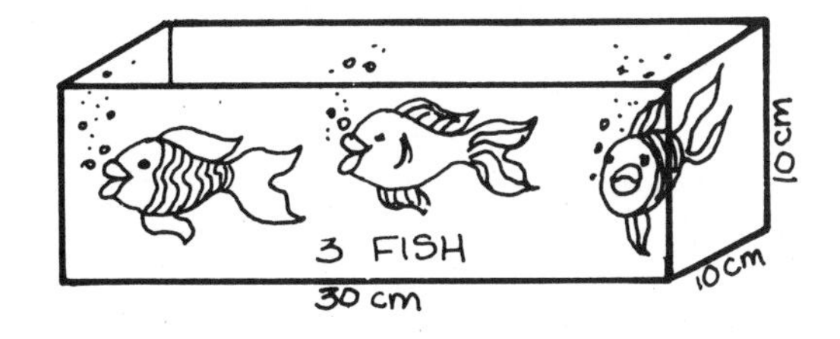

30 cm x 10 cm x 10 cm =3000 cm^3 or
3000 ml or 3 liters

You might want to encourage students to use a calculator to complete the multiplication so they can concentrate on the measurement concept and not be overwhelmed initially by the necessary computation.

CHAPTER 5

Temperature and Time

OVERVIEW

Temperature and time are two commonly used measures, yet both are somewhat more abstract than length, mass, area, and capacity because it is impossible to measure these attributes directly. Temperature is generally measured by calibrating the expansion effect it has on mercury or alcohol. Time is measured by counting the cycles of uniformly recurring events such as the rising of the sun, the period of the moon, the swing of a pendulum, the unwinding of a spring, or the vibration of a quartz crystal.

Both attributes are used in our daily lives, but neither can be seen. Temperature can be felt, however, and apparently it is possible to have a "sense of time." Because no direct measure is possible, care should be taken when introducing these concepts to children. Give them an opportunity to develop an understanding of time and temperature at the comparison and nonstandard unit levels prior to measuring with a thermometer and a timepiece.

Five temperature and five time activities are given in the temperature activity sequence charts. These experiences should be appropriate for any grade level although some adaptation may be needed for younger children. We suggest working through the activities in sequence, allowing ample opportunity for independent investigation at each level.

TEMPERATURE ACTIVITY SEQUENCE

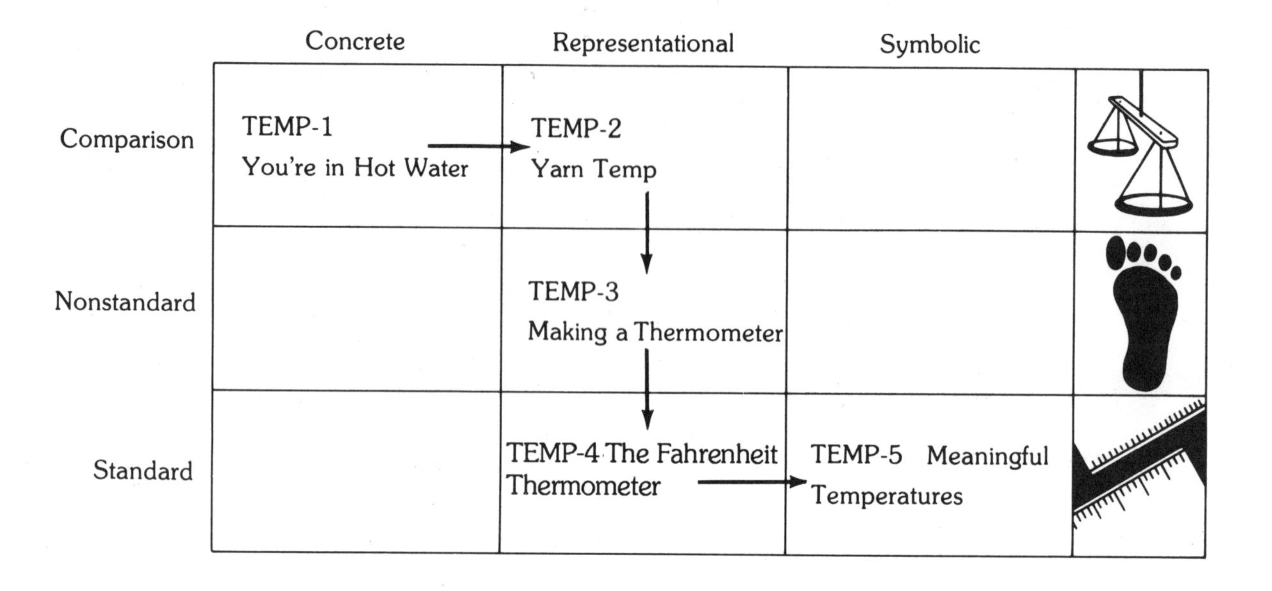

	Concrete	Representational	Symbolic
Comparison	TEMP-1 You're in Hot Water →	TEMP-2 Yarn Temp ↓	
Nonstandard		TEMP-3 Making a Thermometer ↓	
Standard		TEMP-4 The Fahrenheit Thermometer →	TEMP-5 Meaningful Temperatures

DEVELOPMENTAL ACTIVITY SEQUENCE

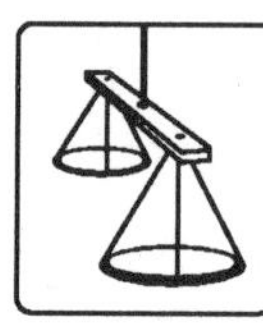

Activity TEMP-1: You're in Hot Water

What You Need: A container of water at room temperature and Record Sheet TEMP-1.

How to Do It: Place a container of water (at room temperature) in front of your classroom. Have one child at a time stick one hand in the water and find things in the room by touch that are colder and hotter than the water. Have children record their results on Record Sheet TEMP-1.

EXTENDED ACTIVITY:

Ms. Wizard In order to give students experience with the relativity of temperature, set up an experiment. You will need three dishes of H_2O (one hot, one cold, and one room temperature) and two unsuspecting victims. Don't tell the students about the relative temperatures of the water in the various containers. Just have one child place a hand in the hot water and another child place a hand in the cold. After the children's hands have been immersed in the two extremes, have them place the same hands in the middle bowl and ask them both to tell the class about the temperature of the water in that bowl. (One will undoubtedly say it is hot and the other that it is cold.) Ask your class why this happened. An interesting discussion of how people see things from various points of view might ensue.

Activity TEMP-2: Yarn Temp

What You Need: Large thermometer with numbers covered up, string, and a chart.

How to Do It: Reading a thermometer is difficult for young children and the resultant numeric values allow for little direct comparison of temperature variation. Here's an activity that provides such an opportunity.

Every day for one week, have your students go to the outdoor thermometer and examine the mercury line at the same time of day. Have them cut a piece of string the height of the mercury column. This string can then be labeled and placed on a weekly chart for comparison.

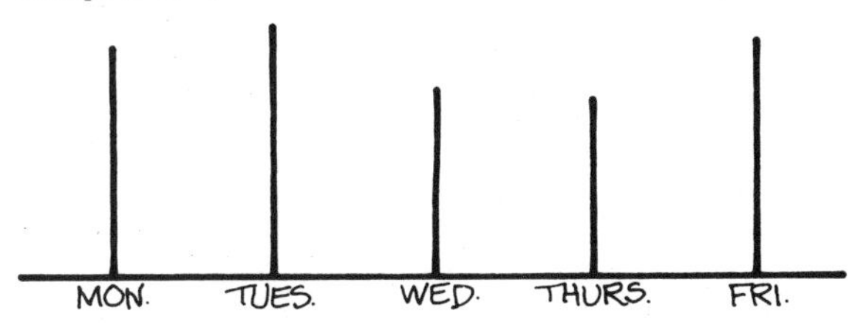

On Friday, students can be asked which day was hottest, coldest, etc.

NOTE: If the temperature is below 0°C, children should use a different color string and place it below the base line:

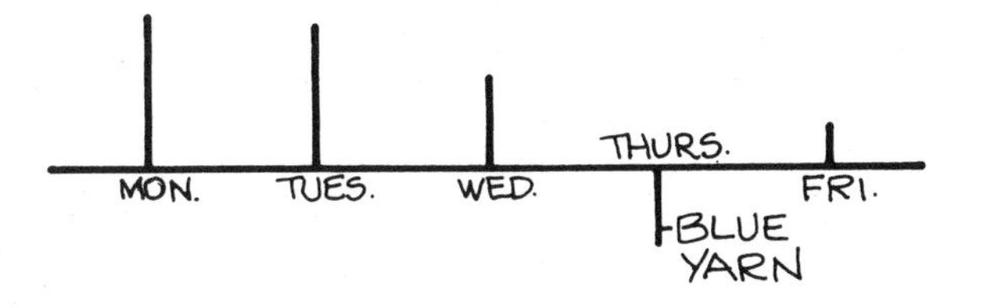

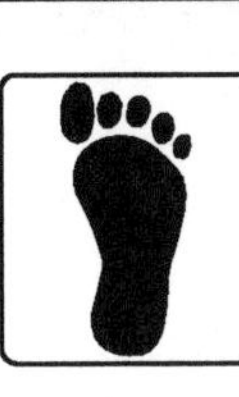

Activity TEMP-3: Making a Thermometer

What You Need: Yarn records from Activity TEMP-2, thermometer, and lima beans.

How to Do It: Soon children will want to know how *much* hotter or colder it is from one day to the next. To introduce the concept of a unit of temperature, have children lay lima beans end to end along their yarn records:

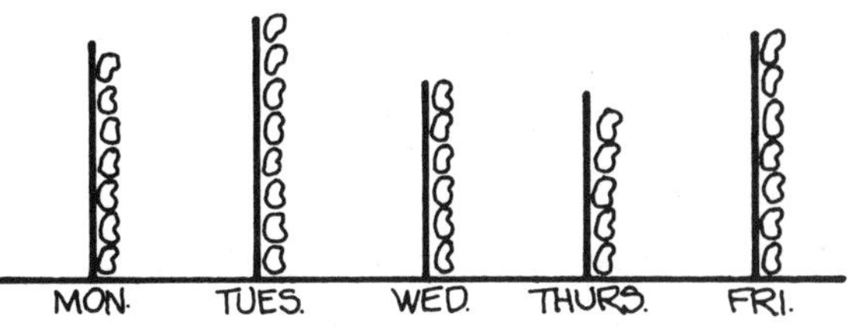

They can then count the beans and record how hot it was in lima bean units: "Wednesday it was eight lima beans hot." Soon, children can skip the yarn stage and lay lima beans directly next to the mercury column on the thermometer.

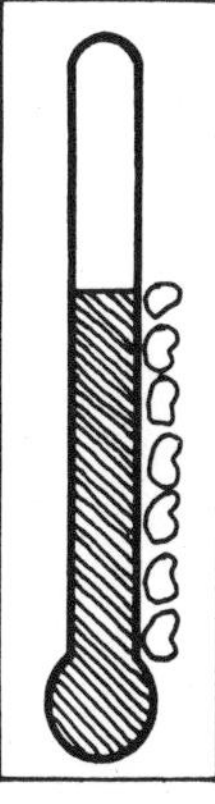

Activity TEMP-4: The Fahrenheit Thermometer

What You Need: Thermometers, Record Sheet TEMP-4, (p. 123), and felt pen.

How to Do It: This activity provides an opportunity for children to practice using the customary temperature scale. Select as many "data collectors" as you have thermometers and construct a graph of the outdoor temperature over the school day. Then ask your students the following kinds of questions: At what time is the temperature the highest?

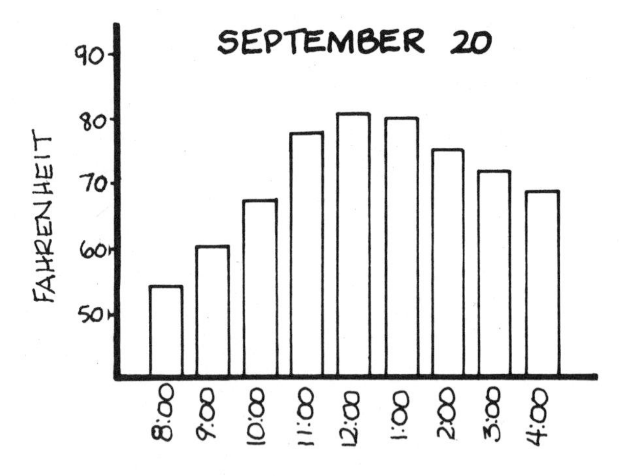

Is it the same time every day? What happens on cloudy days? Develop graphs over the school year and observe changes. Does the temperature ever go below 0°? How could we show a temperature below zero on our graph? Have students complete Record Sheet TEMP-4.

NOTE: We included the following activity to help familiarize your students with metric units. Remember you may easily change this activity to customary units by using Fahrenheit degrees instead Celsius degrees.

EXTENDED ACTIVITY:

Mr. Celsius In order to help your students to discover how Mr. Celsius developed his temperature scale, locate a thermometer that will measure 0°C to 100°C. (Check with a local high school science laboratory.) Have each student measure the temperature of a bucket of ice water (0°C) and a pan of boiling water (100°C). Dividing this difference into 100 equal parts gives us the Celsius scale. Other temperatures can be measured as well, such as body temperature, tap. water (hot and cold), and room temperature. Additional activities to suggest might include finding the temperature of the class hamster, a frog, a dog, a cat, a family member, a plant, a tire (after a long ride), or a skateboard. Have the students use their imaginations in thinking of temperatures to measure and how to measure them.

Activity TEMP-5: Meaningful Temperatures

What You Need: Activity Sheets , TEMP-5A and TEMP-5B (pp. 124 and 125), and pencils.

How to Do It: This activity provides practice interpreting and internalizing the Celsius temperature scale. Distribute copies of Activity Sheets TEMP-5A and TEMP-5B and ask students to choose appropriate clothing or draw an appropriate scene for the temperature indicated.

For example:

TIME ACTIVITY SEQUENCE

	Concrete	Representational	Symbolic
Comparison	TIME-1 What Takes Longer?		
Nonstandard	TIME-2 Making Your Own Clock		
Standard	TIME-3 Making a Sundial →	TIME-4 Just-a-Second →	TIME-5 Time Flies

DEVELOPMENTAL ACTIVITY SEQUENCE

Activity TIME-1: What Takes Longer?

What You Need: Pencils, scissors, paper, Record Sheet TIME-1 (p. 126).

How to Do It: Have your students work in pairs and complete the tasks on Worksheet TIME-1. After completing each set of tasks, they should record which took more and which took less time to finish. Clocks should not be used. Pairs of students should "race," each beginning a different task at the same time. Whoever finishes first did the task which took the least amount of time.

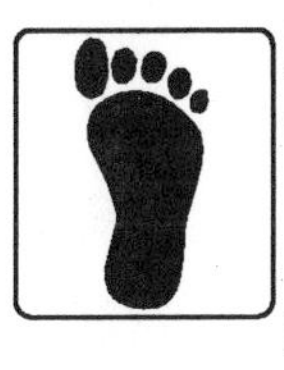

Activity TIME-2: Making Your Own Clock

What You Need: Containers (not glass), H_2O, Activity Sheet TIME-2 (p. 127).

How to Do It: Understanding that time is measurable in distinct, arbitrary units can be a difficult notion to teach children. In order to facilitate this knowledge, have your students design their own time-telling mechanisms.

A simple device that is fun to make and use is a water clock. Punch a tiny hole in a plastic container near the bottom, fill the container with water, and let it drain out. The time the container takes to empty is your nonstandard unit of time. This unit can then be used to time any activity. To avoid having to refill the container each time it empties in order to keep your clock running, set up a series of identical containers with identical holes. To determine the amount of elapsed time, simply count the empty containers from top down. To time longer events, use more containers, one on each stair.

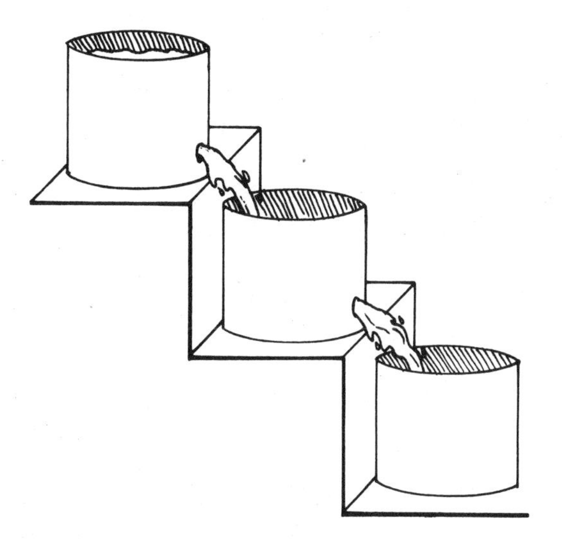

After a period of free exploration, have children try Activity Sheet TIME-2.

EXTENDED ACTIVITY:

Sweet-Smelling Time There are many ways to mark time. The sun and moon have been used for centuries to simplify units of time. In certain areas seasonal variations have provided for longer demarcations of time's passing. Nature also provides us with an hourly time keeper that not only looks beautiful and smells sweet, but is an amazing phenomenon to witness in action. It's a "flower clock" found even today in many formal English gardens. Have your class plant one and see if it works. The following flowers are accurate to the $\frac{1}{2}$ hour on sunny days and work in North America.

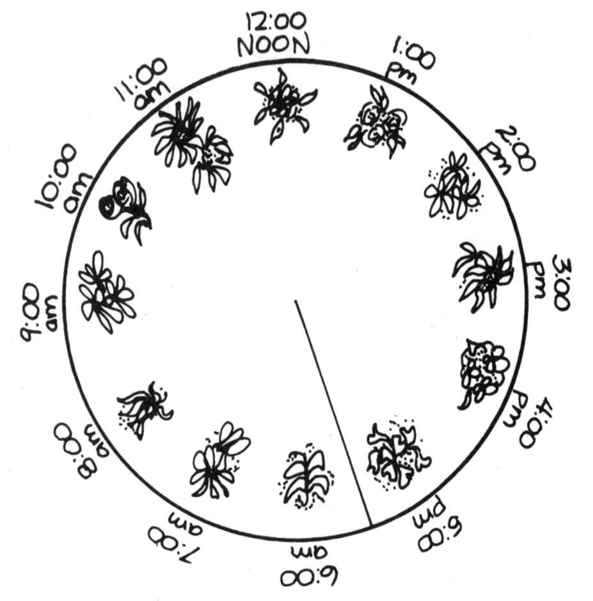

6:00 A.M. Spotted Cat's Ear opens
7:00 A.M. African Marigolds open
8:00 A.M. Mouse-ear Hawkweed opens
9:00 A.M. Prickly Sow Thistle closes
11:00 A.M. Star of Bethlehem opens
12:00 P.M. Passion Flowers open
1:00 P.M. Childing Pink closes
2:00 P.M. Scarlet Pimpernel closes
4:00 P.M. Small Bindweed closes
5:00 P.M. White Water Lily closes
6:00 P.M. Evening Primroses open

Activity TIME-3: Make a Sundial

What You Need: Your city's latitude, cardboard, protractor, scissors, pencils, a table, and sunshine.

How to Do It: After students find their city's latitude on a map, have each of them construct two angles out of cardboard that are equal to 90° minus their present latitude. This can be done using a protractor. If your city has a latitude of 40° North, then,

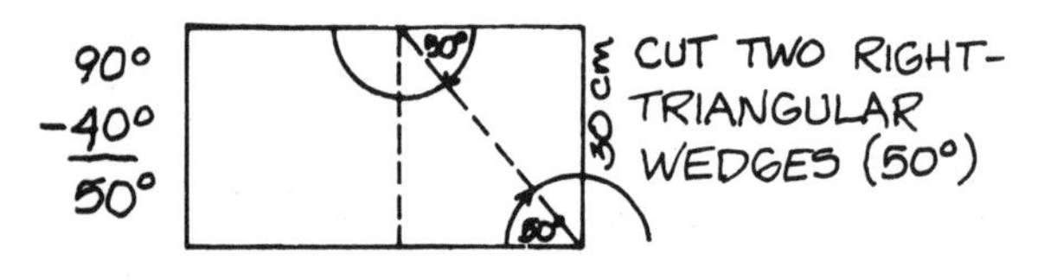

Next, have each child make a flat rectangle for the face of the sundial. Have them mark off the hours on their rectangles using a protractor. Each hour should be 15° apart.

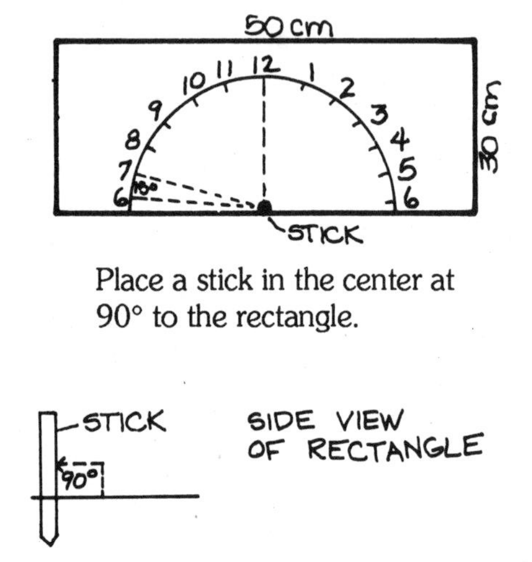

Place a stick in the center at 90° to the rectangle.

Students should then glue the rectangles onto their wedges and the sundials are finished. Students may then take turns placing their sundials on a table outside. With the wedge pointing north, the shadow tells the time (if the sun is shining, of course.) Teachers may also want to make a larger sundial for the classroom.

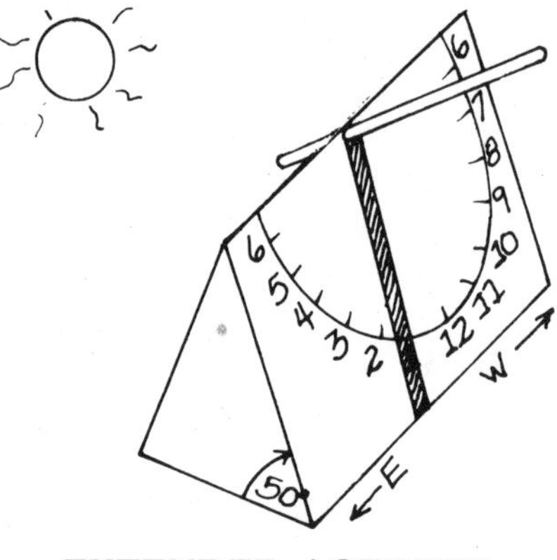

EXTENDED ACTIVITY:

Sunset This activity is a great one to involve students' parents and friends in, since it must be done at home near the end of the day. The problem students must solve is to figure out how to tell how many minutes are left until sunset, without using a watch or clock.

To do this, students should go outside 30–45 minutes before the sun is due to set. If they hold their hands directly in front of them at arm's length, they can measure how many fingers "fit" between the bottom of the sun and the horizon (caution them not to stare directly at the sun but to keep their eyes in the shadow of their hands.)

Once they've measured this distance, they need to clock the time it takes for the sun to set. If it takes 1 hour and 4 fingers fit between the horizon and the sun, then know that each finger was worth 15 minutes. After they clock this occurrence once (and "calibrate" their fingers) they will never again need a watch to determine how many minutes until the sun goes down. Try it!

Activity TIME-4: Just a Second

What You Need: Stopwatch, Record Sheet TIME-4 (p. 128) and pencil.

How to Do It: To practice keeping track of the time, teach your class how to use a stopwatch. Using Record Sheet TIME-4, have each student carefully record the elapsed times of the various events. If you can locate several timepieces, have the students break up into groups for this activity.

Some interesting events to time might include:
1. Writing something backwards.
2. Saying the alphabet forward (or backward).
3. Tying a shoe five times.
4. Running the 100-meter dash.
5. Putting a Tangram puzzle (see Appendix II) together into a square.
6. Putting a deck of cards in order by suit (1, 2, 3, , , Q, K).
7. Have your students think up others.

Activity TIME-5: Time Flies

What You Need: Watch the second hand and Record Sheet TIME-5 (p. 129).

How to Do It: Sharpening the accuracy of our internal clock can lead to several interesting activities. Cover the face of the classroom clock and with your class in their seats, say: "When I say begin, estimate how long it will take for a minute to go by, then stand up." The first time you try this activity, estimates will range from ten seconds to several minutes. Try this activity three or four times and you should notice an improvement in your students' time estimation skills.

Further experience with estimating time should be encouraged. Ask students to try estimating the elapsed time of familiar events such as: washing dishes, transition between classes, walking home, a run around the track, waiting in line at the grocery store, or the commercial time in one hour of TV viewing (Record Sheet TIME-5).

EXTENDED ACTIVITY:

Metric Clock Little serious thought has been given to converting standard time to a base 10 system of keeping time. It might be fun, however, for upper-grade children to try to develop a metric time system for seconds, minutes, hours, days, weeks, and years. It might be helpful to use a calculator for this problem. An interesting question might be "How old will you be in Metric time?"

Record/Activity Sheets and Other Materials

SELECTED BIBLIOGRAPHY

Selected Childrens' Literature Involving Measurement

Childrens' literature books like those included in the following collection can be used to introduce units on measurement concepts. These stories serve to motivate learning about measurement attributes and help to integrate language arts into your mathematics and science curriculum. Have fun!

Linear Measurement

Ernie and the Mile Long Muffler by Marjorie Lewis (Putnam Publishing Group, 1982) is a story about a young boy who is determined to knit a world record muffler (scarf). Classes might actually knit pieces of a muffler, keeping track of the time to estimate how long it would take to knit one mile. Other investigations could involve determining how many times this muffler would wrap around the classroom, or carpet the walkway to the office. Students could determine if it would reach from school to their homes.

Jim and the Beanstalk by Raymond Briggs (Puffin, 1986) is a sequel to *Jack and the Beanstalk*. Jim gets involved in actually measuring the giant for things like eyeglasses and dentures! The concept of ratio can be explored through the hands-on activities introduced in the story.

My Tower by Beverly Randell (Nelson Windmill, 1986) is a primary level book in which children are involved in building towers equal to their height. Your students could also build towers and compare them with each other, drawing a graph to show the relationship between the towers and themselves.

Mass Measurement

In *Dad's Diet* by Barbara Comber (Martin Educational Bookshelf, 1985), Dad's weight is compared to the weights of other members of the family and he decides to go on a diet. Investigations could include comparing masses of the family members in the book with the actual mass of your students' family members. Also, weight ratios can be explored—for example, who in the family weighs about twice as much or one-half as much as each student?

Sizes by Jan Pienkowski (Puffin, 1983) is a primary level book that is excellent for introducing the concept of mass as a size attribute, as well as for motivating investigations of mass comparisons.

Volume

Mr. Archimedes' Bath by Pamela Allen (Collins, 1985) offers an excellent illustration of how to determine volume by displacement. Students can be encouraged to do experiments measuring the volume of solids using the displacement method.

Who Sank the Boat? by Pamela Allen (Nelson, 1985) is a wonderful story about volume and mass and their relationship to the displacement of boats. In the book, animals step one-by-one into a boat until it sinks. Children can perform similar experiments utilizing pennies and boats made of aluminum foil.

Area

Something Absolutely Enormous by Margaret Wild (Ashton Scholastic, 1984) motivates investigations of area, height, and volume. This book encourages children to create their own problems and develop critical thinking skills.

The Hilton Hen House by Jo Hinchliffe (Ashton Scholastic, 1987) explores counting, ratios, and area. The relationship between area and scale drawing is developed in a way that can be easily incorporated into your classroom.

Time

A Day on the Avenue by Robert Roennfeldt (Viking Kestrel, 1983) is a non-text book that promotes investigations of time and sequencing.

All in a Day by Mitsumasa Anno (Bodley Head, 1986) delivers a powerful message about peace for young children through a motivating exploration of time.

Microcomputer Software

Bumble Games (The Learning Company). Practice locating positions on coordinate graphs.

Clock (Hartley Software). Practice reading time on a simulated clock face.

Geometric Supposer: Points and Lines, Triangles, Quadrilaterals, and *Circles* (Sunburst). A versatile series of software tools for evaluating conjectures about area formulae and geometric relationships.

Magic Cash Register (Avant-Garde). Practice making change for simulated purchases.

Metric and Problem Solving (MECC). Practice estimating lengths and logic games.

Micros for Micros: Estimation (Lawrence Hall of Science, UC Berkeley). Practice estimating length, number, and time.

Money and Time Adventures of the Lollipop Dragon (Society for Visual Communication). Practice telling time using digital and traditional clocks, counting money, and making change.

Money Matters (MECC). Primary-age children can learn to recognize money (US or Canadian), count money, and make change.

Playing With Science: Temperature (Sunburst). Students conduct experiements that require the measurement of temperature using computer-controlled thermistors.

Title 4C Microcomputer Math Instruction Project (San Diego City Schools, Computer Resource Dept., 4100 Normal St., San Diego, CA 92103). Set of 243 math activities including length, area, volume, map reading, temperature, time, and measurement applications.

References and Readings

Baffington, A. (1973). *Meters, Liters and Grams.* New York: Random House.

Barnett, C., Judd, W., & Young, S. (1976). *Measure Matters.* Palo Alto, CA: Creative Publications.

Bates, J. (1972). *Exploring Metric Measure—Primary Teacher's Source Book.* New York: McGraw-Hill Book Co.

Bitter, G., Mikesell, J., & Maurdeff, K. (1976). *Activities Handbook for Teaching the Metric System.* Boston, MA: Allyn and Bacon.

Cavanaugh, M. (1977). *Metric Madness.* Denver, CO: Scott Resources.

Christopher, L. (1982). Graphs Can Jazz Up the Mathematics Curriculum. *Arithmetic Teacher,* 30(1), 28-30.

Clements, D., & Battista, M. (1986). Geometry and Geometric Measurement. *Arithmetic Teacher,* 33(6),29-32.

Elementary Science Study (1966). *The Balance Book.* New York: McGraw-Hill Book Co.

Harrison, W. (1987). What Lies Behind Measurement? *Arithmetic Teacher,* 34(7), 19-21.

Hart, K. (1984). Which Comes First – Length, Area, or Volume? *Arithmetic Teacher,* 31(9), 16-18, 26-27.

Hildreth, D. (1983). The Use of Strategies in Estimating Measurements. *Arithmetic Teacher,* 34(7), 50-54.

Horak, V., & Horak, W. (1983). Teaching Time with Slit Clocks. *Arithmetic Teacher,* 30(5), 8-12

Johnson, E. (1981). Bar Graphs for First Graders. *Arithmetic Teacher,* 29(4), 30-31.

Mullen, G. (1985). How Do You Measure Up? *Arithmetic Teacher,* 33(2), 16-21.

National Council of Teachers of Mathematics (1976). *Measurement in School Mathematics: 1976 Yearbook.* D. Nelson & R. Reys (Eds.). Reston, VA: NCTM.

Nibbelink, W. (1982). Graphing for Any Grade. *Arithmetic Teacher,* 30(3), 28-31.

Roper, A. (1977). *Metric Recipes for the Classroom.* Palo Alto, CA: Creative Publications.

Thompson, C., & Van de Walle, J. (1985). Learning about Rulers and Measuring. *Arithmetic Teacher,* 2(8), 8-12.

SI METRIC SYSTEM

SI METRIC SYSTEM

A summary of the Standard International (SI) Metric System is included on page vi for your reference. Some rules regarding editorial style and the use of symbols are listed here.

1. Avoid capitalizing unit names or commonly used symbols except Celsius (either l or L can be used for liter).

   i.e., gram not Gram

2. Never use the plural form of symbols.

   i.e., 5 kg not 5 kgs

3. Never put a period after a symbol except at the end of a sentence.

   i.e., km not km.

4. Leave a space between the digit and the symbol.

   i.e., 4 cm not 4cm

5. Never use a prefix alone.

   i.e., kilogram not kilo

6. Include a zero before the decimal point when the measure is less than one unit.

   i.e., 0.42 cm not .42 cm

7. Use a space instead of a comma when writing large numbers. Some countries use the comma as a decimal point and this might lead to confusion.

   i.e., 2 462 384.42 m not 2,462,384.42 m

8. The metric units can be spelled as follows:

   metre — foreign usage
   meter — common usage

METRIC PREFIXES

Prefix	Factor	Meter (m)		Gram (g)		Liter(L)	
kilo	(1000)	kilometer	(km)	kilogram	(kg)	kiloliter	(kl)
hecto	(100)	hectometer	(hm)	hectogram	(hg)	hectoliter	(hl)
deka	(10)	dekameter	(dam)	dekagram	(dag)	dekaliter	(dal)
base unit	(1)	meter	(m)	gram	(g)	liter	(L)
deci	(1/10)	decimeter	(dm)	decigram	(dg)	deciliter	(dl)
centi	(1/100)	centimeter	(cm)	centigram	(cg)	centiliter	(cl)
milli	(1/1000)	millimeter	(mm)	milligram	(mg)	milliliter	(ml)

Metric Units and Place Value

kg	hg	dag	g	dg	cg	mg
1000	100	10	1	0.1	0.01	0.001

Metric Mass Measures

1000 milligrams (mg)	= 1 gram (g)
100 centigrams (cg)	= 1 gram (g)
10 decigrams (dg)	= 1 gram (g)
1 gram (g)	= 1 gram (g)
10 grams (g)	= 1 dekagram (dag)
100 grams (g)	= 1 hectogram (hg)
1000 grams (g)	= 1 kilogram (kg)
.	.
.	.
.	.
1,000,000 grams (g)	= 1 megagram (Mg) or tonne (t)

Liter and Cubic Unit Equivalents

Liter Units		Cubic Units
1 milliliter (ml)	=	1 cubic centimeter
1 centiliter (cl)	=	10 cubic centimeters (cm^3)
1 deciliter (dal)	=	100 cubic centimeters (cm^3)
1 liter (L)	=	1000 cm^3 or 1 cubic centimeter (dm^3)
1 dekaliter (dl)	=	10 000 cubic centimeters (cm^3)
1 hectoliter (hl)	=	100 000 cubic centimeters (cm^3)
1 kiloliter (kl)	=	1 000 000 cm^3 or 1 cubic meter

TABLE OF COMMON METRIC UNITS AND EQUIVALENCE

	Symbol	Equivalence	Benchmark
LENGTH			
kilometer	km	1 km = 1,000 m	about one-half mile
meter	m		a basketball player is about 2 meters tall
centimeter	cm	100 cm = 1 m	width of a little fingerprint
millimeter	mm	1,000 mm = 1 m	
AREA			
hectare	ha	1 ha = 10,000 m^2	two football fields
square meter	m^2		
square centimeter	cm^2	10,000 cm^2 = 1 m^2	little fingerprint
CAPACITY			
liter	l or L		about 1 quart
milliliter	ml	1,000 ml = 1 L	a thimble full
VOLUME			
cubic meter	m^3	1 m^3 = 1,000 L	
cubic decimeter	dm^3	1 dm^3 = 1 L	
cubic centimeter	cm^3	1 cm^3 = 1 ml	
MASS			
kilogram	kg	approx. mass of 1 L of water (at 4°C)	about two pounds
gram	g	1,000 g = 1 kg	a nickel weights about 5 grams
milligram	mg	1,000 mg = 1 g	
TEMPERATURE			
Celsius (degree)	°C		about 2 degrees Fahrenheit

CUSTOMARY UNITS OF MEASURE

Length		Weight		Capacity	
12 inches	= 1 foot	437.5 grains	= 1 ounce (dry)	3 teaspoons	= 1 tablespoon
3 feet	= 1 yard	16 ounces	= 1 pound	16 tablespoons	= 1 cup
5.5 yards	= 1 rod	100 pounds	= 1 hundredweight	2 cups	= 1 pint
40 rods	= 1 furlong	20 hundred-weights	= 1 ton	2 pints	= 1 quart
8 furlongs	= 1 mile			4 quarts	= 1 gallon
				2 gallons	= 1 peck
				4 pecks	= 1 bushel

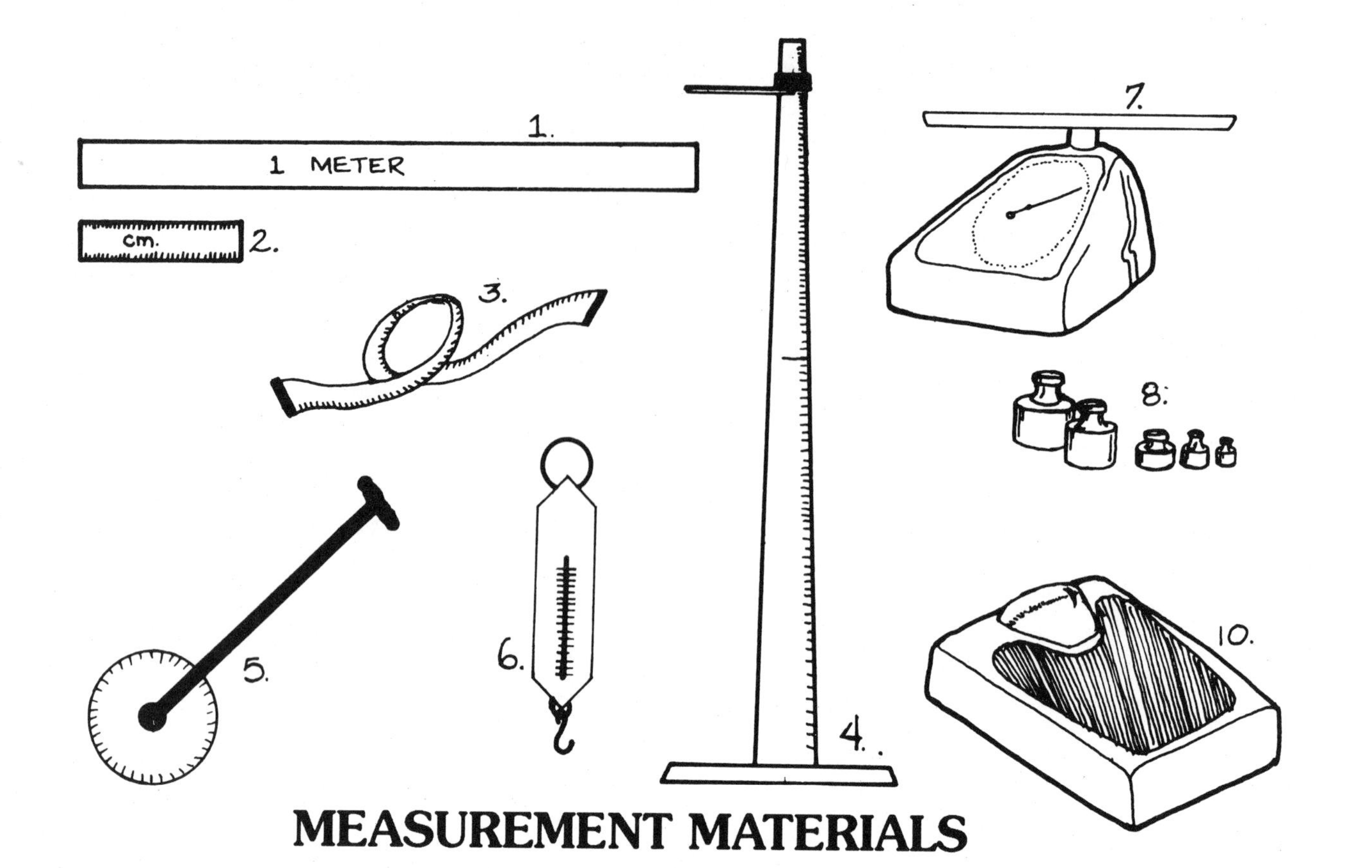

MEASUREMENT MATERIALS

LENGTH

1. *Yard and metersticks:* These can be purchased unmarked, calibrated in only inches, centimeters, and/or decimeters. Qualities to look for are clarity and simplicity of unit markings appropriate for your grade level.

2. *Foot and centimeter rulers:* These rulers are usually 25 to 30 cm or 12 inches long. They prove useful for your standard classroom ruler. The most efficient ruler is marked in centimeters on one side and millimeters on the other (decimeter distinctions are all right,too).

3. *Measuring tapes:* These are cloth tapes marked in customary metric units. They are useful for measuring curves and corners or any uneven surface.

4. *Height measures:* These come in two types: (1) the wall measure, which is usually a paper strip marked off in meters and centimeters and affixed to the wall; (2) the free-standing height measure, which is similar to those found in doctors' offices. It consists of a calibrated pole with a sliding bar that comes to rest atop an individual's head, thereby delineating his or her height.

5. *Trundle wheel:* The metric trundle wheel is a very useful device for measuring longer distances. It is a wheel that "clicks" every time one yard or meter is traveled (i.e., a wheel with the circumference of 1 yd).

MASS

6. *Spring scales:* Spring scales are calibrated in grams and kilograms and are used by hanging the object to be weighed by the hook on the scale (similar to fish-weighers).

7. *Single pan metric scales:* These are scales with a single pan for the object and a dial-type scale for the measure (similar to baby scales).

8. *Customary metric weights:* A variety of metric weights are available commercially. A classroom should have at least one commercial set to provide the standard for "homemade" weights that can be made by pouring appropriate amounts of sand into milk cartons and then sealing them shut. These weights are used with a double-pan balance.

9. *Invicta balance:* Commercial balance with numbered pegs and plastic mass pieces.

10. *Personal scales:* These are typical bathroom scales with metric readout. They can be purchased through most educational supply dealers.

AREA

11. *Squared paper:* This paper comes in $\frac{1}{8}$ in, $\frac{1}{4}$ in, 1 in, 1 cm^2 and 2 cm^2 sizes, either in sheets or on a roll. The roll of squared paper is extremely useful for all

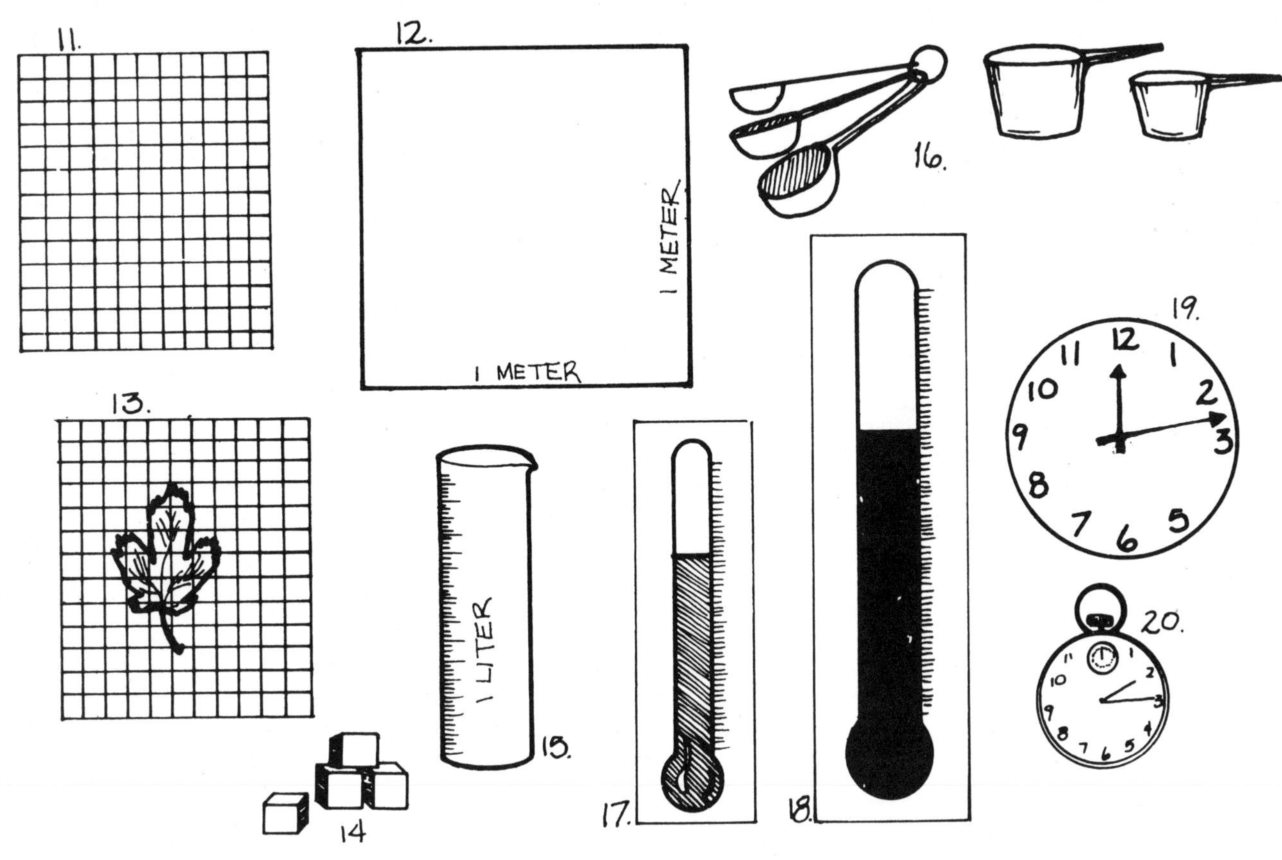

area activities as well as for making graphs.

12. *Square yard or meter:* This is used to measure large areas like carpets, basketball courts, etc. Although available commercially, it can be easily made by connecting four sticks, each 1 yd or m long, into a square.

13. *Transparent grids:* These grids are marked on clear plastic sheets and are useful for laying over actual objects in order to find their area or for use with overhead projectors.

CAPACITY

14. *Inch or centimeter cubes:* These wood or plastic cubes play an integral part in developing the concept of volume and its algorithms.

15. *Graduated containers:* It is extremely useful to have at least one set of standard capacity measures in your class. These can then be used to create "homemade" pint, quart, liter, or milliliter measurement containers.

16. *Spoon and dry measure sets:* These are your "cooking" measures, such as standard cups, tablespoons, etc. Although these can be purchased through educational supply houses, they are now available at a much more reasonable price through discount stores or supermarkets.

TEMPERATURE

17. *Thermometers:* Thermometers are available in all sizes and shapes in Fahrenheit or Celsius scales for your classroom walls.

18. *Classroom demonstration thermometer:* This is a giant thermometer on which you manually move the red line to correspond to any temperature desired. It is very useful for comparison activities.

TIME

19. *Demonstration clocks:* These cardboard, plastic-handled clocks are very useful for time-telling practice. Available commercially, they can also be constructed by students from paper plates and cutout hands secured by a brass brad.

20. *Stopwatches:* These are available through discount stores and sporting goods stores as well as educational supply houses.

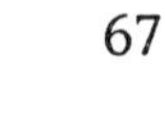

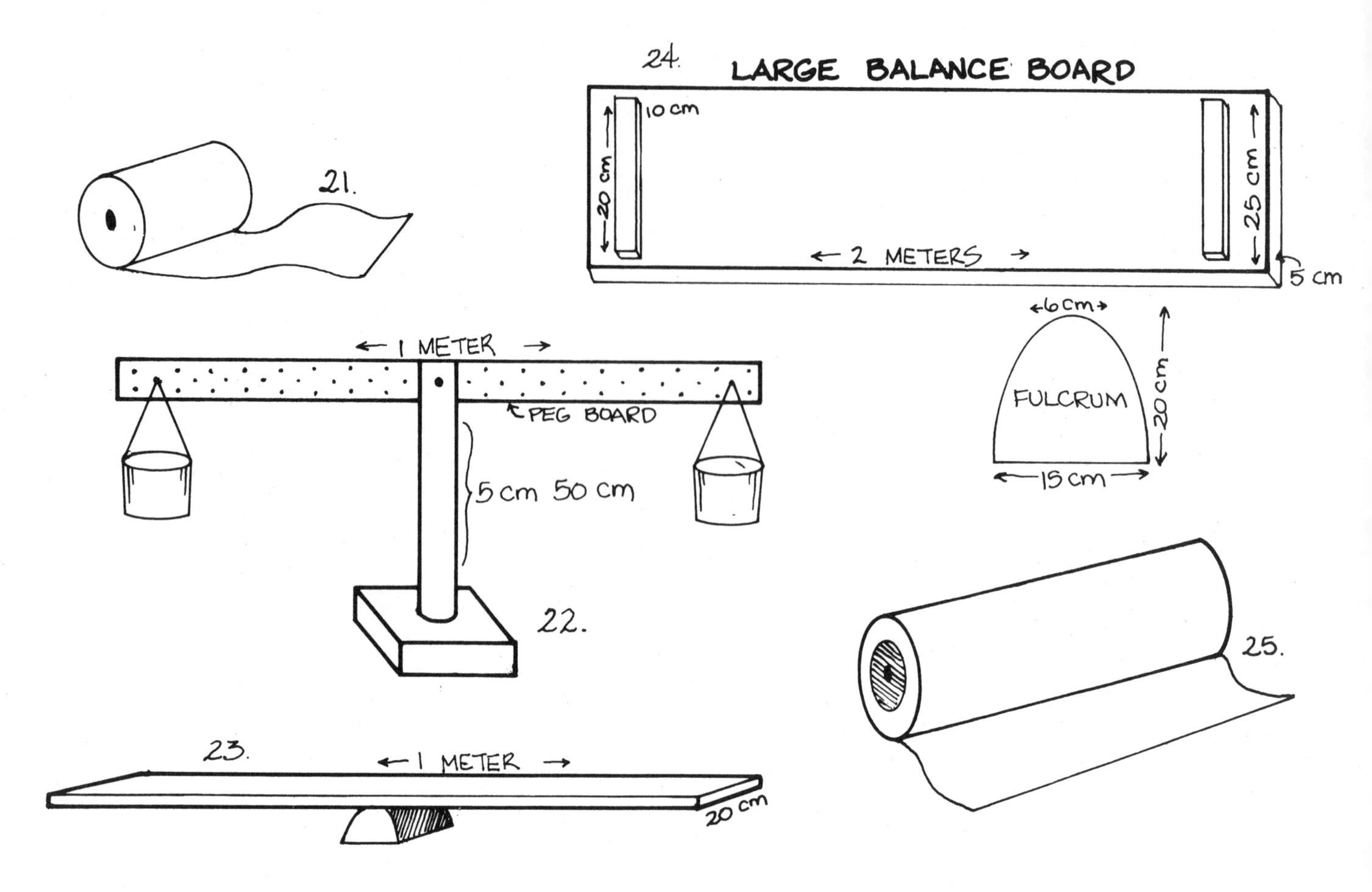

MISCELLANEOUS MATERIALS

21. ***Adding machine tape:*** For your thumb print, this tape may be purchased at most office supply stores or stationers.

22. ***Balances:*** The double-pan balance can be purchased commercially, but is very easily constructed. It is a simple balance system that has no readout scale. The example shown above is one that you can build.

23. ***Seesaw balances:*** This is another type of balance without a scale that can be made very simply from the above plans.

24. ***Large balance board:*** This balance should be very sturdy as it must support the weight of your children. Although these boards can be purchased commercially, they can be easily made following the above plans. If additional safety features are desired, you may wish to add strips of wood set in around the bottom of each end. This reduces the potential for smashed fingers.

25. ***Footprint rulers:*** The paper required for this activity is most effective at 6 in width. This can be obtained by cutting inexpensive, white rolls of shelf paper in half. Computer rolls also work well if you have access to these supplies.

26. ***Homemade yard or metersticks:*** These are a necessity for any classroom. For primary grades, yardsticks should have only inch markings and metersticks should have only centimeter markings. For older children, fractional parts of an inch and decimeter and millimeter demarcations may prove useful. At least one should be purchased commercially to use as a model. Individual yardsticks and metersticks can easily be made from scrap lumber strips obtained free of cost (or very reasonably) from a local lumber yard. Each student should be given a stick longer than one yard or meter. Using a commercially obtained meterstick, students can measure and if possible saw off their own sticks to the appropriate length. These can then be calibrated according to your classroom needs. Again, use a commercial yardstick or meterstick as the marking model.

27. ***Household washers:*** These washers can be purchased at a local hardware store. The "large" washers referred to in the mass section are 1" and the small washers are 1/2".

28. ***Large classroom graphs:*** These graphs can be made by appropriately marking off construc-

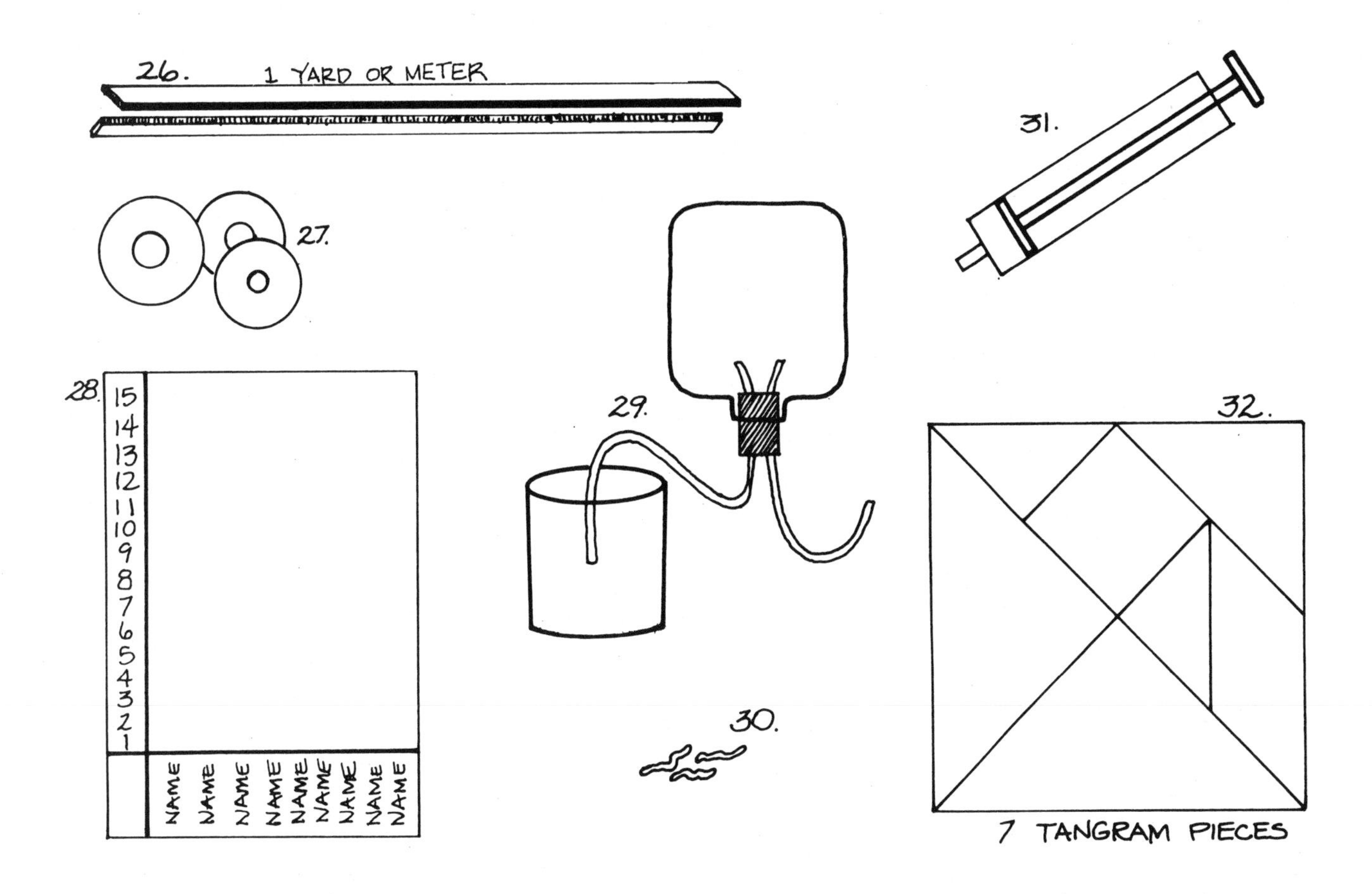

tion paper with a base line and scale. However, to simplify this process, the centimeter graph paper that comes on rolls can be used. This is available through Creative Publications.

29. *Lung capacity measurer:* The surgical tubing and two-hole corks required for this device can be purchased at a good craft or hobby store or at a medical supply house. The bottle used as the reservoir can be simply a gallon jug that many juices come in at a local supermarket.

30. *Mealworms:* These worms are the larvae of a large dark brown beetle. They can be purchased at any local pet store, since they are more traditionally used for feeding pet lizards. (They should be stored in a refrigerator.)

31. *Syringes:* These syringes, which may be used in the bottle-graphing activity, may be purchased from a medical supply house.

32. *Tangrams:* These are ancient seven-piece Chinese puzzles that can be used to develop the concept of area as well as shape, congruence, similarity, perimeter, and other geometric principles. They are available commercially through Creative Publications. An excellent source book for tangrams is *Tangramath* by Dale Seymour, also available through Creative Publications.

COMMERCIAL SOURCES OF INSTRUCTIONAL MATERIALS

Creative Publications
5040 West 111th Street
Oak Lawn, IL 60453
800-624-0822

Cuisenaire Company of America
12 Church Street, Box D
New Rochelle, NY 10802
800-237-3142

Dale Seymour Publications
P.O. Box 10888
Palo Alto, CA 94303-0879
800-222-0766 (California)
800-872-1100 (All Others)

Although there are many distributors of materials, these national companies are reliable and offer a comprehensive selection of measurement instructional materials.

CENTIMETER AND INCH RULERS

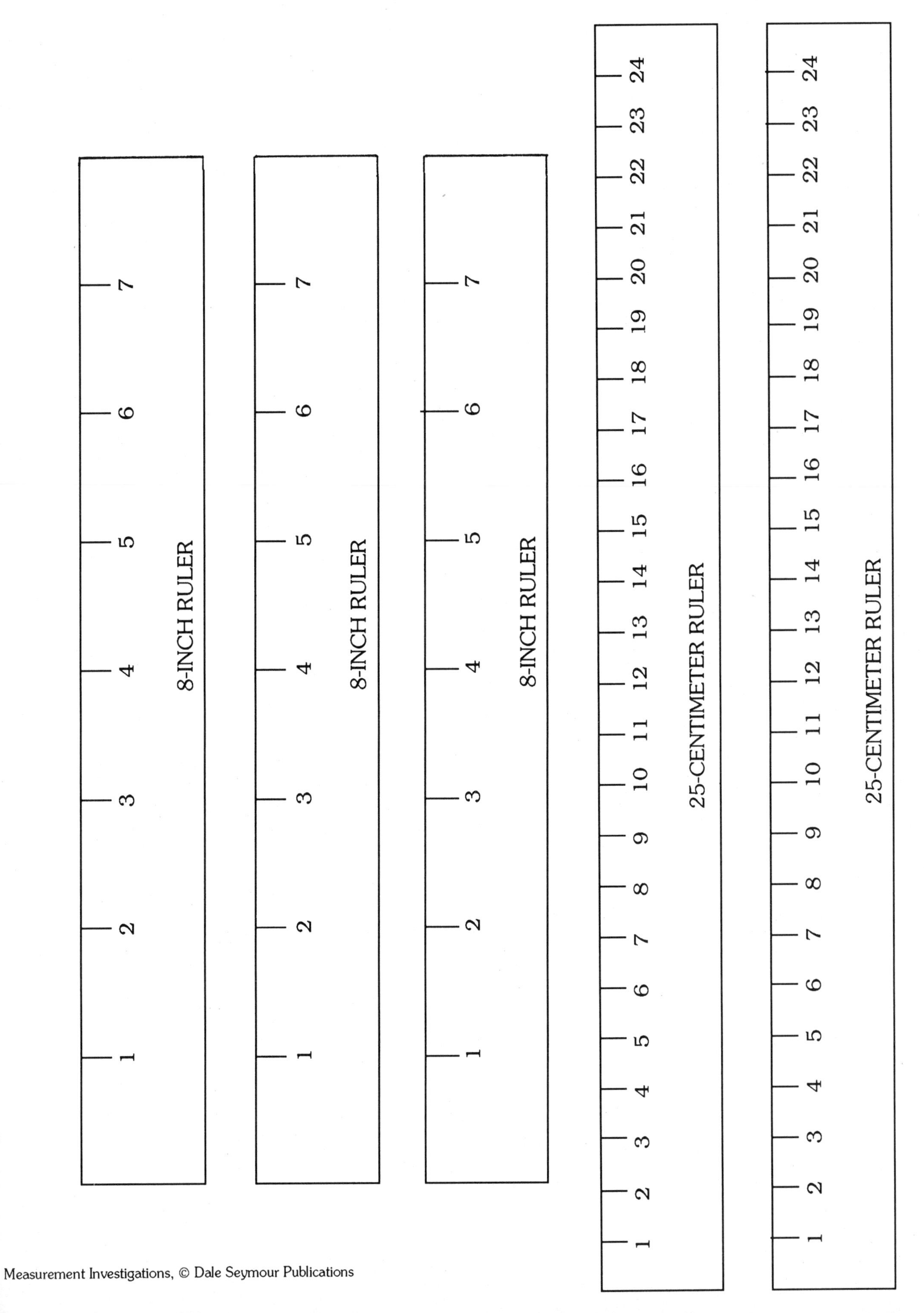

INCH SQUARED (in^2) GRAPH PAPER

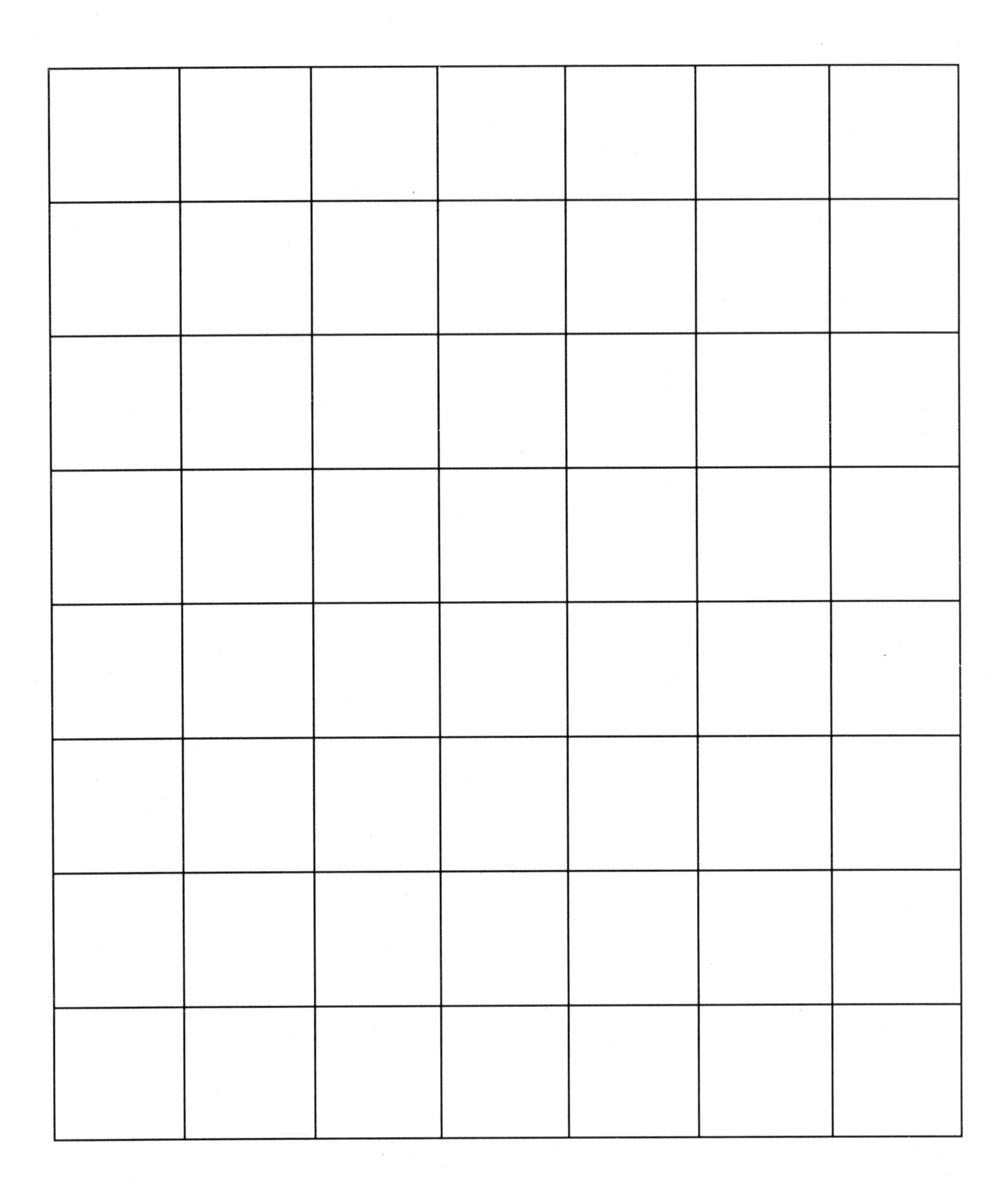

Measurement Investigations, © Dale Seymour Publications

CENTIMETER SQUARED (cm^2) GRAPH PAPER

Measurement Investigations, © Dale Seymour Publications

GEOBOARD TEMPLATE

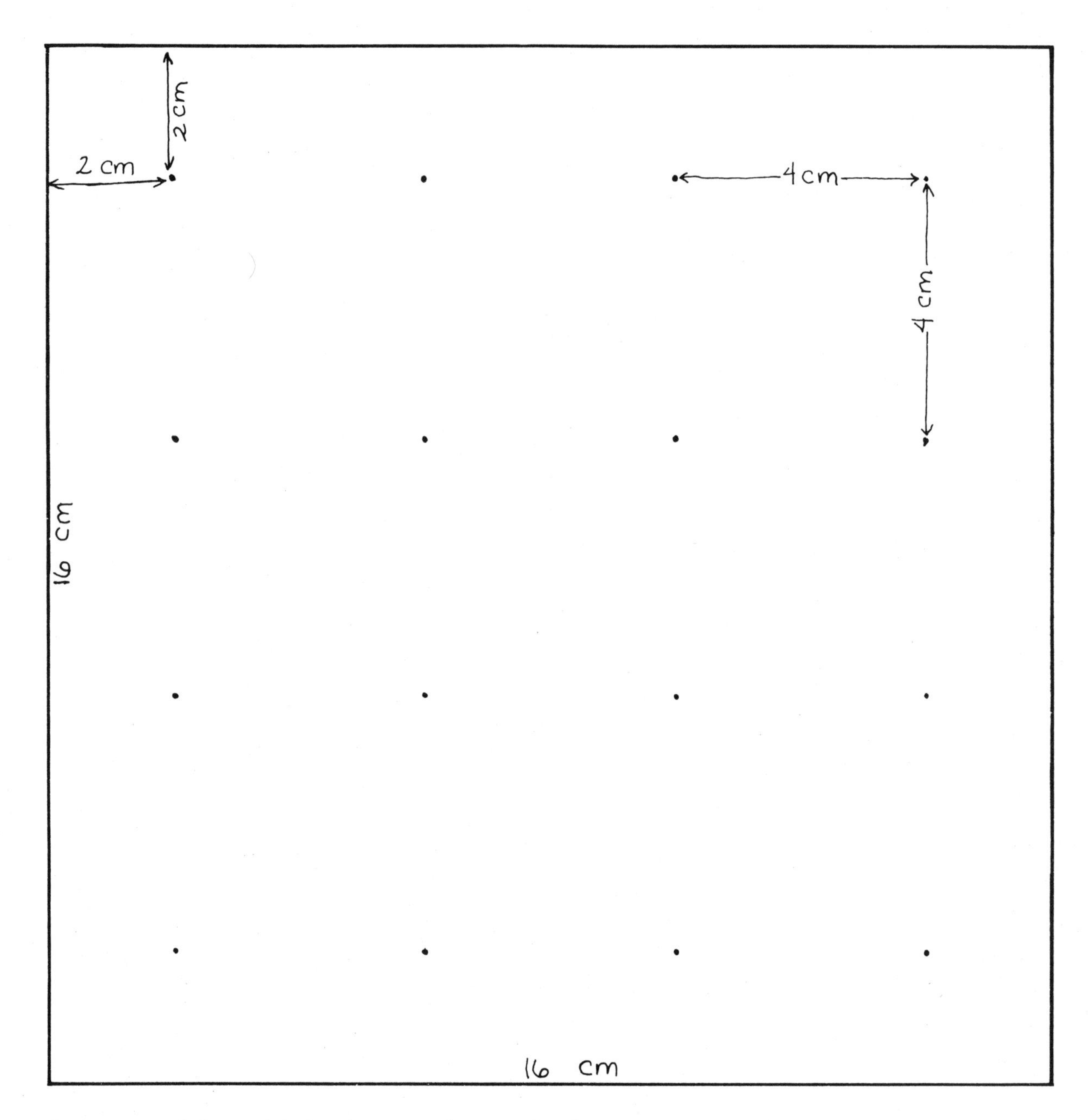

Cut squares of plywood to the above specifications, lay the template over the square, and drive small finish nails through each dot.

GEOBOARD DOT PAPER

Measurement Investigations, © Dale Seymour Publications

TOPIC CHECKLIST

(K–3)

Class List

Topic	Activity																										
Length	Warm-up																										
	P-L1																										
	P-L2																										
	P-L3																										
	P-L4																										
	P-L5																										
Mass	Warm-up																										
	P-M1																										
	P-M2																										
	P-M3																										
	P-M4																										
	P-M5																										
Area	Warm-up																										
	P-A1																										
	P-A2																										
	P-A3																										
	P-A4																										
	P-A5																										
Capacity	Warm-up																										
	P-C1																										
	P-C2																										
	P-C3																										
	P-C4																										
	P-C5																										
Temperature	TEMP-1																										
	TEMP-2																										
	TEMP-3																										
	TEMP-4																										
	TEMP-5																										
Time	TIME-1																										
	TIME-2																										
	TIME-3																										
	TIME-4																										
	TIME-5																										
Class List																											

Measurement Investigations, © Dale Seymour Publications

TOPIC CHECKLIST

(3–6)

Class List

Topic	Activity
Length	Warm-up
	I-L1
	I-L2
	I-L3
	I-L4
	I-L5
	Measurement Check
Mass	Warm-up
	I-M1
	I-M2
	I-M3
	I-M4
	I-M5
	Measurement Check
Area	Warm-up
	I-A1
	I-A2
	I-A3
	I-A4
	I-A5
	Measurement Check
Capacity	Warm-up
	I-C1
	I-C2
	I-C3
	I-C4
	I-C5
	Measurement Check
Temperature	TEMP-1
	TEMP-2
	TEMP-3
	TEMP-4
	TEMP-5
	Measurement Check
Time	TIME-1
	TIME-2
	TIME-3
	TIME-4
	TIME-5
Class List	

Measurement Investigations, © Dale Seymour Publications

TUG OF WAR

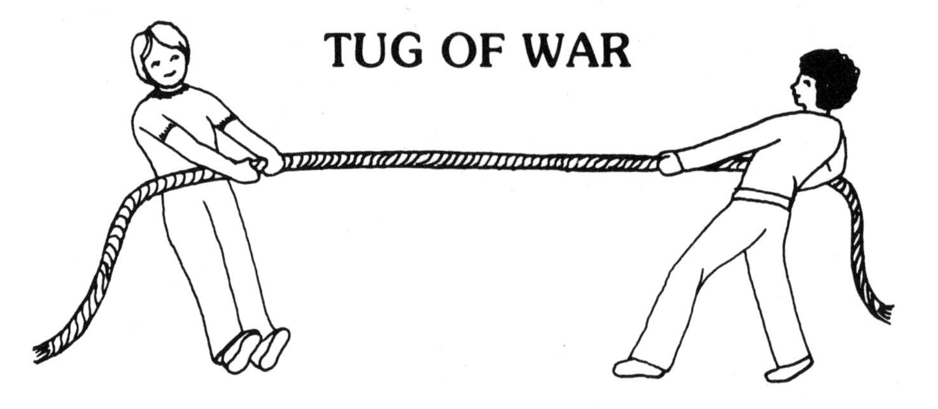

Construct the gameboard shown here and write the six common prefixes (milli, centi, deci, deka, hecto, kilo) on two different colored wooden cubes—one prefix on each face. These cubes now serve as dice.

A marker is placed in the center position to start. To play, a pair of students each roll one die. The one with the most "powerful" prefix (i.e., representing the largest factor) "tugs" the marker one space toward his or her end of the board. A tie is simply rerolled. The player who tugs the marker to the end of the board wins.

Advanced players can try moving a distance proportional to the relative "power" of the dice each time they roll. For example, if the dice showed *centi* and *hecto*, the second player could tug the marker 4 jumps since *hecto* represents a factor 10^4 times larger than *centi*. For *deci* and *deka*, the second players could tug 2 places since *deka* represents a factor 10^2 times larger than *deci*.

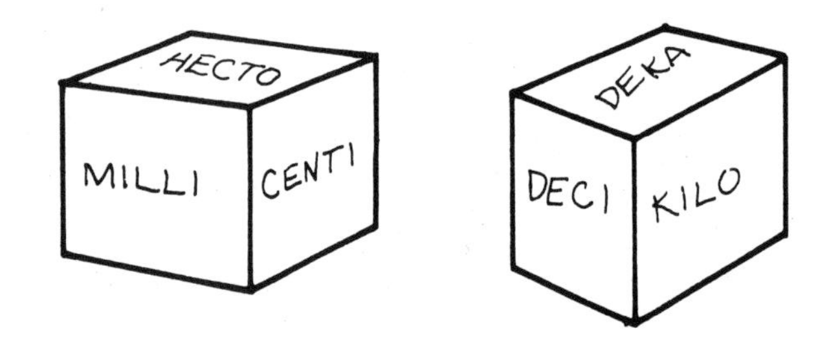

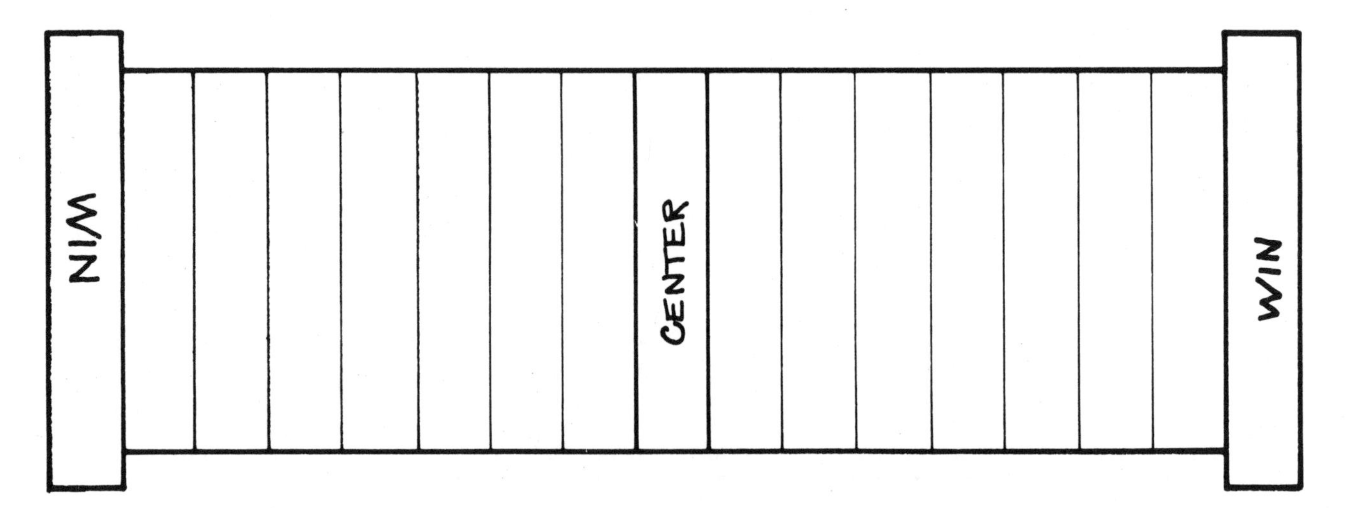

METRIC HEX

Laminate the puzzle below onto heavy tagboard and cut out the hexagons. The object is to try and put the puzzle back together so that equal measures touch everywhere.

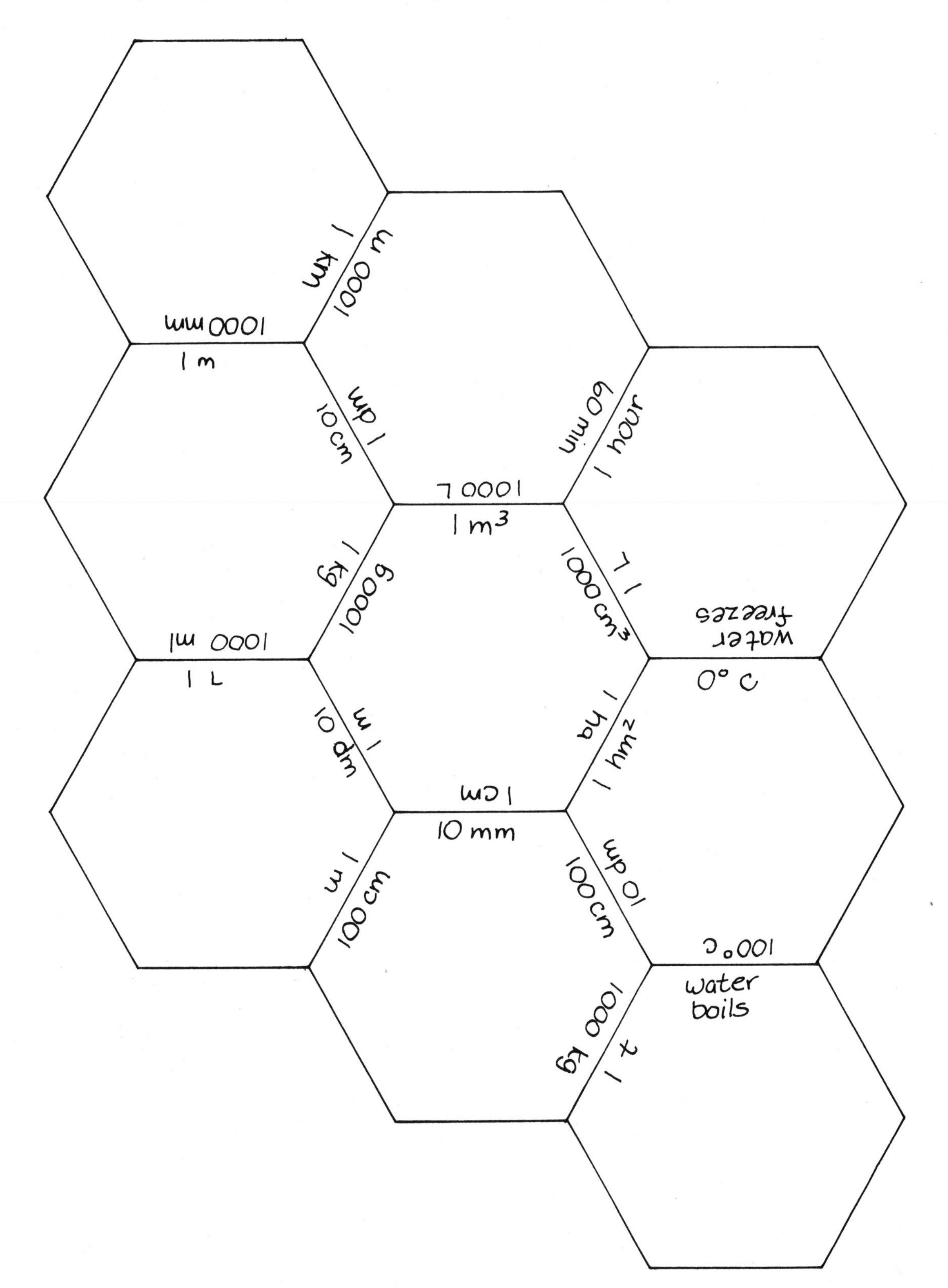

MEASUREMENT HEX

Have your students make their own hex puzzle using customary or metric units.

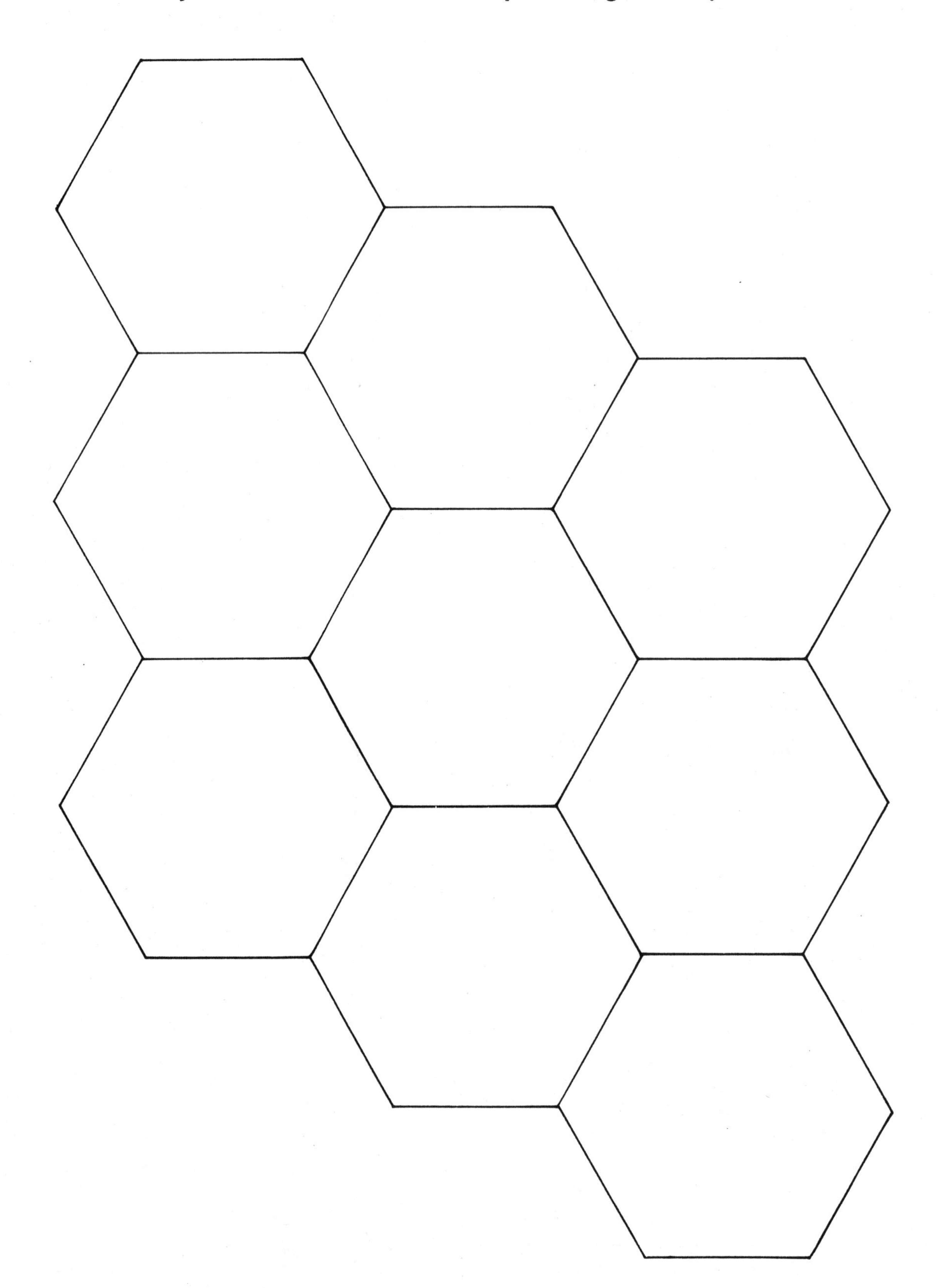

BULLETIN BOARD IDEAS

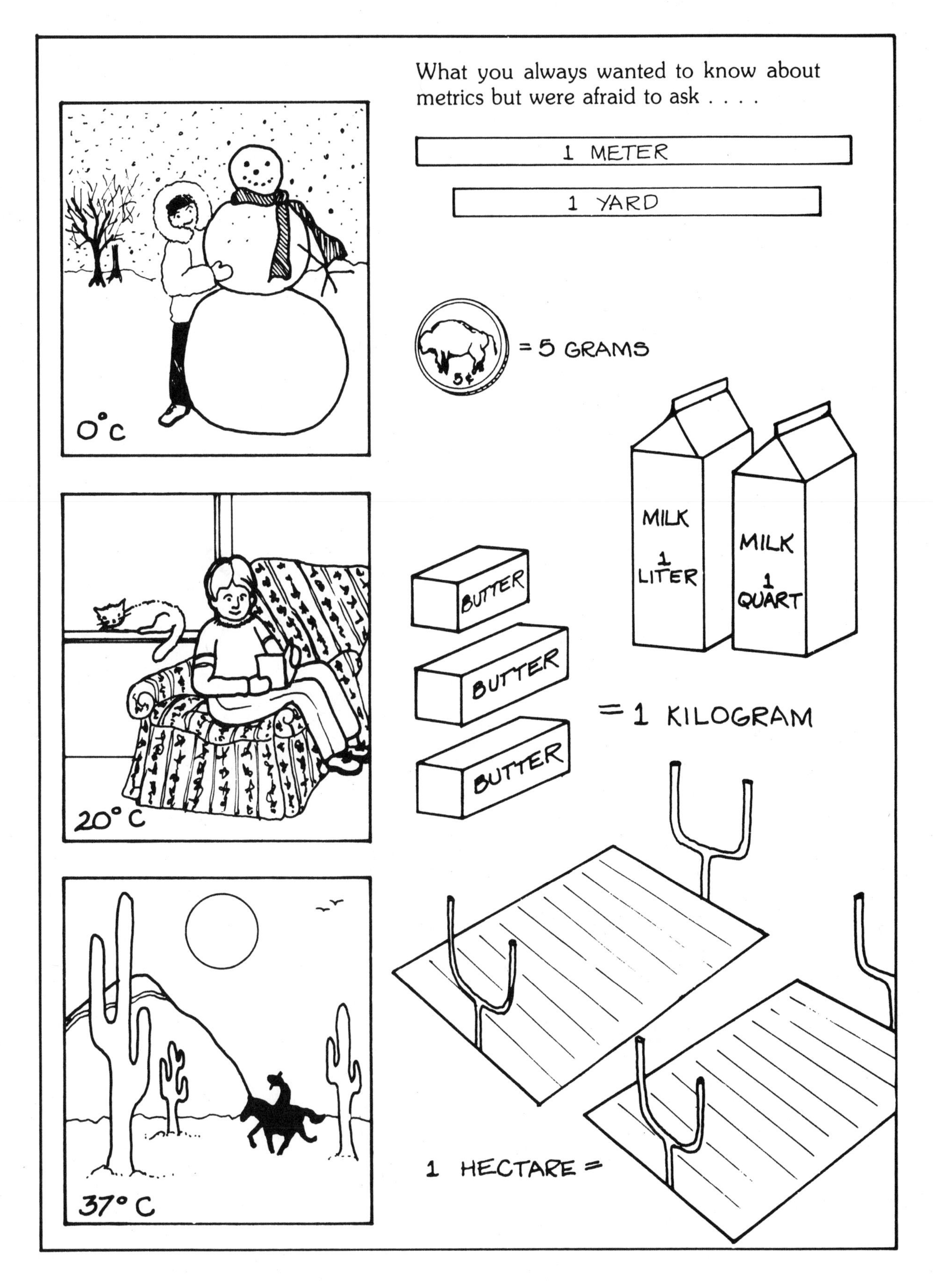

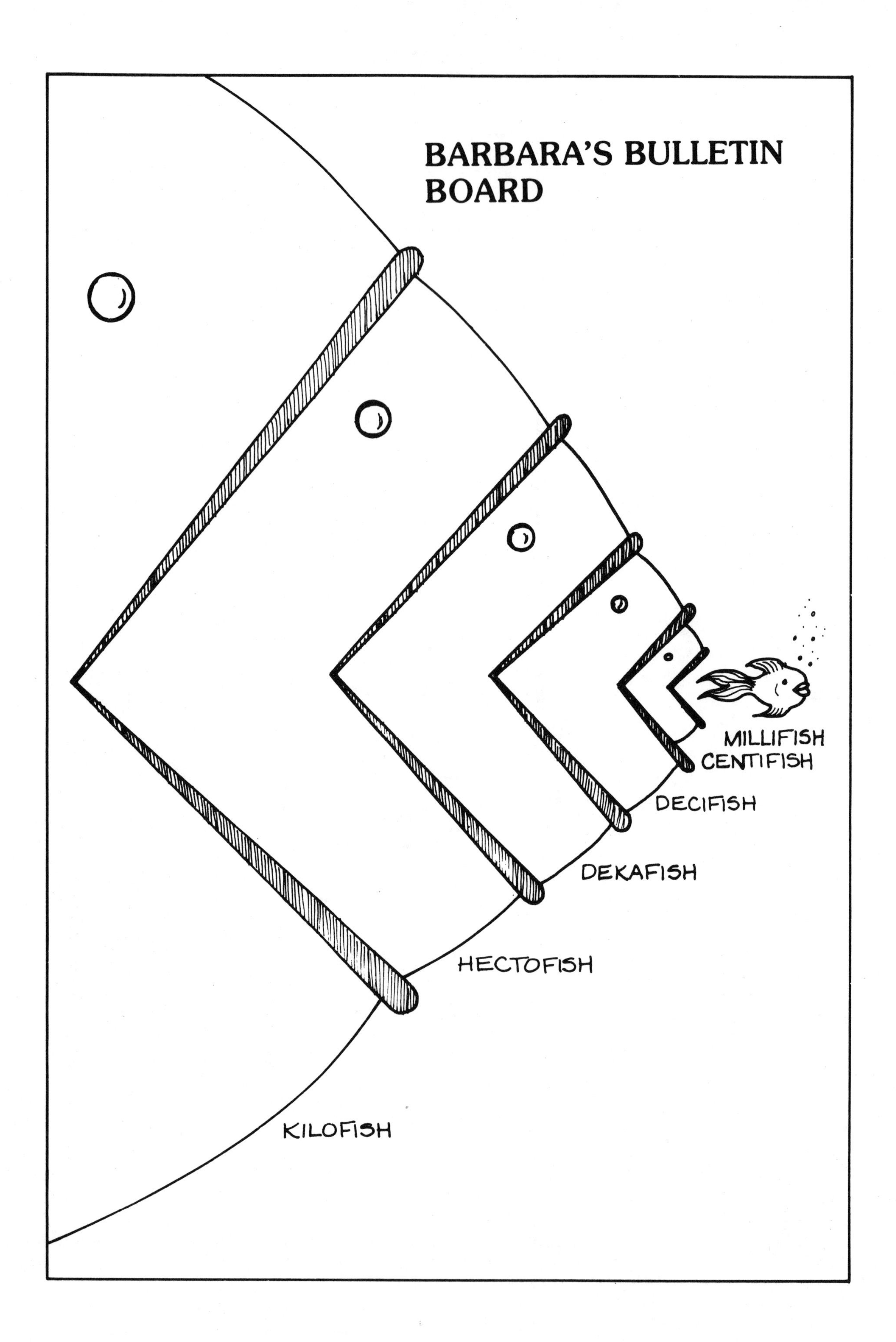
BARBARA'S BULLETIN BOARD
MILLIFISH
CENTIFISH
DECIFISH
DEKAFISH
HECTOFISH
KILOFISH

FOOTPRINT RULER

Record Sheet P-L3 Name ____________________

1. Find two things that are 1 2 3 of your own feet long.

    1. ____________________

    2. ____________________

2. Find something longer than 1 2 but shorter than 1 2 3 4 of your own feet long.

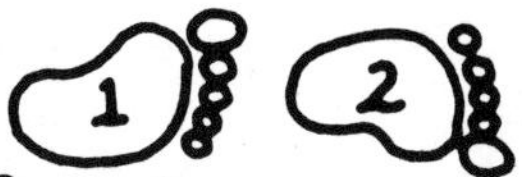

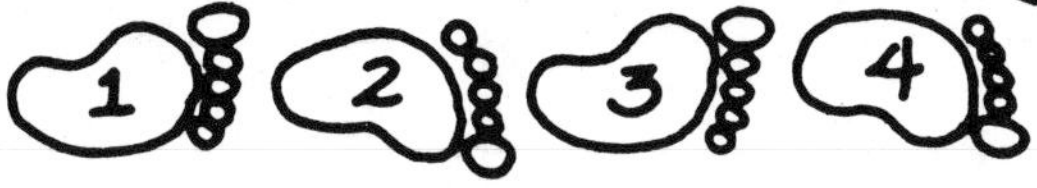

    1. ____________________

Now measure: estimate first!

3. My desk is (guess) ________ of my own feet long.

    (measure) ________

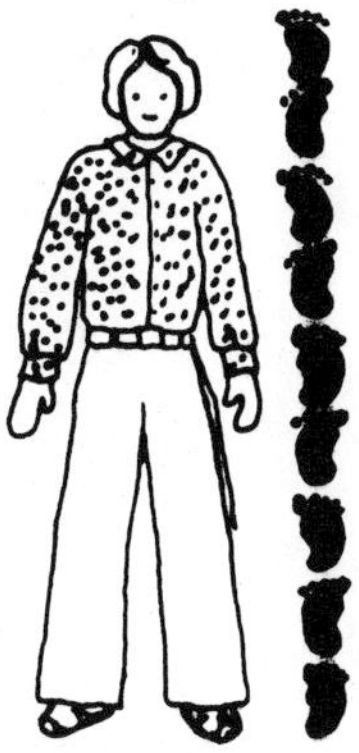

4. I am (guess) ________ of my own feet tall.

    (measure) ________

5. The door is (guess)________ of my own feet long.

    (measure) ________

Measurement Investigations, © Dale Seymour Publications

BODY BUNDLE MEASURE

Record Sheet P-L4 Name ______________________

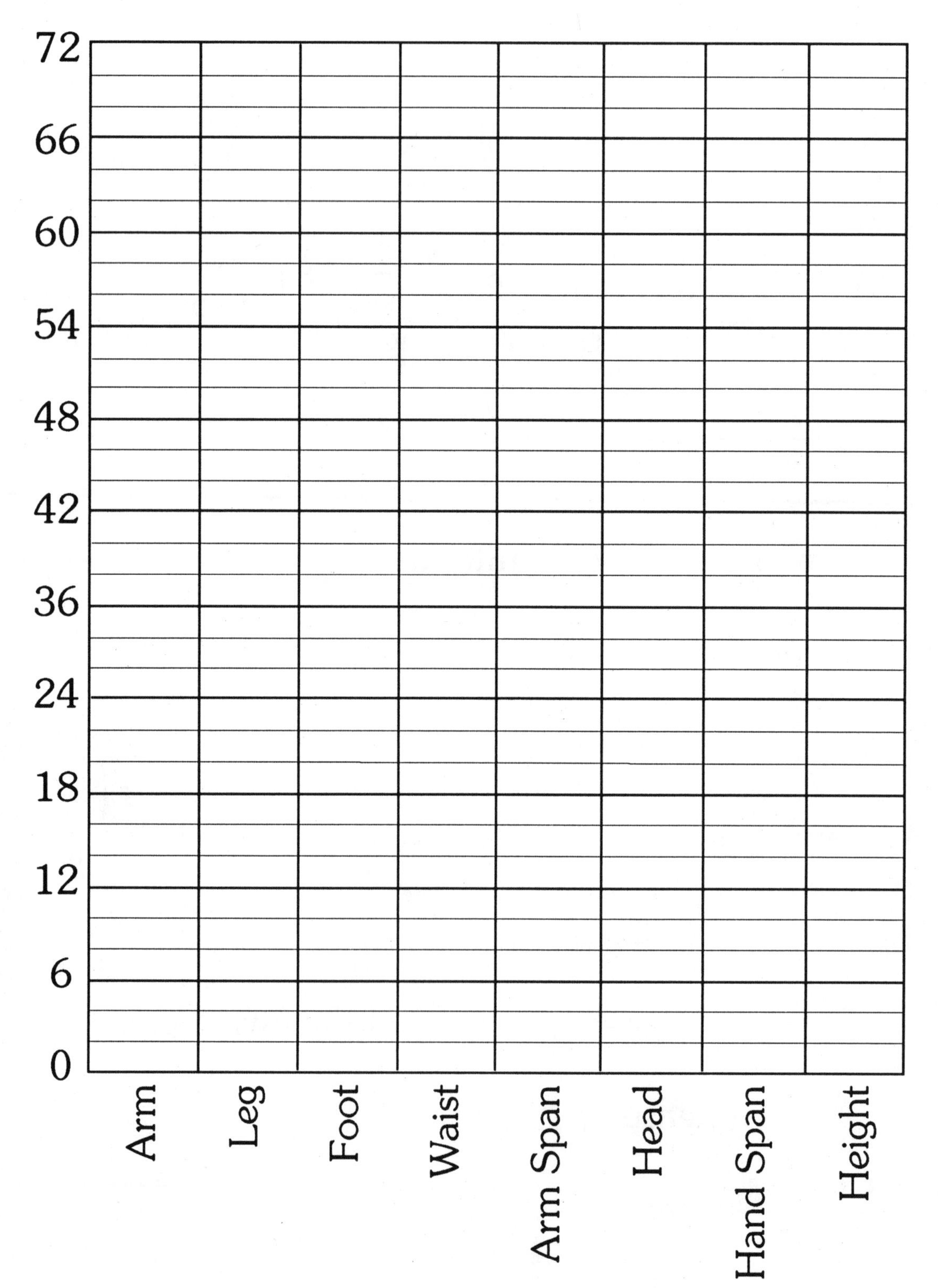

Measurement Investigations, © Dale Seymour Publications

MEASUREMENT SCAVENGER HUNT

Record Sheet P-L5 Name ________________

Look around your classroom and find objects:

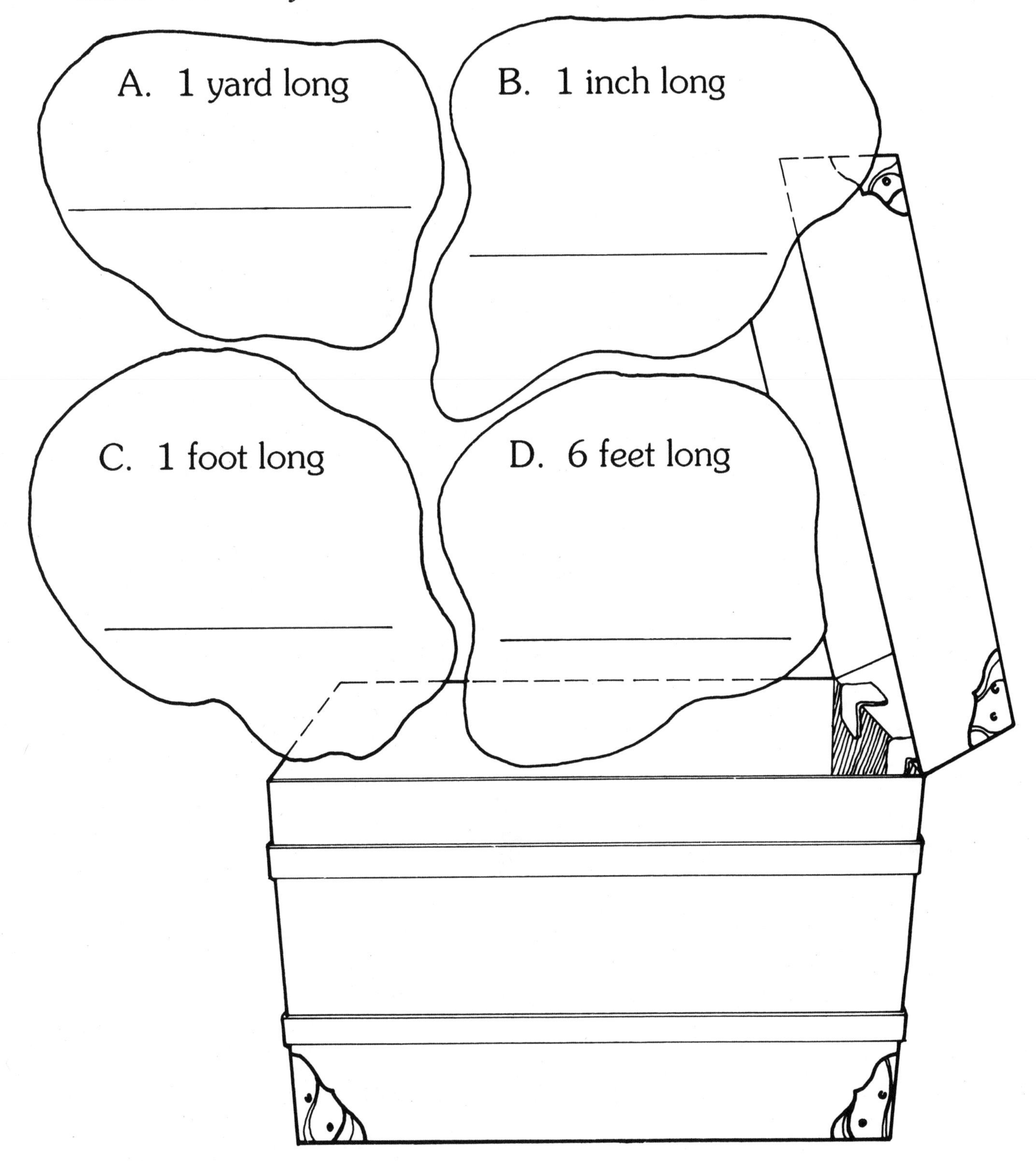

BALANCE BOARD BONANZA

Activity Sheet P-M1 Name ____________________

Use:

Find someone who weighs the *same* as you do:

1. ____________________ weighs the same as I do.

Find someone who is heavier and someone who is lighter than you.

2. ____________________ is heavier than I am.

3. ____________________ is lighter than I am.

____________________ is my measurement partner.
#1

Measurement Investigations, © Dale Seymour Publications

ORDERING OBJECTS

Record Sheet P-M1A Name ____________________

Draw pictures or write the names of ordered objects below:

Heavier	Lighter
1.	
3.	
5.	
7.	
9.	

Heavier	Lighter
2.	
4.	
6.	
8.	
10.	

Measurement Investigations, © Dale Seymour Publications

ORDERING PICTURES

Record Sheet P-M1B Name________________________

Glue your picture sets in the appropriate places below:

Heavier	Lighter
1.	
3.	
5.	
7.	
9.	

Heavier	Lighter
2.	
4.	
6.	
8.	
10.	

Measurement Investigations, © Dale Seymour Publications

ORDERING PICTURES

Record Sheet P-M1B Name________________________

Cut out each set of pictures and glue them on Record Sheet P-M1B in the correct order.

MASS UNITS

Record Sheet P-M2A Name ____________________

Select some objects and find the mass of each, using your favorite unit. Record your results.

Objects	Mass	
	Estimate	Measure
1. Chalkboard Eraser	15 Pencils	20 Pencils
2.		
3.		
4.		
5.		
6.		
7.		
8.		
9.		
10.		

Measurement Investigations, © Dale Seymour Publications

WASHER MANIA

Record Sheet P-M2B Name ______________________

Find the mass of five objects in the classroom.
First estimate and then measure, using washers as your unit of mass measure.

Objects	Number of Washers	
	Estimate	Measure
1.		
2.		
3.		
4.		
5.		

Measurement Investigations, © Dale Seymour Publications

MASS GRAPH

Record Sheet P-M3 Name ______________________

Glue graph strips here.

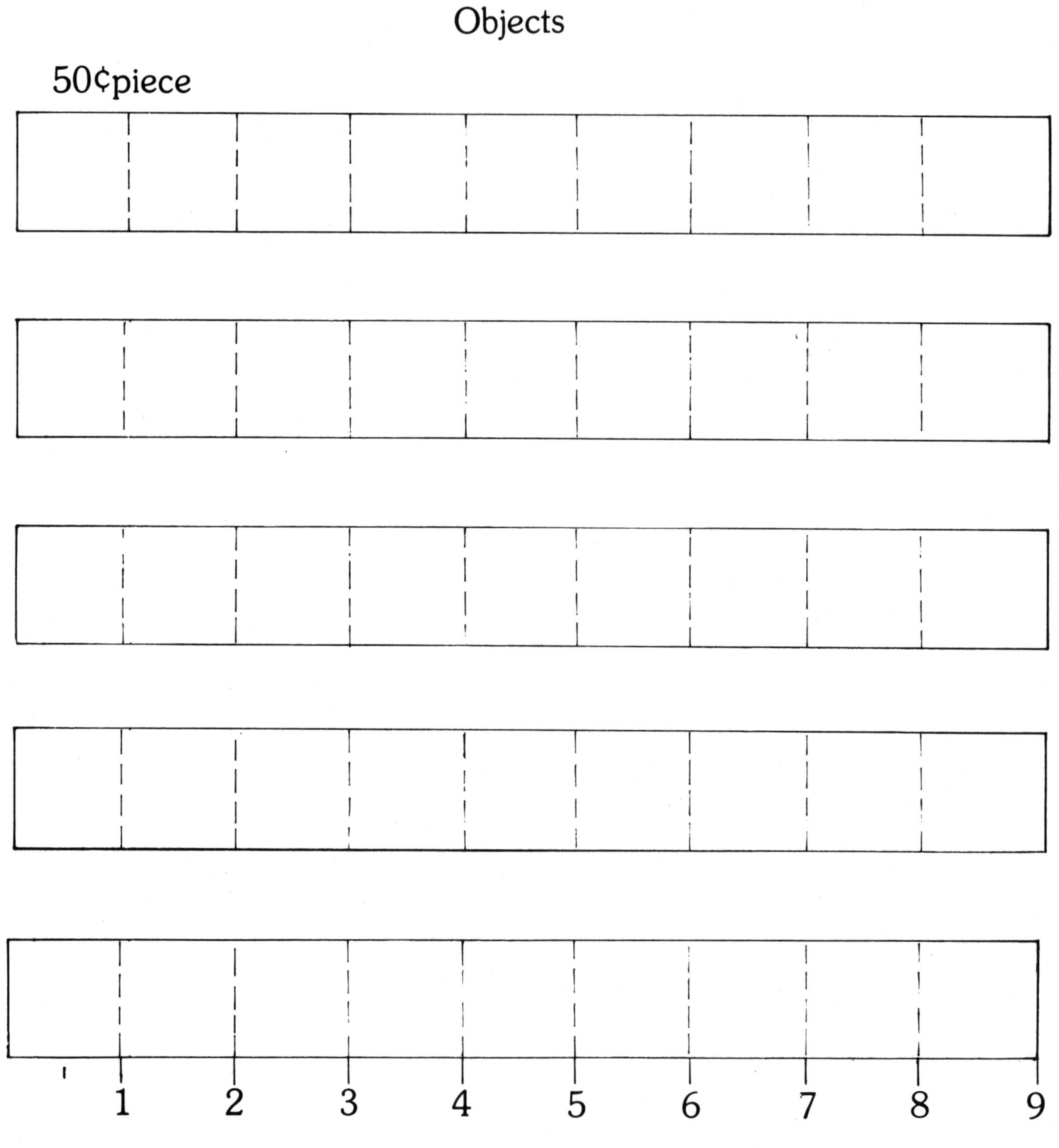

Measurement Investigations, © Dale Seymour Publications

MEASURE YOUR MASS

Record Sheet P-M4 Name ____________________

Find your mass in pounds.

1. I weigh ________________ pounds.

Find someone 5 pounds lighter than you.

2. ____________________ is 5 pounds lighter than I am.

Find someone 5 pounds heavier than you are.

3. ____________________ is 5 pounds heavier than I am.

MASS MEASURE

Record Sheet P-M5 Name ______________________

Find some objects in your classroom and measure their mass with ounces. Fill in the table below:

Picture or Name of Object	Ounce Estimate	Ounce Measure
1. chalk	6 oz.	1 oz.
2. board eraser	25 oz.	8 oz.
3.		
4.		
5.		
6.		
7.		
8.		
9.		
10.		

HOW BIG IS YOUR KISS?

Record Sheet P-A2 Name ____________________

1. Kiss the paper here, trace around your kiss and determine the area by laying split peas over its surface area.

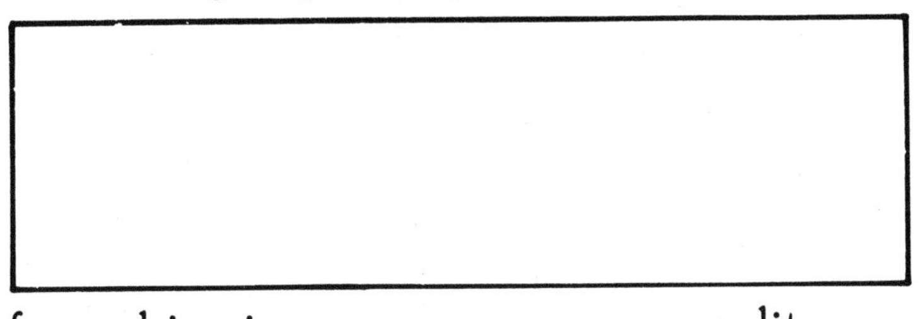

The area of my kiss is ____________ split peas.

2. Make a record of your classmates' kisses from smallest to largest:

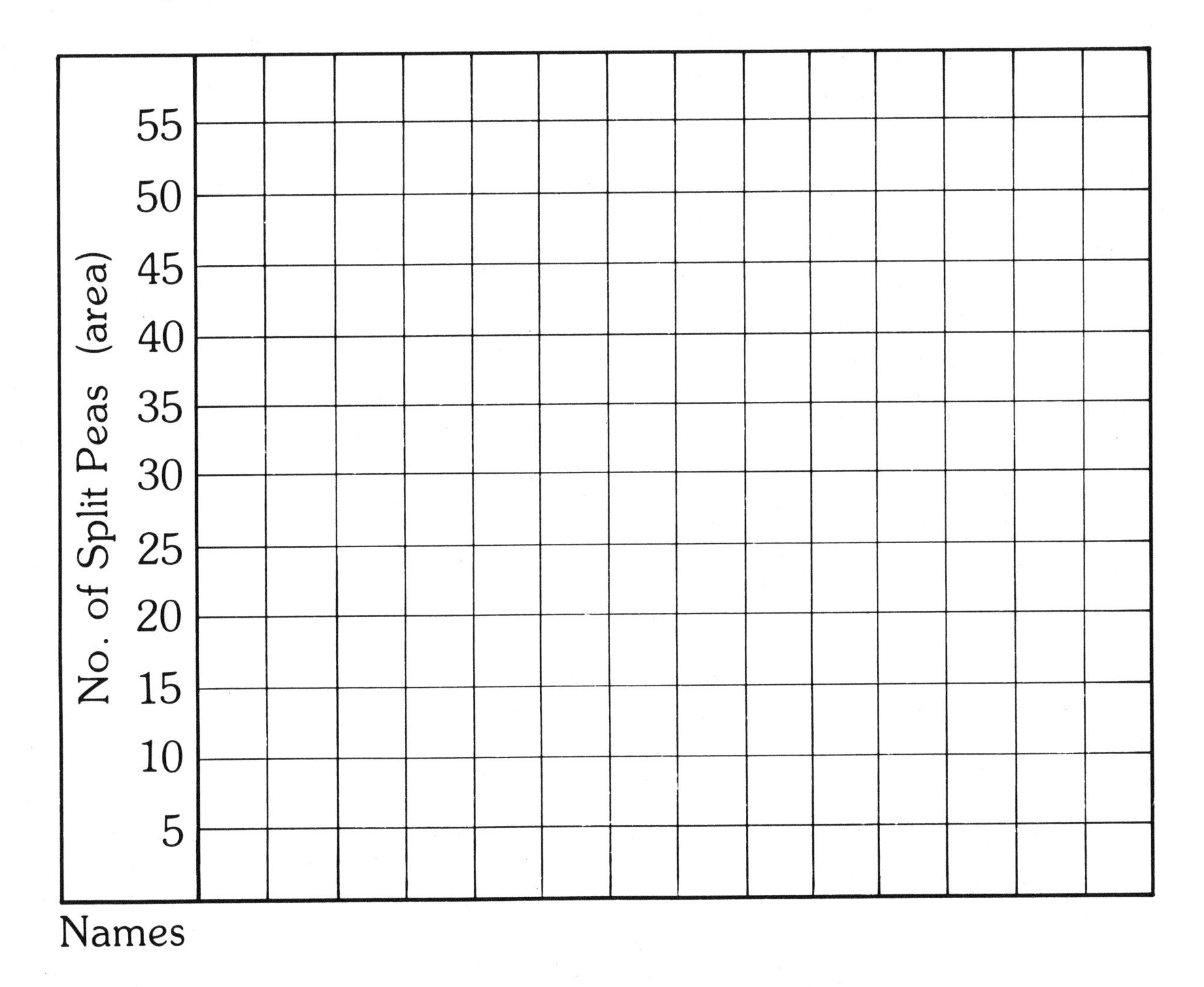

Measurement Investigations, © Dale Seymour Publications

BIG FOOT

Record Sheet P-A3 Name ____________________

1. On construction paper, find the area of your footprint, using thumb prints as a unit.

The area of my footprint is ____________ thumb prints.

2. Order your classmates by footprint area from smallest to largest.

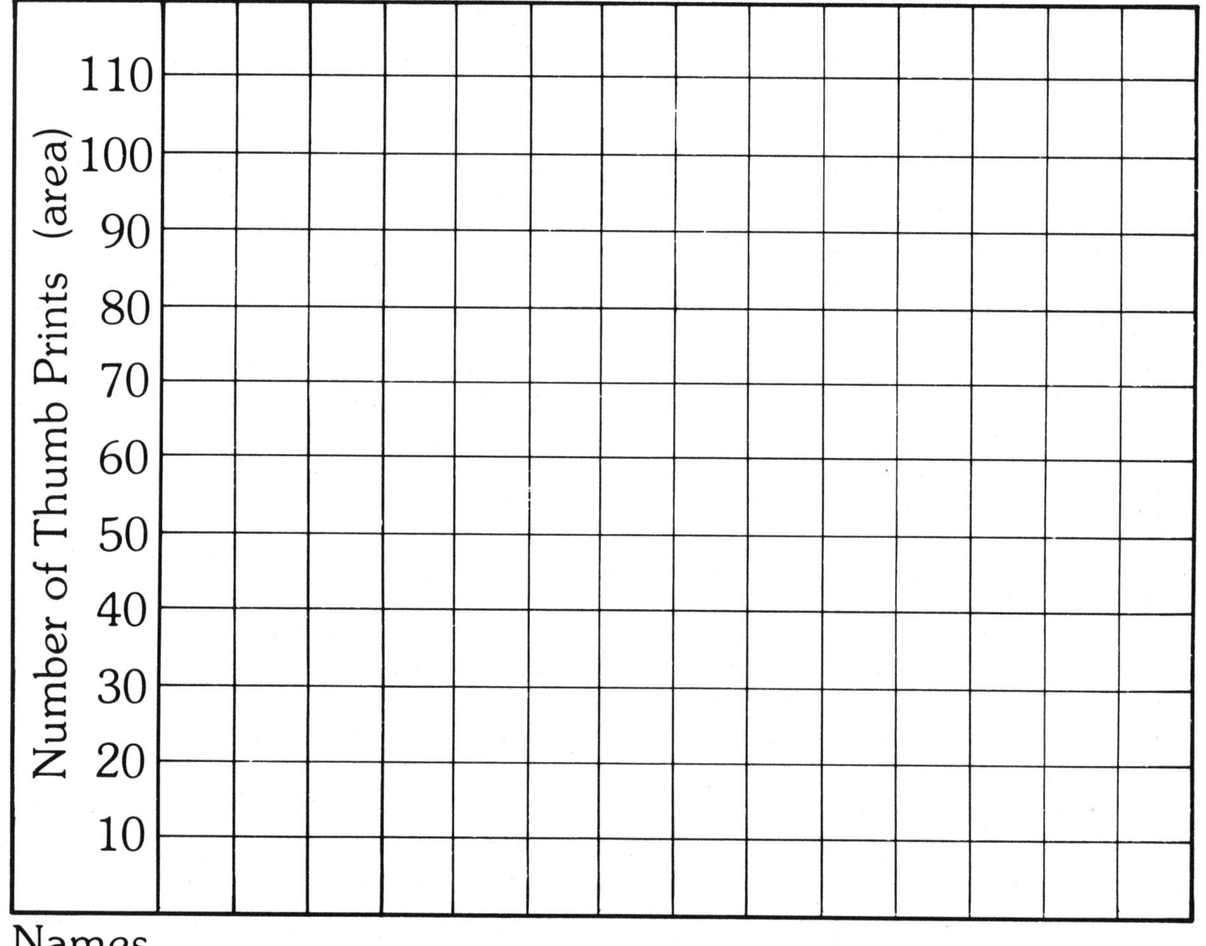

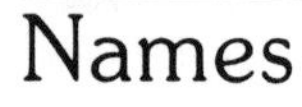

FOOTPRINTS

Activity Sheet P-A4 Name________________________

Trace around your foot or hand and count the number of square inches inside to find the area. You will have to combine pieces of squares around the edge.

The area of my foot is approximately ________________ in^2.

The area of my hand is approximately ________________ in^2.

Measurement Investigations, © Dale Seymour Publications

AREA FORMULAS

Activity Sheet P-A5 Name____________________

Find the area of each rectangle:

Example: ? in^2 = 6 in^2

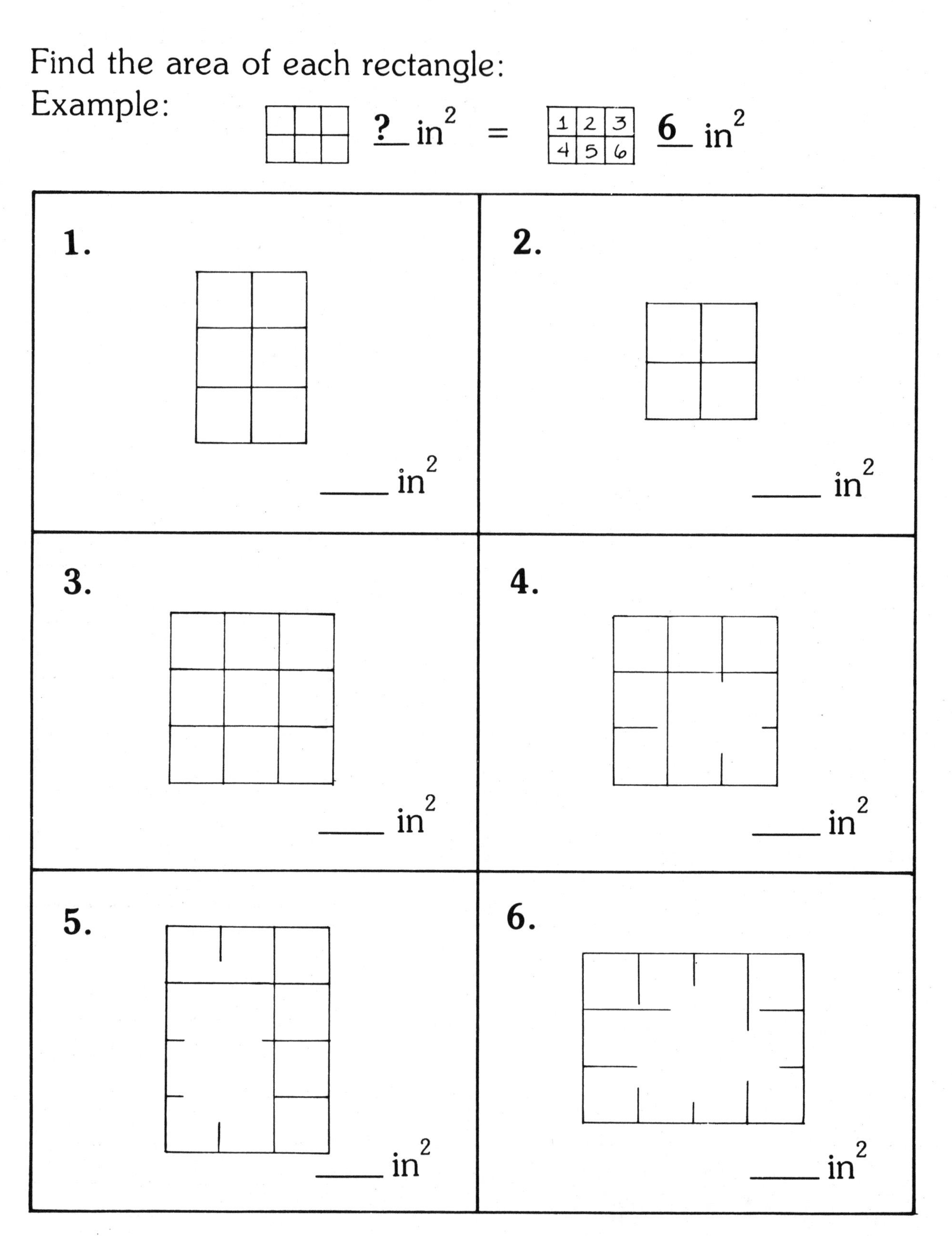

MARSHMALLOW MOUTH

Record Sheet P-C3 Name ____________________

1. I can fit ______________ marshmallows in my mouth.

2. My class of big mouths:

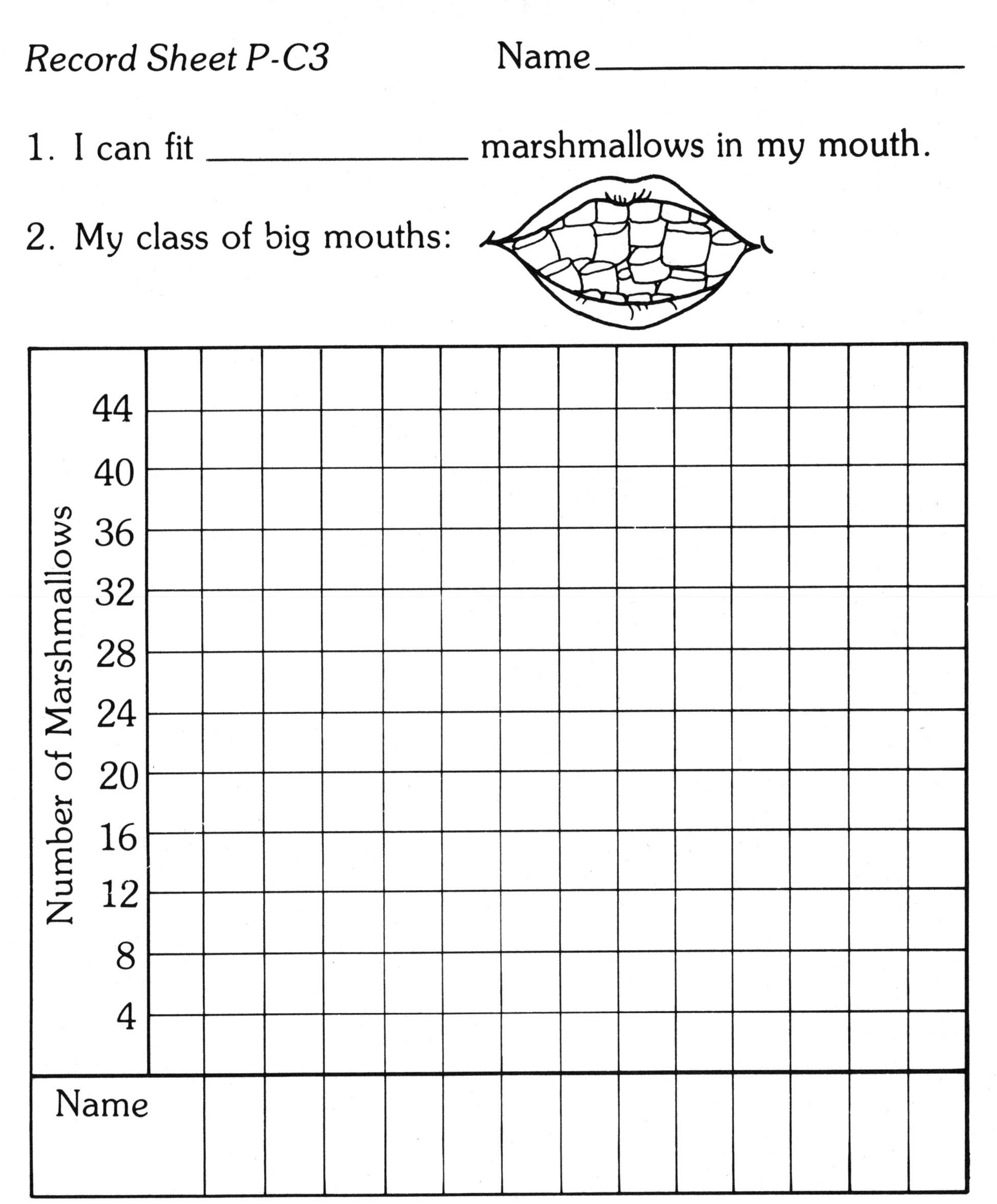

3. Who has the biggest mouth ? ____________________

4. Who has the smallest mouth ? ____________________

Measurement Investigations, © Dale Seymour Publications

MILK CARTON LITER

Record Sheet P-C4 Name______________________

Find the capacity of several containers in quarts and graph your results.

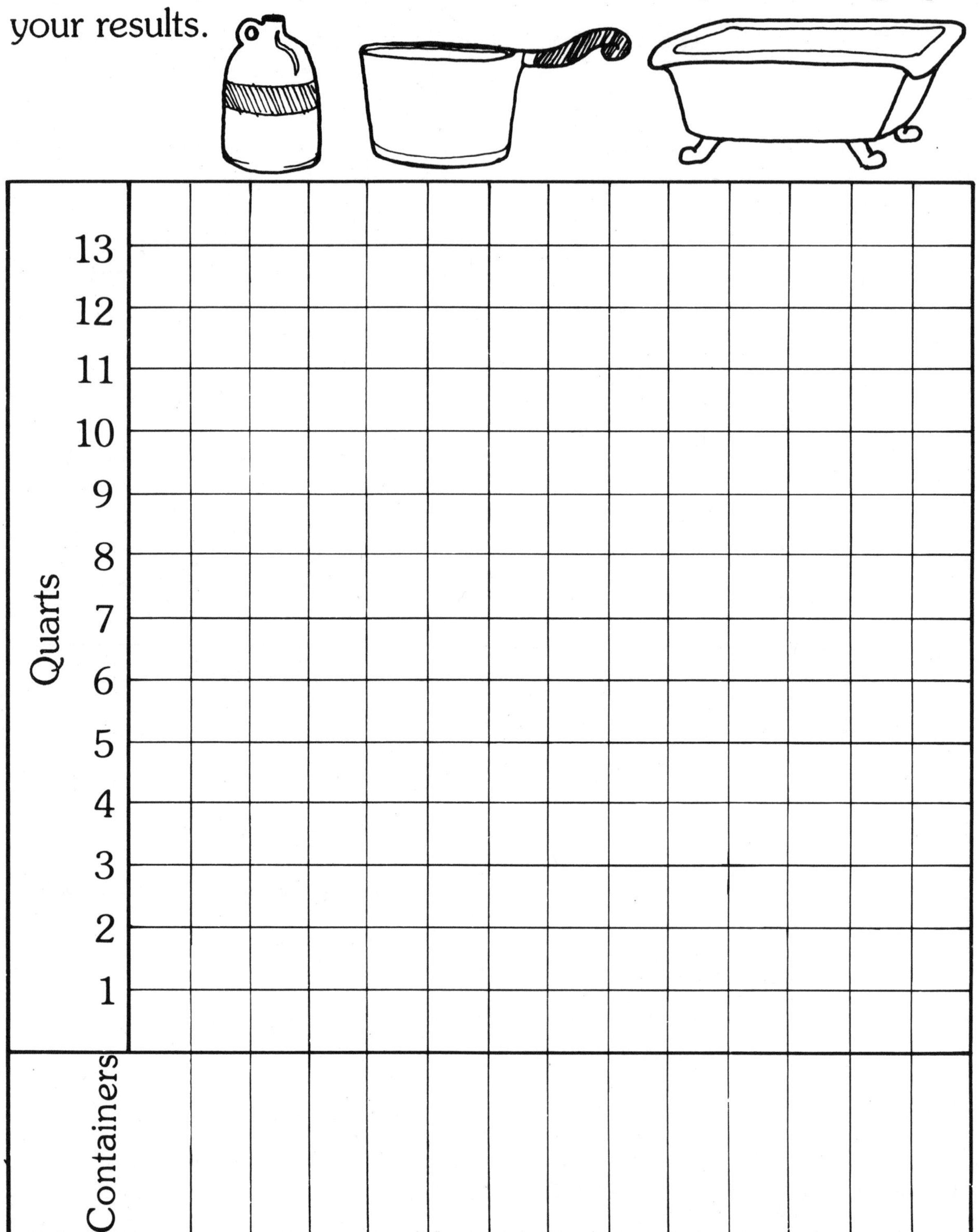

LITER RECIPES

Activity Sheet P-C5 Name ____________________

1. Today we made ____ Metric Lemonade
   ____ Strawberry Smoothies
   ____ Other

2. Here's how we did it: (Draw and label each step you took.)

Measurement Investigations, © Dale Seymour Publications

TIDDLY CLIPS GRAPH

Record Sheet I-L2 Name ___________________________

Graph how far you and your friends can "tiddly" a clip.

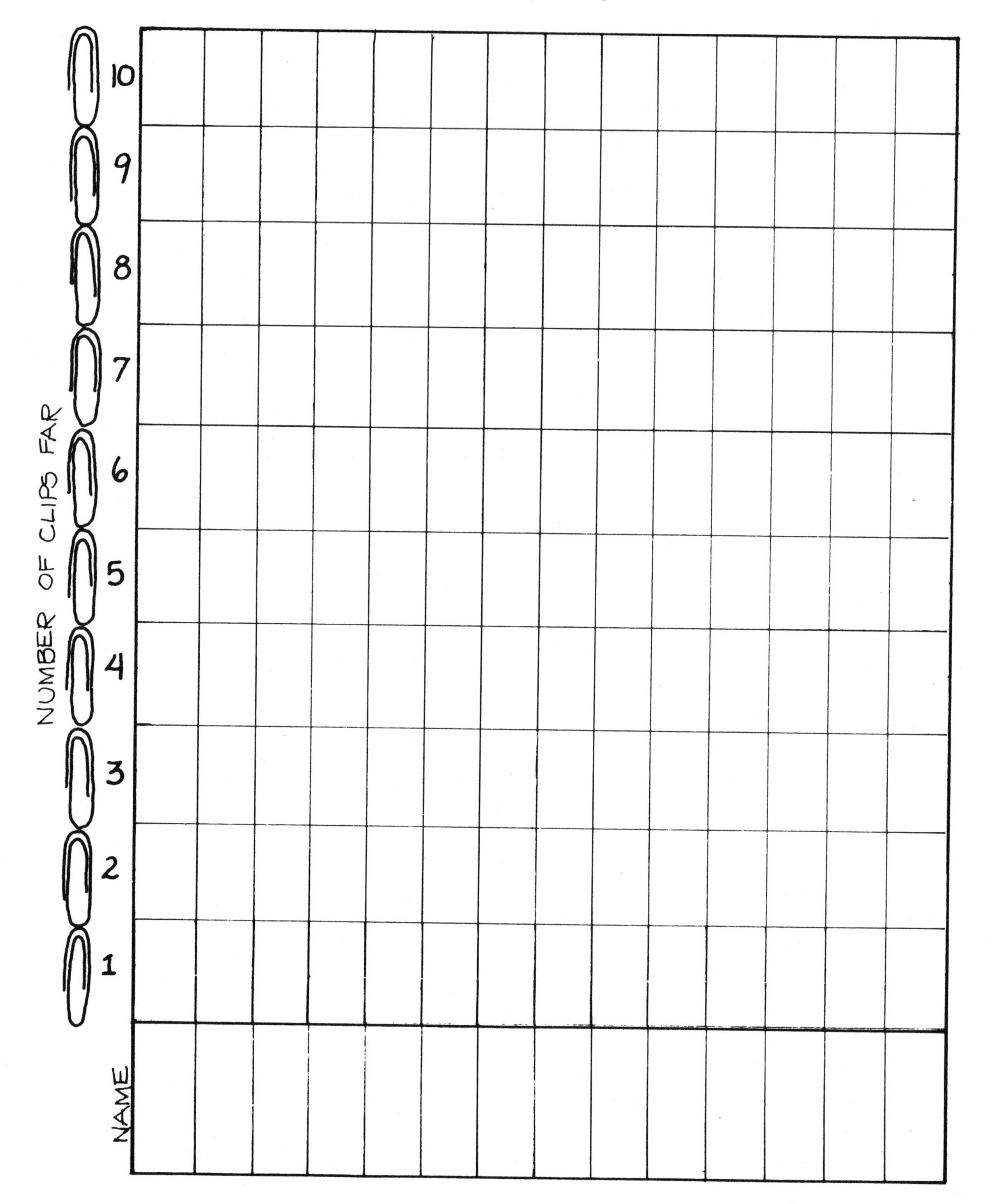

Measurement Investigations, © Dale Seymour Publications

PACE-ON

Record Sheet I-L2A Name ____________________

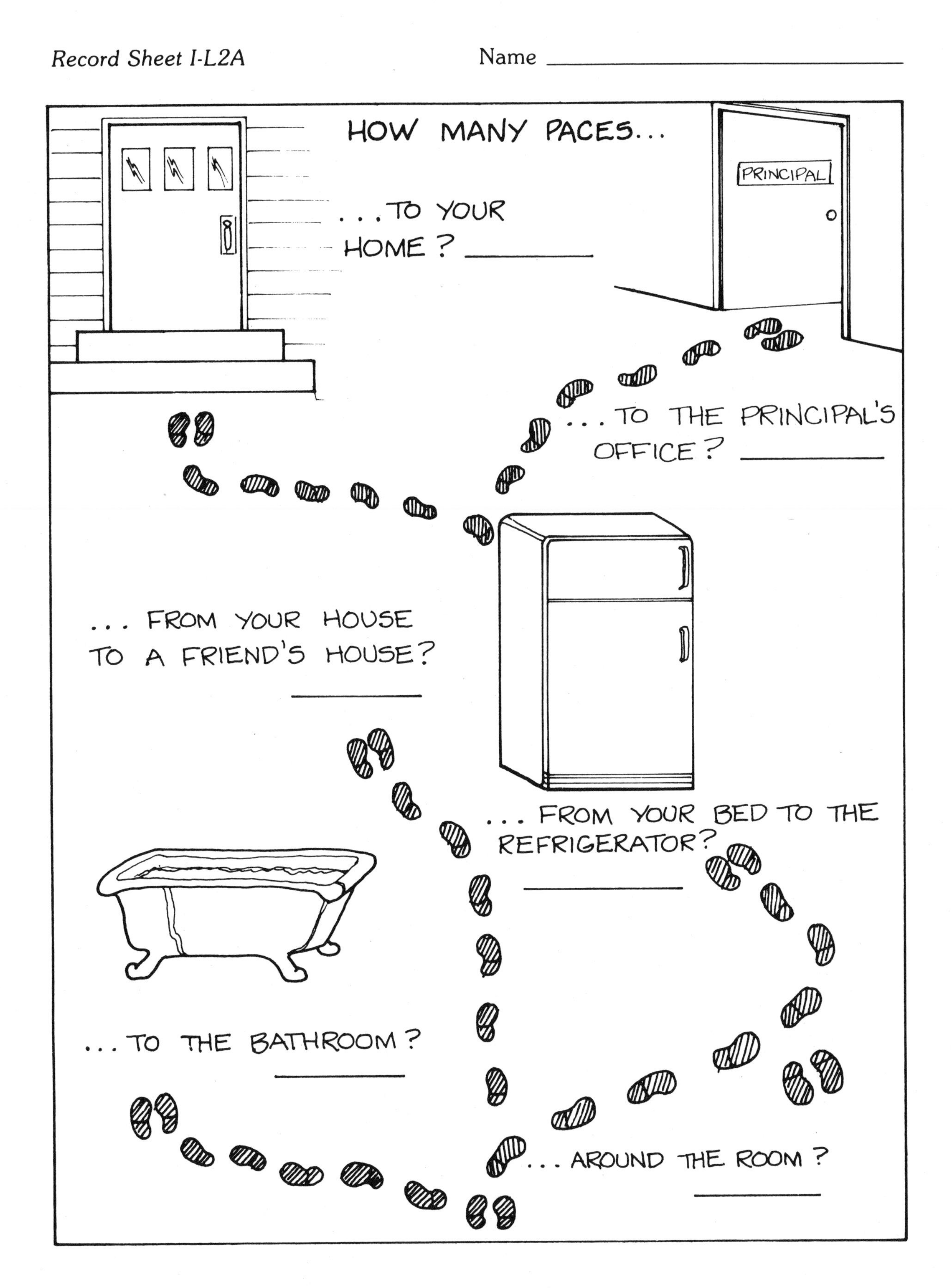

MEALWORM MANIA

Record Sheet I-L2B Name ______________________

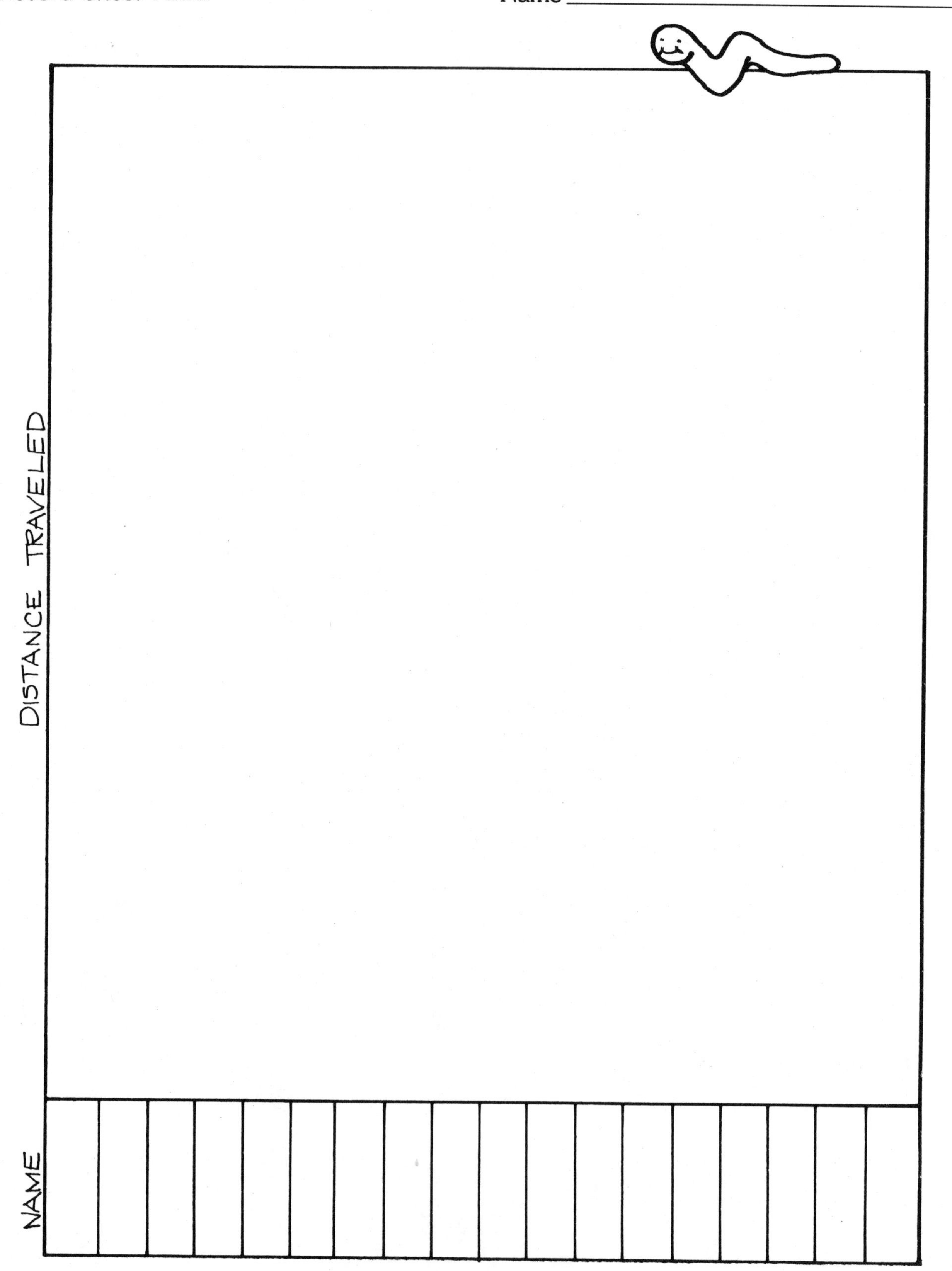

THUMBS UP

Record Sheet I-L3

Name ______________________________

Remember: Estimate first!

1. How wide is your smile?

estimation: __________ thumbprints.

measure: __________ thumbprints.

2. How long is your tongue?

estimation: __________ thumbprints.

measure: __________ thumbprints.

3. How long is your hair?

estimation: __________ thumbprints.

measure: __________ thumbprints.

4. How far can you shoot a marble?

estimation: __________ thumbprints.

measure: __________ thumbprints.

5. How wide is the room?

estimation: __________ thumbprints.

measure: __________ thumbprints.

TREASURE MAP

Record Sheet I-L4 Name ______________________

Coast Route __________cm__________mm

Jungle Route __________cm__________mm

River Route __________cm__________mm

Measurement Investigations, © Dale Seymour Publications

METRIC SCAVENGER HUNT

Record Sheet I-L5 Name ______________________

Look around your classroom and find objects:

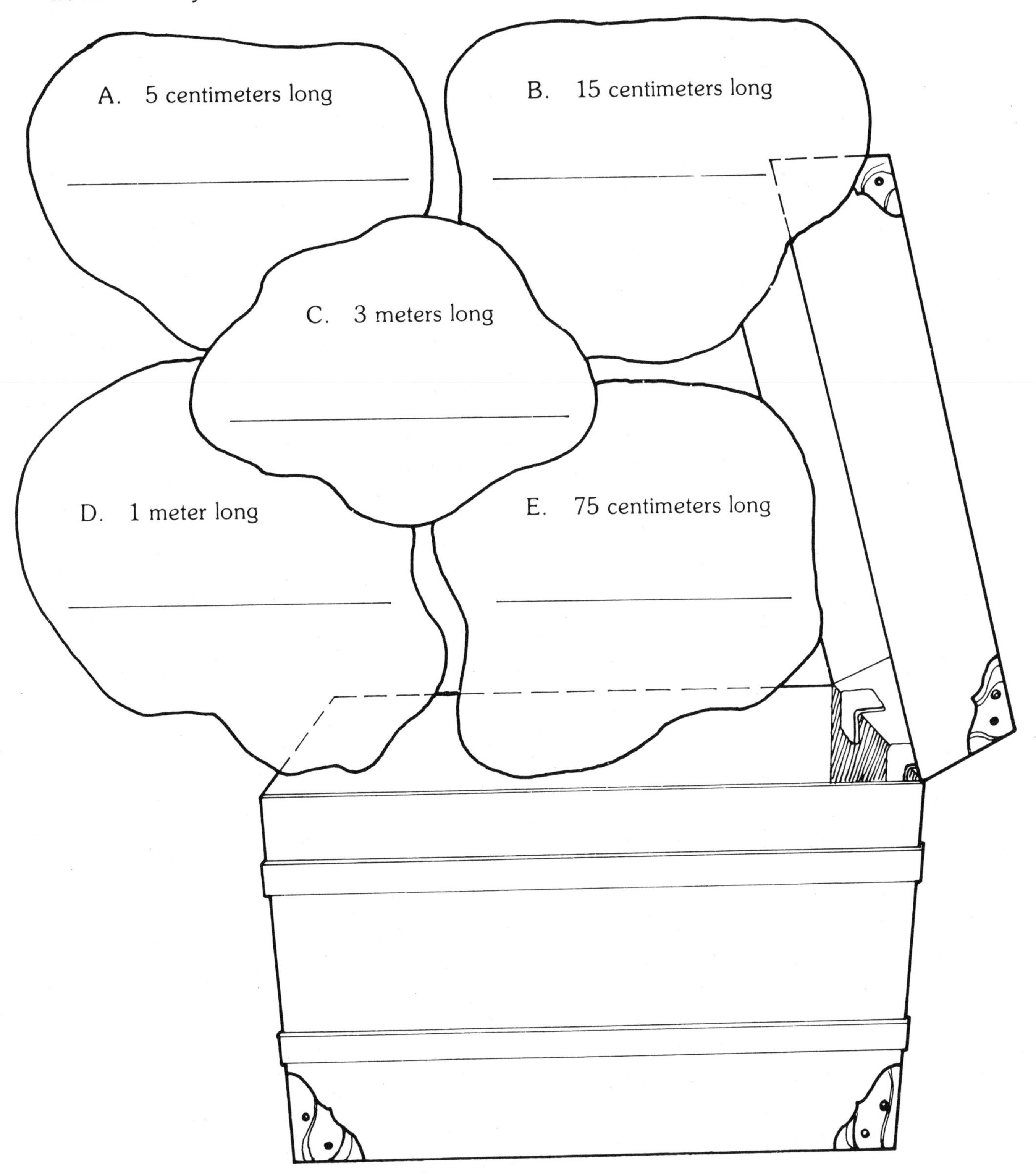

BODY BALANCE

Activity Sheet I-M1 Name ______________________

Find someone the same mass as you are.

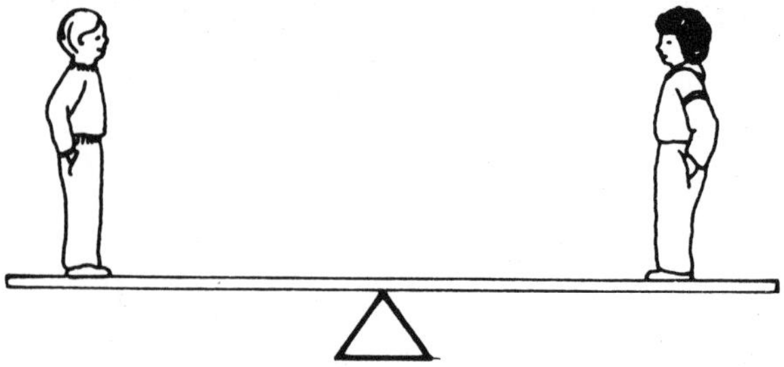

1. ______________________ is the same mass as I am.

Find someone with a greater mass and someone with less mass than you.

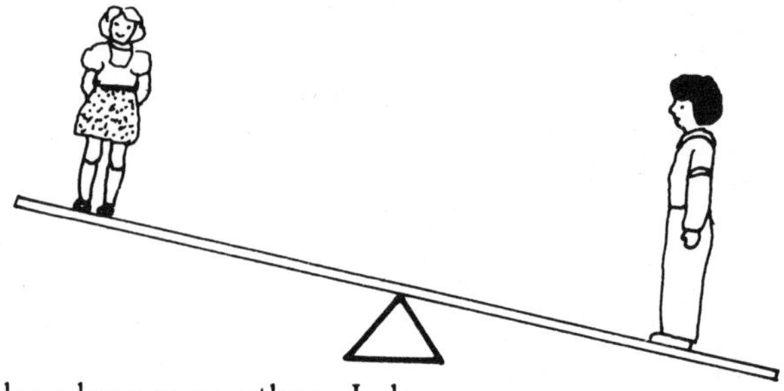

2. ______________________ has less mass than I do.

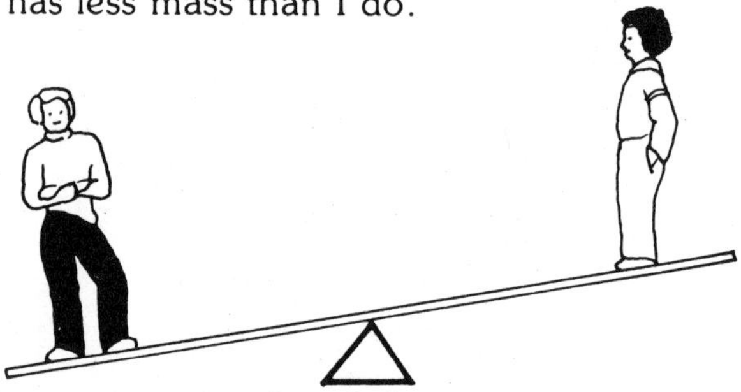

3. ______________________ has more mass than I do.

Order the mystery boxes from lightest to heaviest:

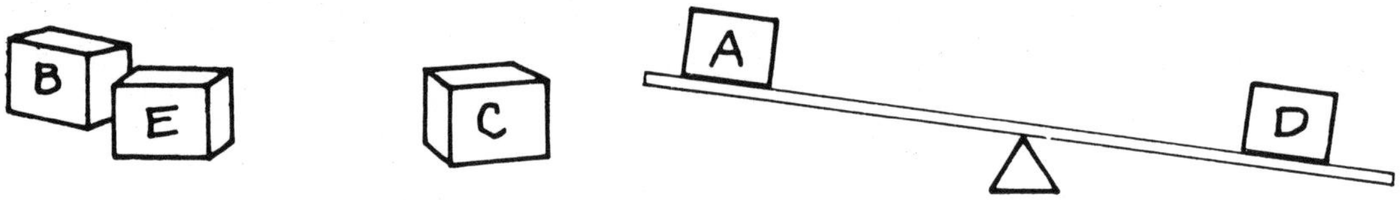

B E C A D

______ ______ ______ ______ ______

lightest heaviest

WASHER WEIGHTS

Record Sheet I-M2 Name ______________________

Find ten objects in your classroom, estimate their mass, in washers, then use a balance to measure their mass.

OBJECT	ESTIMATE	MASS MEASURE
1.		
2.		
3.		
4.		
5.		
6.		
7.		
8.		
9.		
10.		

Measurement Investigations, © Dale Seymour Publications

WASHER RECORDS

Record Sheet I-M3 Name ______________________

Graph your results from the previous activity. Order them from lightest to heaviest.

Objects

50¢ Piece

1 2 3 4 5 6 7 8 9 10 11 12 13 14 15 16 17 18

Number of Washers

Measurement Investigations, © Dale Seymour Publications

WEIGHING IS BELIEVING!

Record Sheet I-M4 Name ____________________

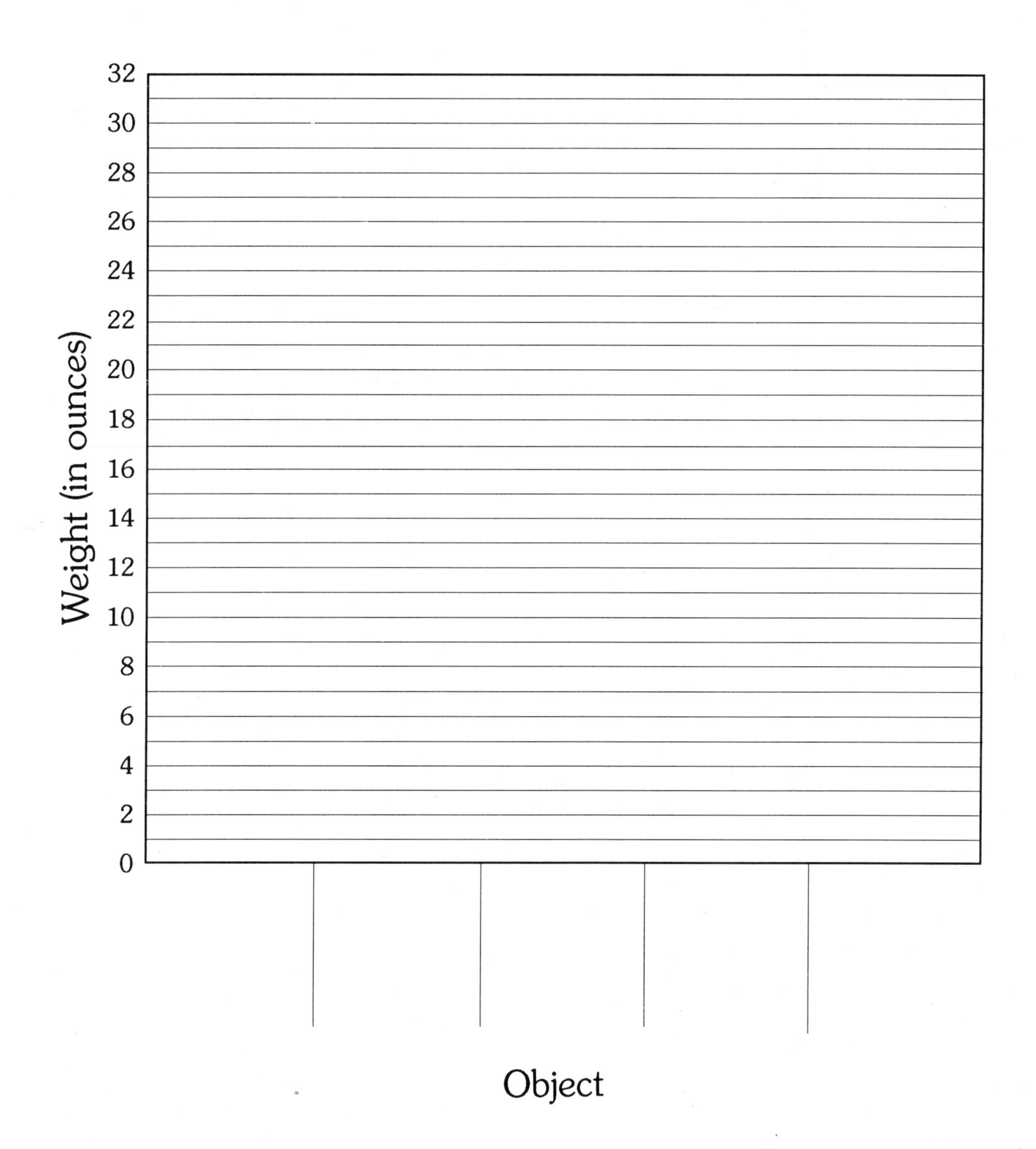

Measurement Investigations, © Dale Seymour Publications

MASS TIME

Record Sheet I-M5 Name ______________________

Find ten objects in your classroom and find the mass of each in kilograms and grams, using a balance and mass pieces.

Object	**Mass**	
	Kilograms	**Grams**
(example) *Hamster and Cage*	*3 kg*	*450 g*
1.		
2.		
3.		
4.		
5.		
6.		
7.		
8.		
9.		
10.		

Measurement Investigations, © Dale Seymour Publications

ORANGE PEEL MANIA

Record Sheet I-A2 Name ____________________

1. Determine the surface area of your orange peel in lima bean units.
   My orange peel has an area of __________ lima beans.
2. Order your classmates' orange peels from least surface area to greatest (get your information from the class graph).

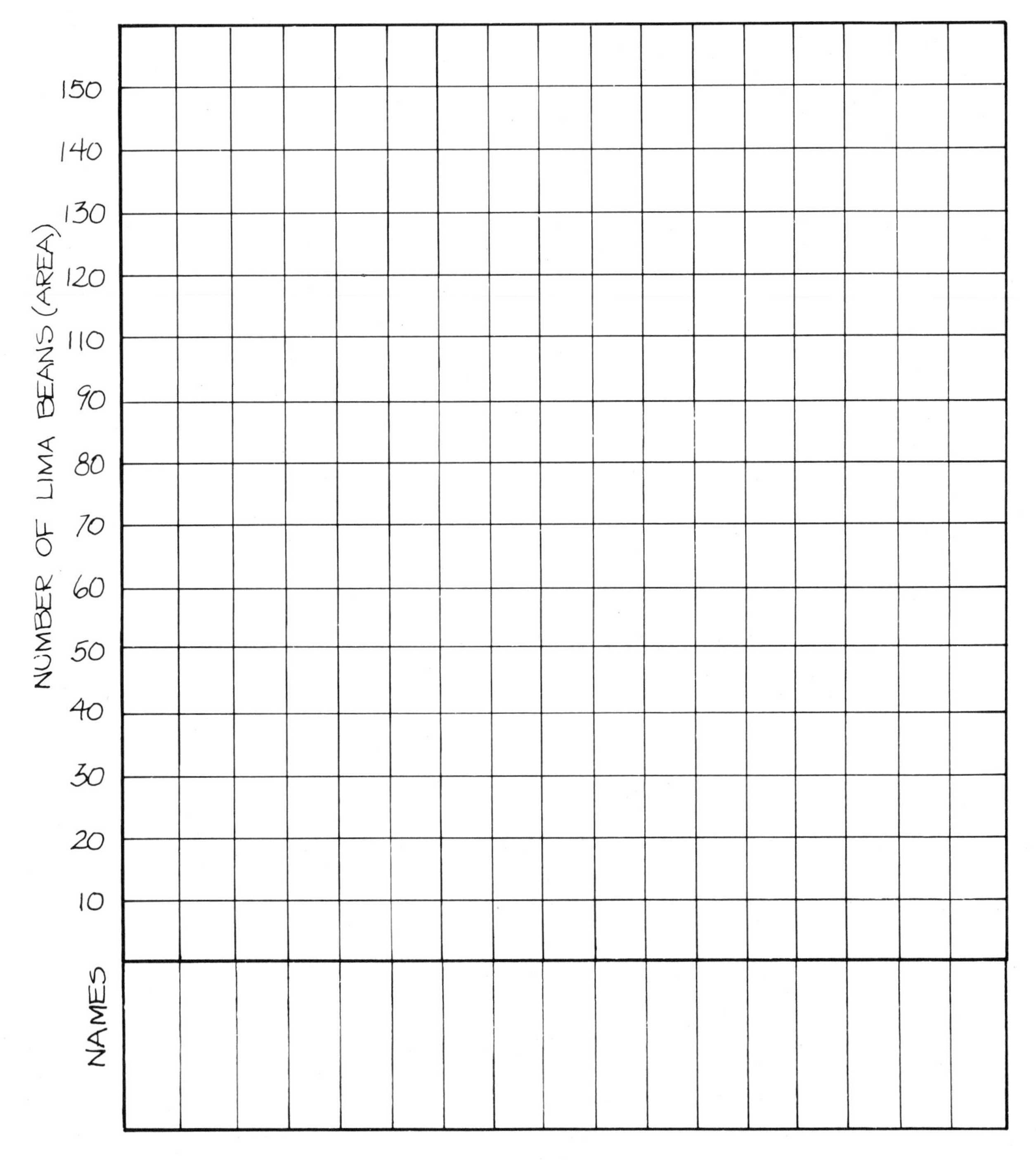

Measurement Investigations, © Dale Seymour Publications

GEOBOARD DOT PAPER

Record Sheet I-A3 Name ____________________

ORANGE PEEL MAP

Record Sheet I-A4 Name ____________________

Carefully peel an orange and trace around it on the in^2 graph paper below.
You may need to use two pieces of graph paper for a large orange.

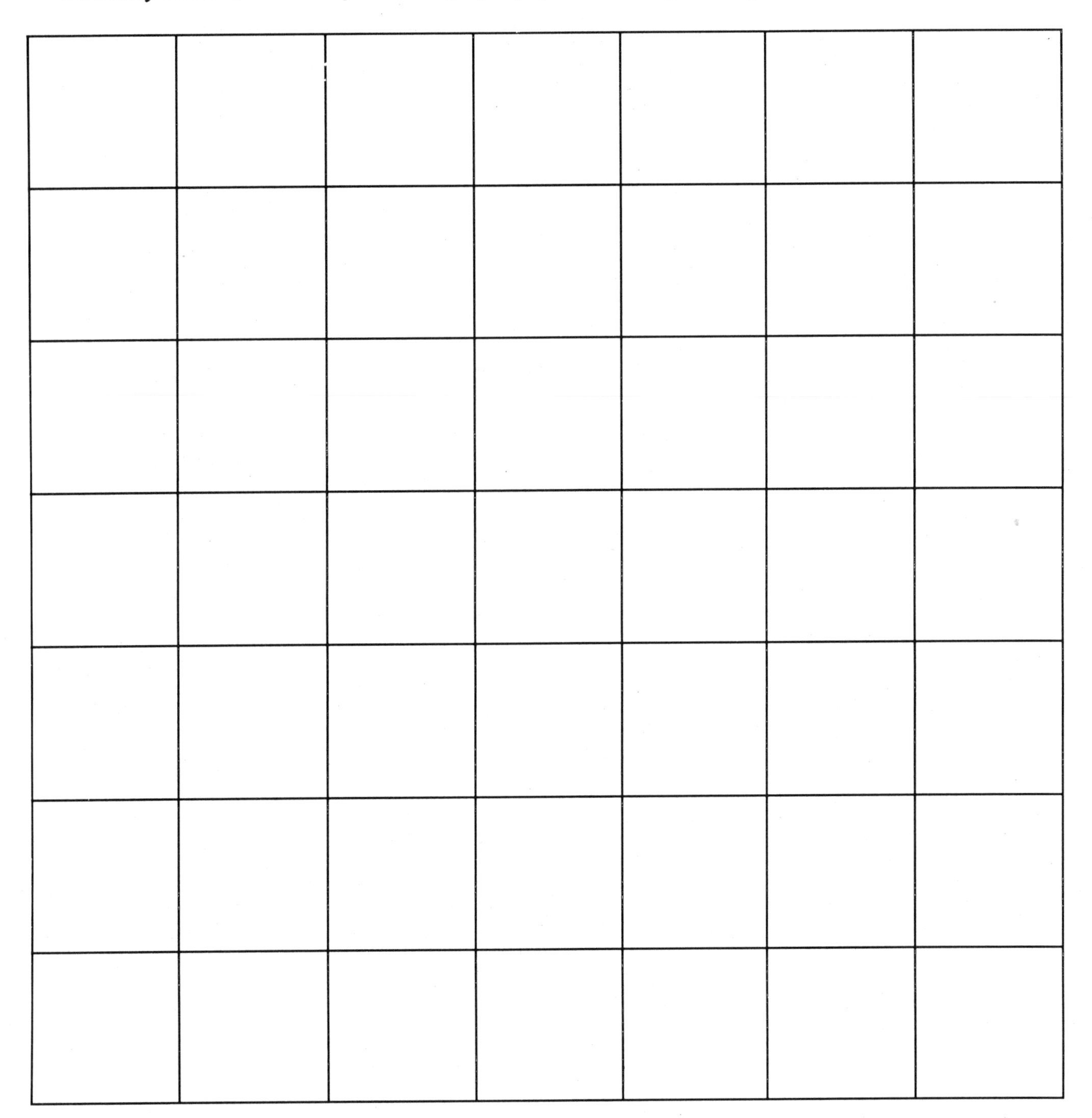

How many squares are covered by your orange peel map? ________ Area
(Parts of squares around the edge of your map should be put together to make whole squares as much as possible.)

Measurement Investigations, © Dale Seymour Publications

AREA FORMULAS

Record Sheet I-A5 Name ____________________

Find the area of each rectangle:

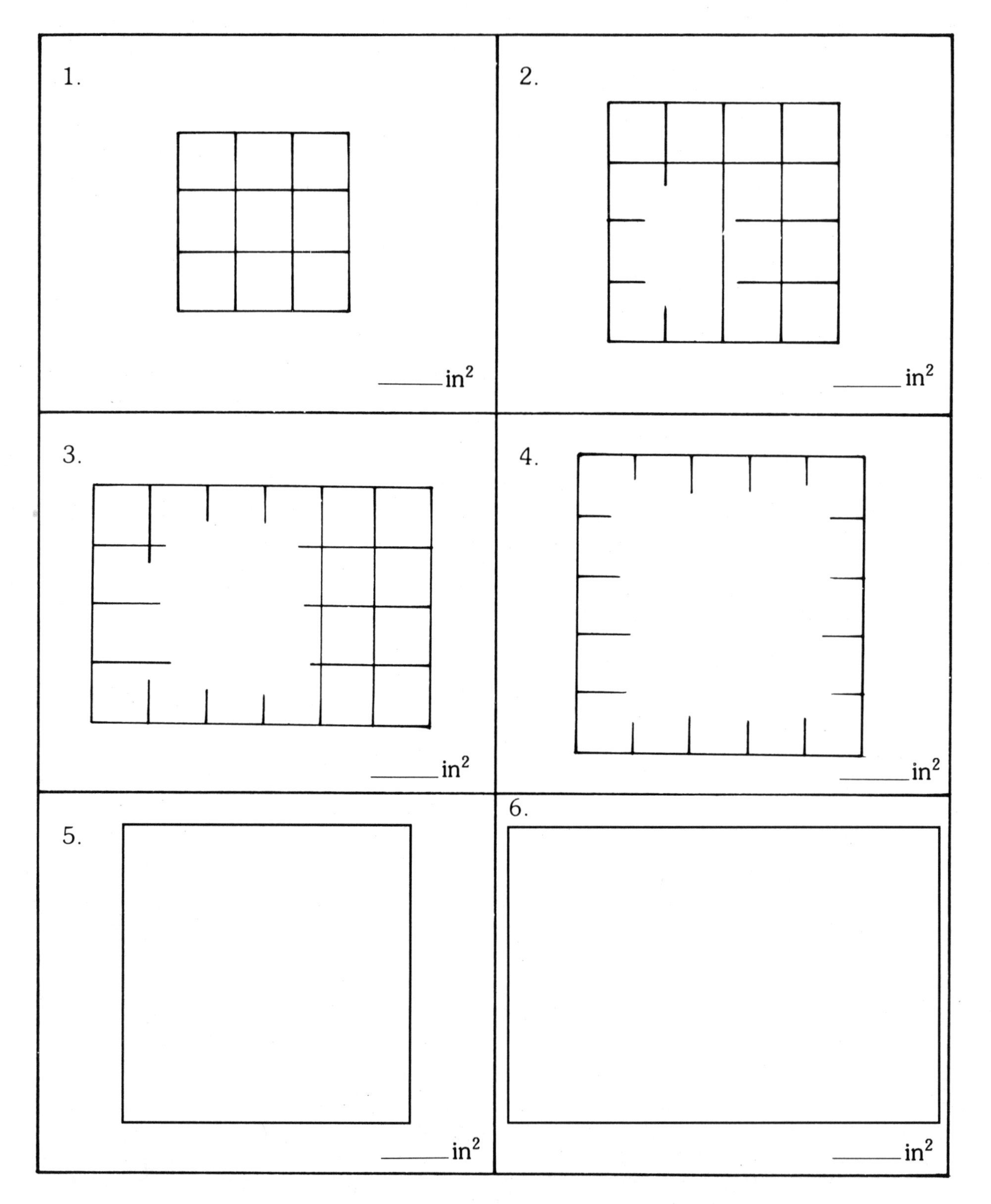

Measurement Investigations, © Dale Seymour Publications

FULL OF HOT AIR

Record Sheet I-C1 **Name** ______________________

Graph the lung capacity of some of your friends.

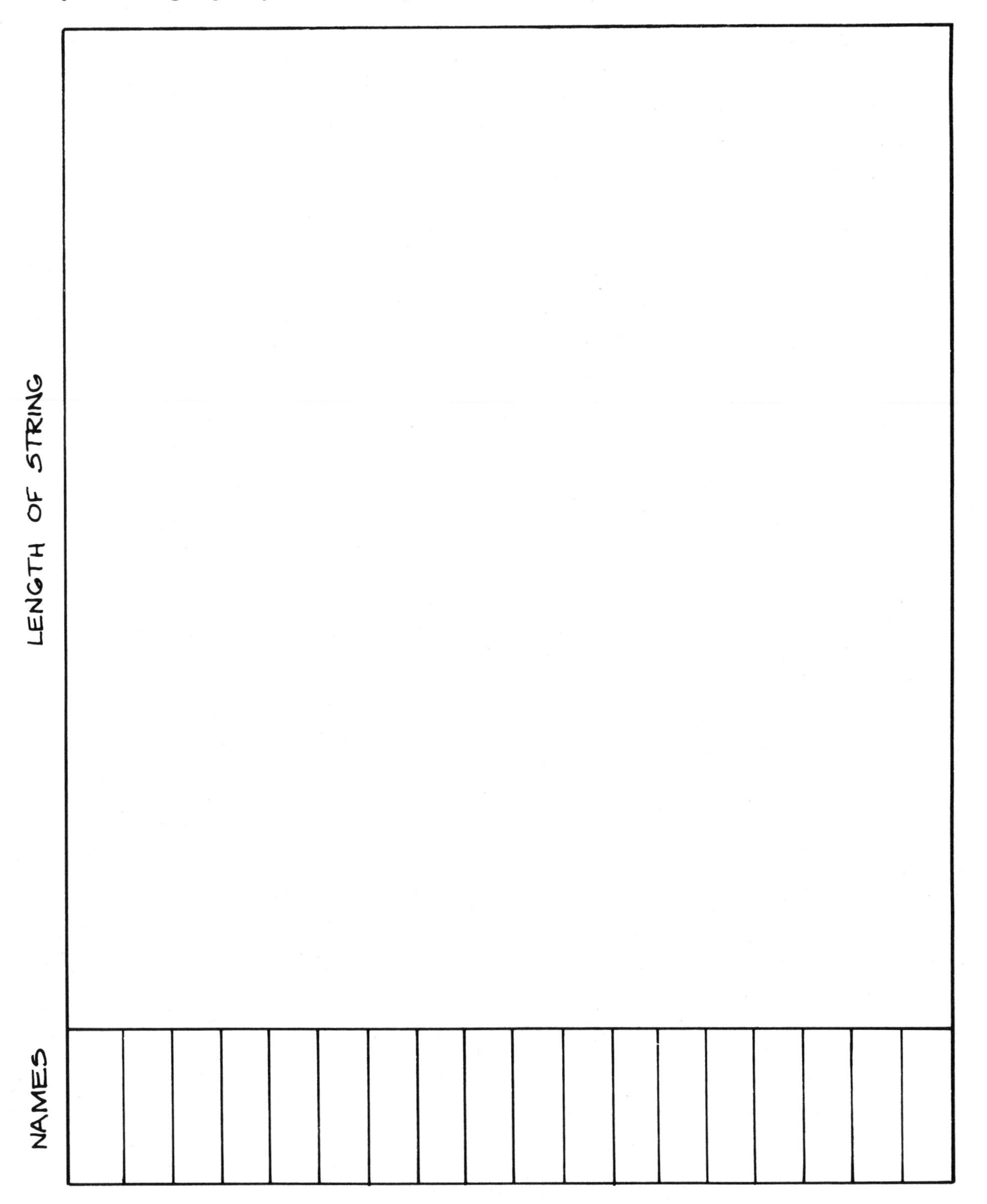

Measurement Investigations, © Dale Seymour Publications

MARBLES IN A SHOE

Record Sheet I-C2 Name ______________________________

1. Find the capacity of your shoe in marble units: __________ marbles.
2. Record below the respective capacities of your classmates' shoes from least to most:

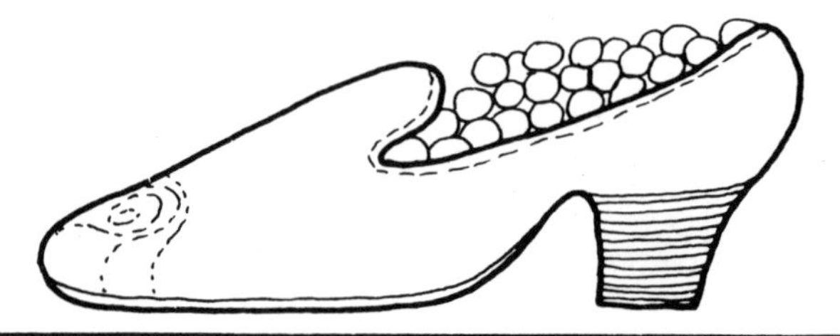

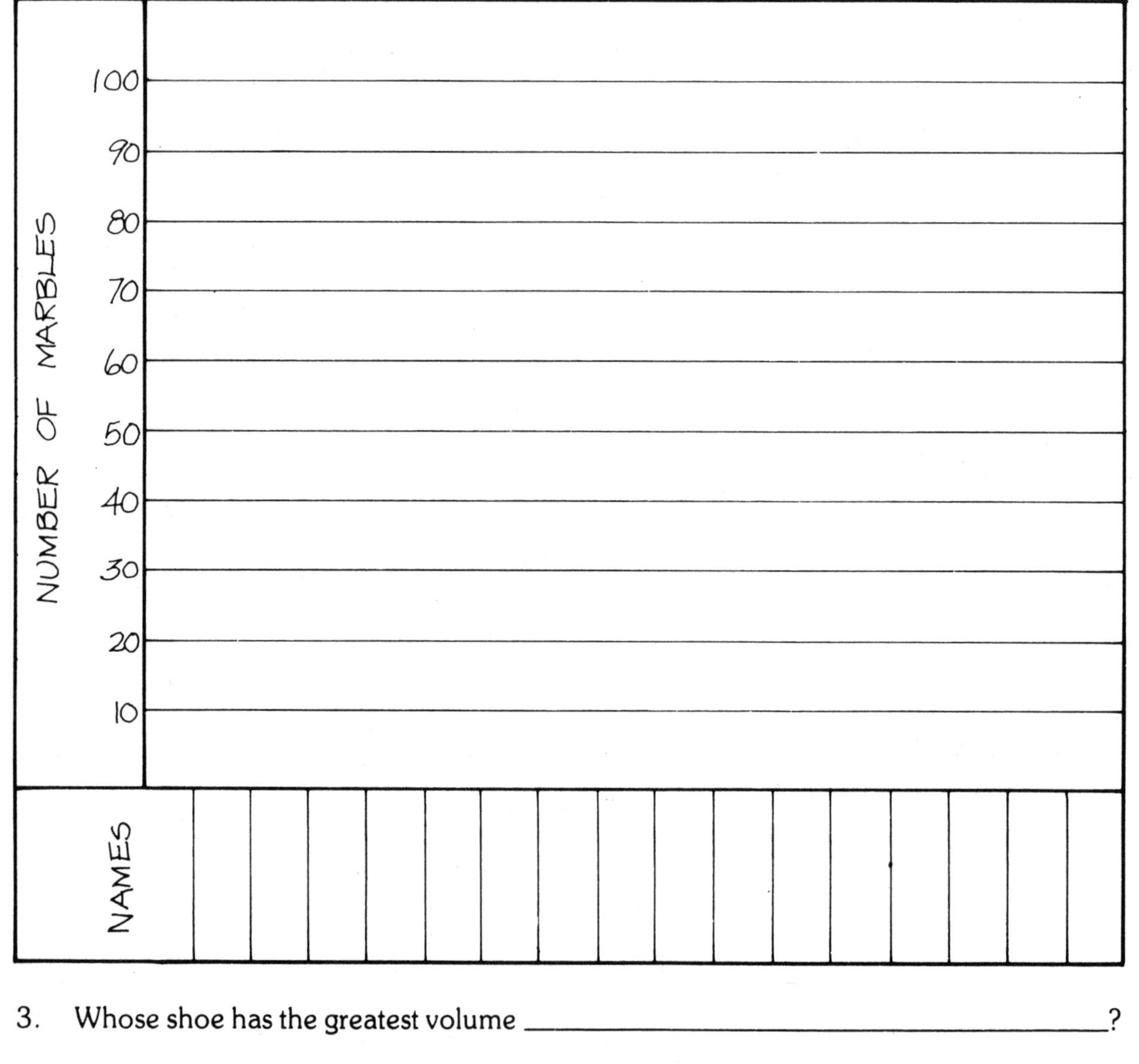

3. Whose shoe has the greatest volume ______________________________?
4. Whose shoe has the least volume ______________________________?
5. Whose shoe has a capacity closest to yours ______________________________?

BOTTLE GRAPHS

Record Sheet I-C3

Name ______________________

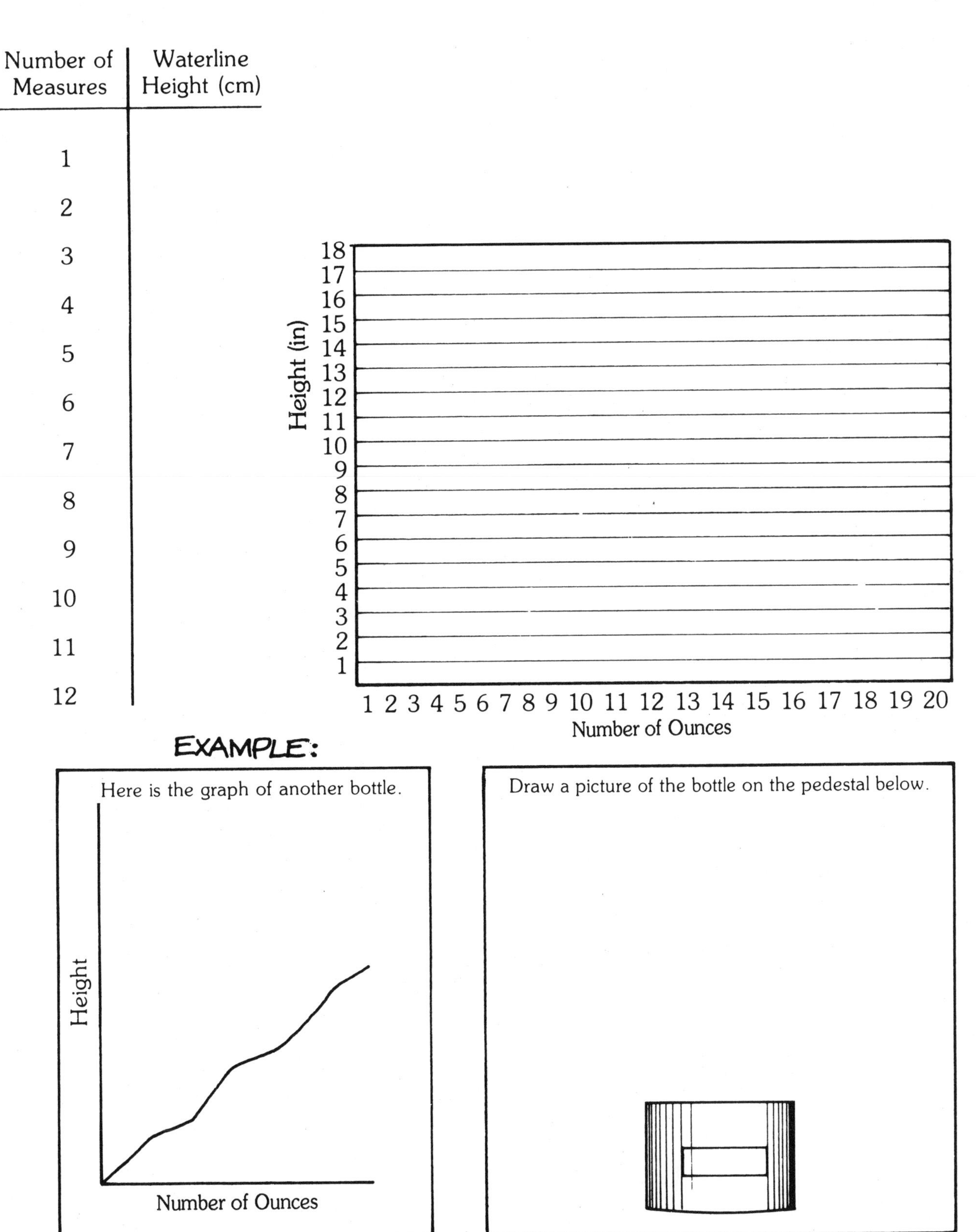

Number of Measures	Waterline Height (cm)
1	
2	
3	
4	
5	
6	
7	
8	
9	
10	
11	
12	

Measurement Investigations, © Dale Seymour Publications

PACKAGING

Activity Sheet I-C4 Name ______________________

Using the square below, cut five similar squares out of centimeter graph paper. Cut a square out of each corner of one piece and form an open-top box. What is the largest box you can make?

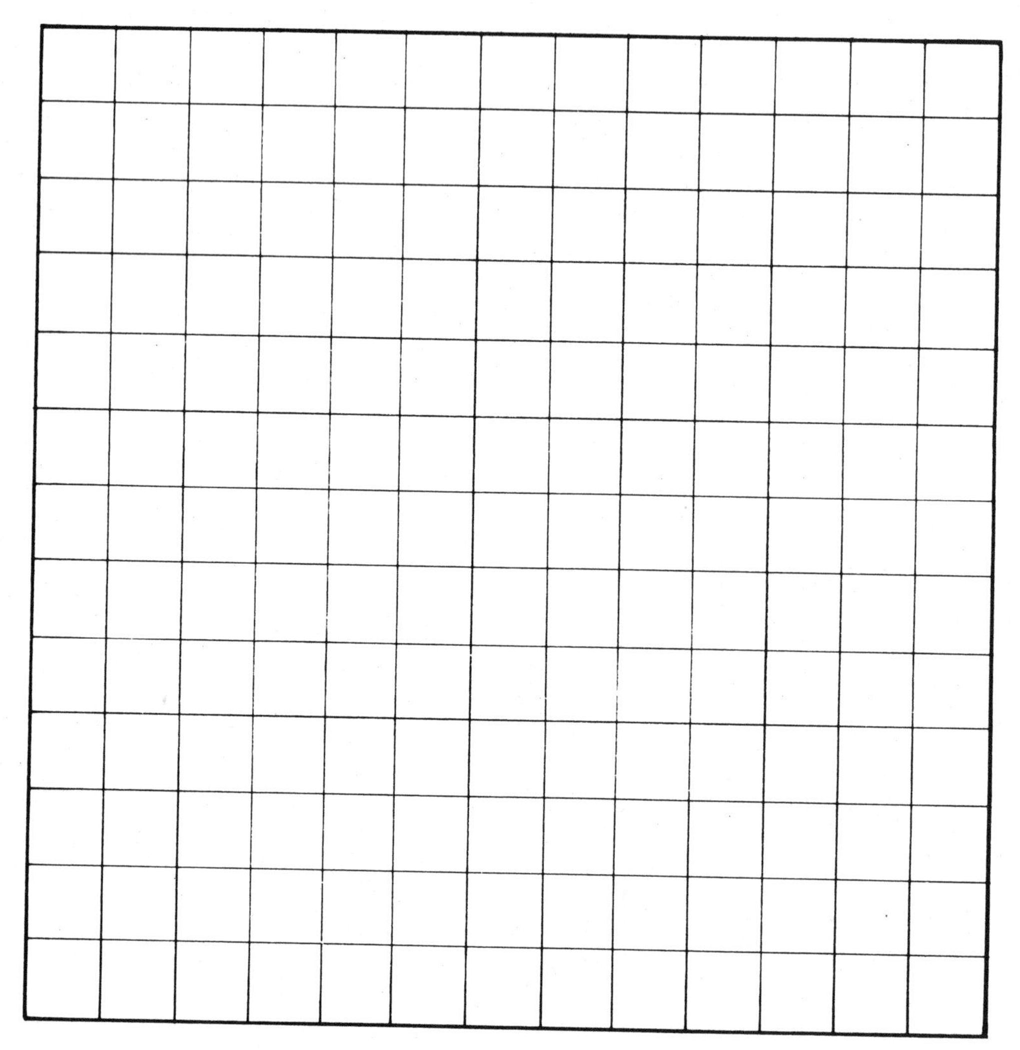

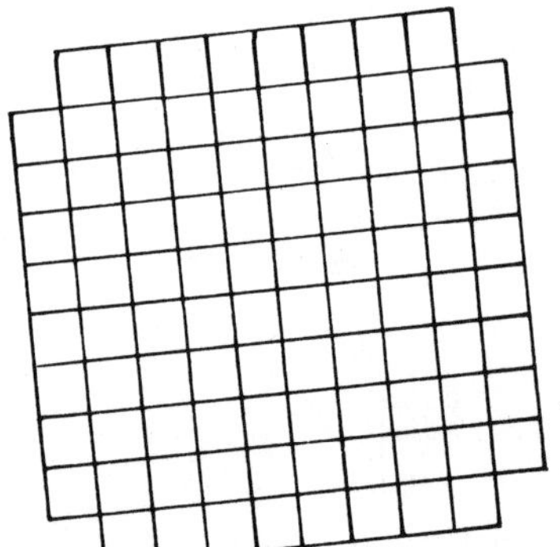

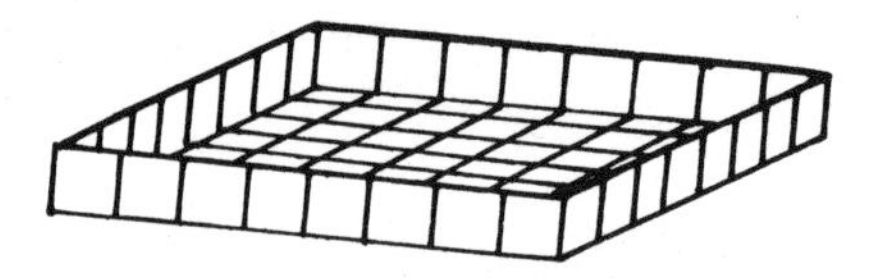

FISH TANKS

Activity Sheet I-C5 Name ______________________________

If each fish needs one liter (1000 milliliters) of water to live, how many fish can live in each tank below? Remember, an easy way to find the capacity of each tank is to multiply the length times the width times the height.

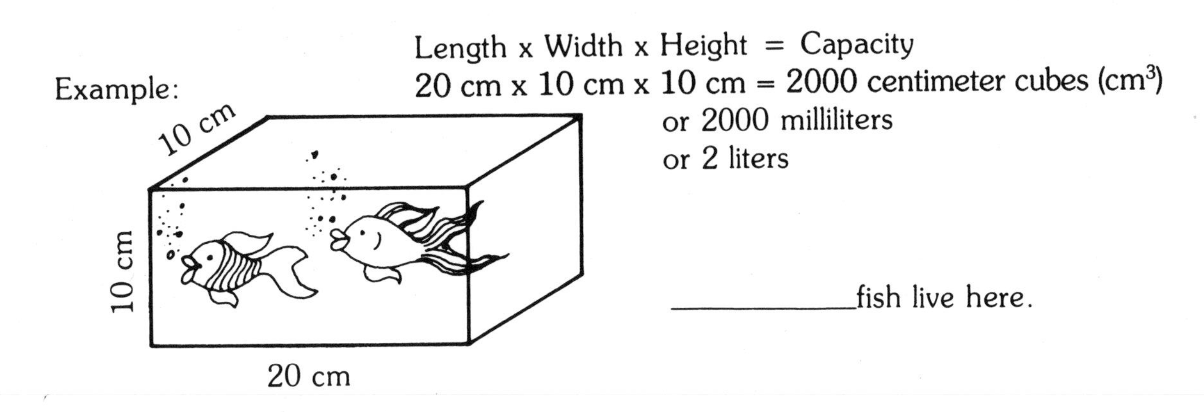

Draw the correct number of fish in each tank.

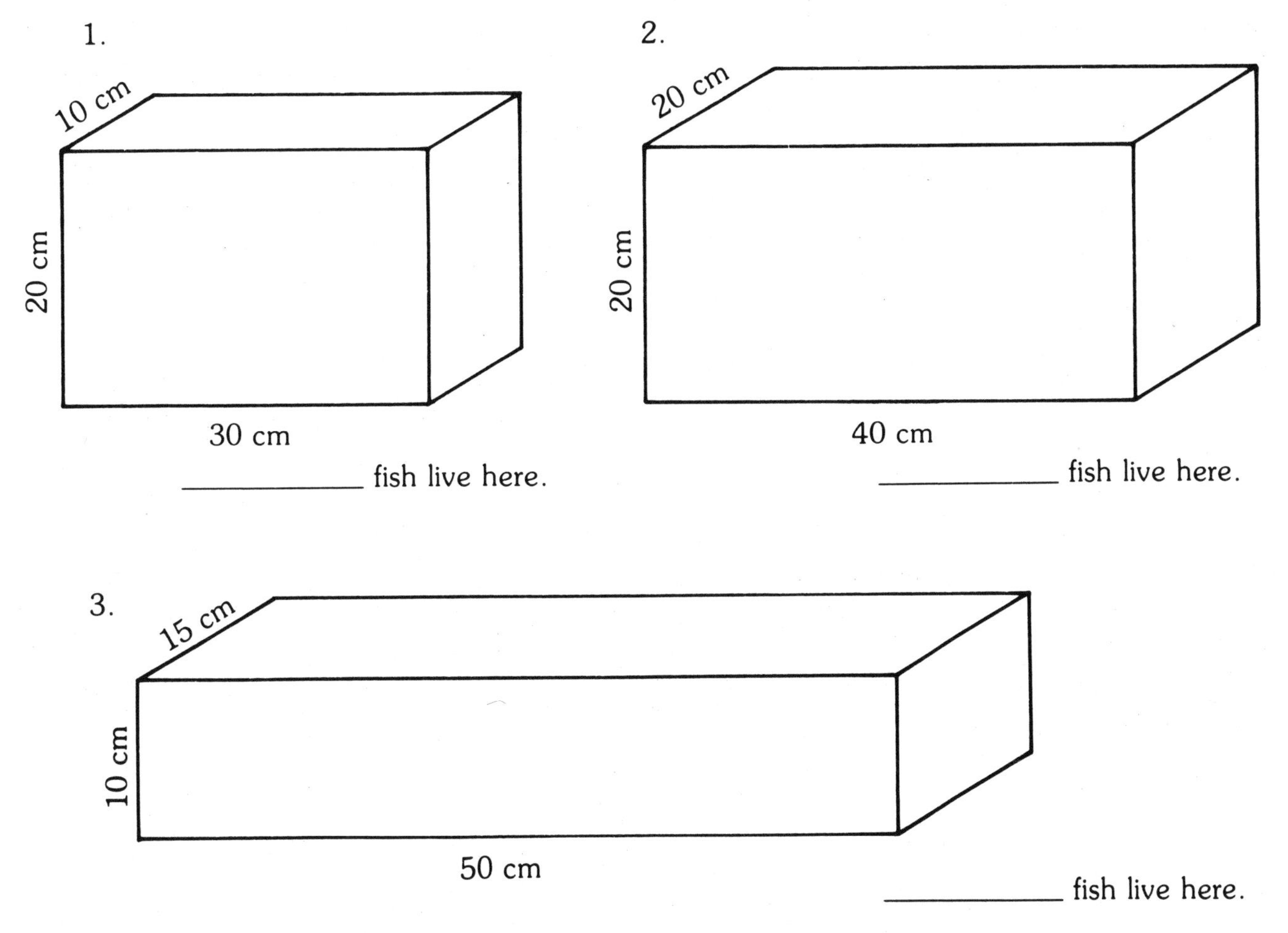

YOU'RE IN HOT WATER

Record Sheet TEMP-1 Name_______________

Find objects that are hotter and colder than your container of water:

THE FAHRENHEIT THERMOMETER

Record Sheet TEMP-4 Name________________________

Using a thermometer, find the temperature of the items below.

Item	Temperature °F
1. Human body temperature	
2. Class hamster	
3. A frog	
4. A dog	
5. A cat	
6. A plant	
7. A tire (before you ride to school).	
8. A tire (after you ride to school).	
9. A skateboard	
10. Your mother	
11.	
12.	

MEANINGFUL TEMPERATURES

Activity Sheet TEMP-5A Name____________________

Circle what you would wear out to play if the temperature outside was:

TEMPERATURE SCENES

Activity Sheet TEMP-5B Name ____________________

Draw a picture of something you would like to do outside when the temperature is:

0 °Celsius

20 °Celsius

Measurement Investigations, © Dale Seymour Publications

WHAT TAKES LONGER?

Record Sheet TIME-1 Name____________________

1. Mark an X under the longest task in each pair.

2. Mark an O under the shortest task in each pair.

ESTIMATE FIRST!

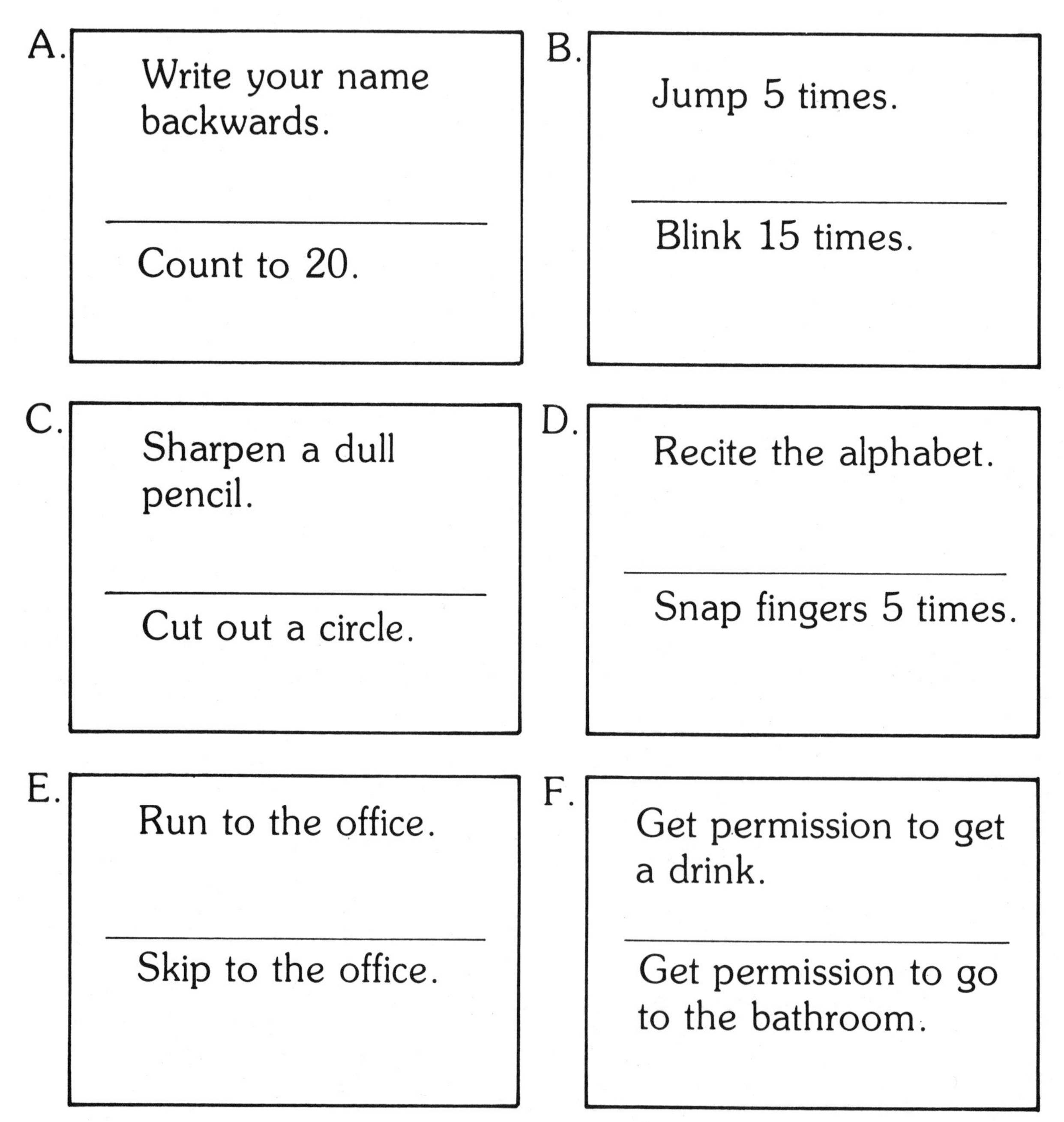

A. Write your name backwards. / Count to 20.

B. Jump 5 times. / Blink 15 times.

C. Sharpen a dull pencil. / Cut out a circle.

D. Recite the alphabet. / Snap fingers 5 times.

E. Run to the office. / Skip to the office.

F. Get permission to get a drink. / Get permission to go to the bathroom.

Measurement Investigations, © Dale Seymour Publications

MAKING YOUR OWN CLOCK

Activity Sheet TIME-2 Name ____________________

Find a partner, and time the following activities using your water clock (estimate first).

1. I estimate it will take me ________ water container units of time to do one page of math homework.

   It took ________ water container units.

2. I estimate it will take me ________ water container units to run all around the perimeter of the school.

   It took ________ water container units.

3. I estimate it will take ________ water container units to get my partner to laugh.

   It took ________ water container units.

4. I estimate it will take ________ water container units to count to one hundred by two's.

   It took ________ water container units.

5. I estimate it will take ________ water container units to walk around the room five times.

   It took ________ water container units.

Measurement Investigations, © Dale Seymour Publications

JUST A SECOND

Record Sheet TIME-4 Name____________________

Time the following events with a watch and graph your results.

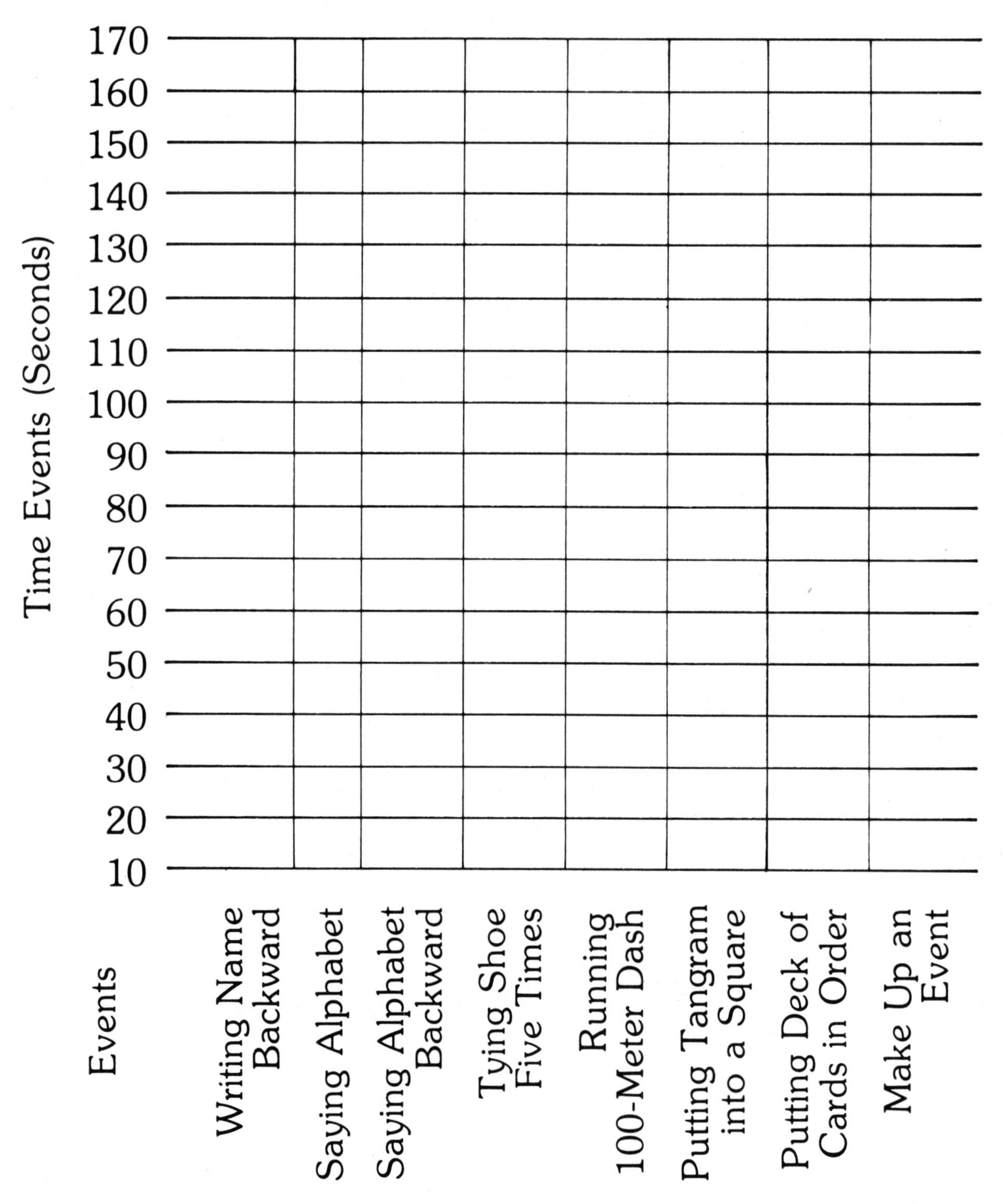

Measurement Investigations, © Dale Seymour Publications

TIME FLIES

Record Sheet TIME-5 Name____________________

Pick a partner, and time the following events. First, you estimate the elapsed time, and then you have your friend time each event with a watch.

Event	Estimated Time	Actual Time
1. Time between two classes		
2. Walking home		
3. One run around the track (you)		
4. One run around the track (your friend)		
5. Waiting in line at grocery store		
6. Waiting in line for lunch		
7. Waiting in doctor's or dentist's office		
8. Commercial time for one hour of TV watching		

Measurement Investigations, © Dale Seymour Publications

METRIC CHECK: LENGTH

Name____________________

Fill in each blank below with the most reasonable metric unit: millimeter (mm), centimeter (cm), meter (m), or kilometer (km).

1. A new pencil is about 15 _______ long.
2. The distance between Los Angeles and San Diego is about 200________________.
3. A basketball player is about 2 _______ tall.
4. One hand span is about 10 ________________.
5. One decimeter equals 10 __________________.
6. The width of a thumb print is about 20____________.
7. The length of a football field is about 90 __________.
8. One mile is a little less than 2__________________.
9. The distance around (circumference) of a basketball is about 1 __________________.
10. Make up a similar problem: ____________________

____

____.

Measurement Investigations, © Dale Seymour Publications

METRIC CHECK: MASS

Name ____________________

Fill in each blank below with the most reasonable metric unit: gram (gr), kilogram (kg), or metric ton (t).

1. A football player weighs approximately 100 ________.
2. The recipe called for 5 ________ of salt.
3. Mr. Brubaker's entire sixth-grade class weighs a little more than 1 ____________________.
4. Renee went to the store to buy 2 ________ of potatoes.
5. Maryann's new truck has a mass of over 2 __________.
6. A nickel has a mass of about 5 ____________________.
7. Together, the authors of this book weigh approximately 126____________________.
8. The class hamster weighs about 150 ____________.
9. Gypsy, the Golden Retriever, weighs about 20 ______.
10. Make up a similar problem: ____________________

____

____

Measurement Investigations, © Dale Seymour Publications

METRIC CHECK: AREA

Name________________________

Fill in each blank below with the most reasonable metric unit: square millimeter (mm^2), square centimeter (cm^2), square meter (m^2), hectare (ha), square kilometer (km^2).

1. The area of a postage stamp is about 4______________.
2. The area of a swimming pool is about 40______________.
3. The area of a thumbnail is about 90 ______________.
4. The area of a large lake would probably be measured in

   ______________________.
5. The area of a footprint is about 45 ______________.
6. The area of a classroom is about 60 ______________.
7. One hectare equals 10,000 ______________.
8. Mrs. Miller has an 8 ______________ ranch.
9. The area of this book is about 300 ______________.
10. Make up a similar problem: ______________

    ____

    ______________________________________.

Measurement Investigations, © Dale Seymour Publications

METRIC CHECK: CAPACITY

Name ______________________

Fill in each blank below with the most reasonable metric unit: milliliter (ml), liter (l), kiloliter (kl).

1. Michelle went to the store and bought 2 ________ of milk.
2. The doctor injected 5 ________ of penicillin.
3. The swimming pool contained 100 ________ of water.
4. One cubic meter is the same as 1 ________________.
5. One cubic decimeter is the same as 1 ______________.
6. One cubic centimeter is the same as 1 ______________.
7. The tank in your family car contains about 50 ________ of gas.
8. The recipe called for 5 ________ of hot mustard.
9. Normal lung capacity is about 3 ________________.
10. Make up a similar problem: ____________________

    ____

    ____.

Measurement Investigations, © Dale Seymour Publications

METRIC CHECK: TEMPERATURE

Name ____________________

Fill in each blank below with the most reasonable Celsius temperature.

1. Your normal body temperature is about__________°C.
2. Normal room temperature is about ____________°C.
3. Water boils at ____________°C.
4. Water freezes at ____________ °C.
5. The temperature of a hot day on the Mojave Desert might

   be__________°C.
6. A cold winter day in Dresden, Maine might be ______°C.
7. The temperature of a snowball would be about _____°C.
8. The temperature of a hot cup of tea would be about

   __________°C.
9. The temperature of a frog is about __________°C. (Good luck on this one.)
10. Make up a similar problem on the back of this page.

Measurement Investigations, © Dale Seymour Publications